THE ROUTLEDGE

HISTORICAL ATLAS

OF

PRESIDENTIAL

ELECTIONS

Routledge Atlases of American History

Series Editor: Mark C. Carnes

The Routledge Historical Atlas of the American Railroads
John F. Stover

The Routledge Historical Atlas of the American South
Andrew K. Frank

The Routledge Historical Atlas of Women in America
Sandra Opdycke

The Routledge Atlas of African American History
Jonathan Earle

The Routledge Historical Atlas of Religion in America
Bret E. Carroll

THE ROUTLEDGE
HISTORICAL ATLAS
OF
PRESIDENTIAL
ELECTIONS

YANEK MIECZKOWSKI

MARK C. CARNES, SERIES EDITOR

ROUTLEDGE

NEW YORK AND LONDON

Published in 2001 by
Routledge
29 West 35th Street
New York, NY 10001-2299

Published in Great Britain in 2001 by
Routledge
11 New Fetter Lane
London EC4P 4EE

10 9 8 7 6 5 4 3 2 1

Library of Congress Cataloging-in-Publication Data

Mieczkowski, Yanek
    The Routledge historical atlas of presidential elections / Yanek Mieczkowski.
        p. cm. — (Routledge atlases of American history)
    Includes bibliographical references and index.
    ISBN 0-415-92133-3 (hardback : alk. paper) — ISBN 0-415-92139-2 (pbk : alk. paper)
    Presidents—United States—Election—History—Maps. I. Title. II. Title. III. Series.

    G1201.S1   M5 2001
    328.973'022'3—dc21

                                                                    00-30014 00051771

To Bogdan, Seiko,
Van, and Dean

Contents

Foreword

The presidential election of the year 2000 turned on Florida. Just before the polls closed there, the major television networks announced that, based on a sampling of those who had just voted, Democratic candidate Al Gore had won the state. Several hours later, the networks retracted their prediction. Now Florida was "too close to call." By three o'clock A.M., after 99 percent of the Florida vote had been counted, the networks announced that Republican George W. Bush had won the state. But as the sun rose over the Everglades and returns trickled in from the remaining precincts, the networks again reversed themselves: Bush's lead in Florida had dwindled to several hundred votes out of six million cast. Florida, the networks sheepishly reported, was again "too close to call." And so it remained for weeks while local, state, and federal courts wrangled over who had won the state—and with it, the presidency.

Nationwide, Gore had received 300,000 more votes than Bush had. But the Constitution provided that the president was not to be chosen directly by the nation's voters, but by an "electoral college." The idea of an electoral college grew out of a heated debate during the Constitutional Convention of 1787. Some delegates had then questioned whether the people of the vast young nation possessed the "requisite capacity" to choose the chief executive; such unlettered and far-flung peoples would likely be swayed by "a few active and designing men." It would be preferable for Congress—either the House of Representatives, the Senate, or both—to select the nation's president. But James Madison and Gouverneur Morris countered that if the president were chosen by the legislative branch, he would become subservient to its wishes. The president should serve the people and be held directly accountable to them. Unable to come to agreement, the delegates eventually turned this contentious matter over to a Special Committee on Postponed Matters, which, after much debate, finally proposed a fateful compromise: neither the American people nor any branch of Congress would choose the president. Instead, each state would select, in a manner of its own devising, presidential "electors" equal in number to the state's total congressional delegation (members of the House of Representatives plus two senators); and the electors of all the states would meet together as an "electoral college" to choose the president.

Whatever the merits of the compromise—James Madison later conceded that the decision had been partly a product of "a degree of the hurrying influence produced by fatigue and impatience"—the electoral college has decisively shaped presidential political campaigns. The election of 2000 was an especially vivid demonstration of this fundamental—some might say peculiar—aspect of American politics. Because politicians were obliged to win states (and thus their electors), presidential candidates have long tailored their speeches and programs to appeal to states whose electoral votes were thought to be decisive. Presidential candidates have fought their battles, inescapably, upon the geographical landscape marked by the boundaries of the states.

In this atlas Yanek Mieczkowski repeatedly illustrates the truth of this assertion. Even a glance at its pages reveals much about our political culture: the continuities of its distinctive regions—New England, the South, the north central Plains, the Far West—and also the historic shifts that have forced new alignments—the breakup of the Federalists, and then of the Whigs; the rise of the Republican Party in the North and Midwest; the way in which the FDR, LBJ, and Reagan landslides obliterated the old political boundaries; the southern strategy of Republicans Richard Nixon and, later, Ronald Reagan; and so on.

This atlas's clarity of purpose is reinforced by Mieczkowski's clean, concise narrative; together, the maps and the text encapsulate millions of words of contentious speeches, party platforms, and political conniving. Casual readers and candidates for a doctoral degree in history alike will find this an indispensable household reference; it may well constitute the best brief guide to American history yet published. It is a worthy and indispensable addition to the Routledge Atlases of American History series.

Mark C. Carnes
Barnard College, Columbia University
Series Editor

Introduction

The presidency is the highest elective office in the United States and, along with the vice presidency, the only one where the winner is not determined through direct popular vote. The Founding Fathers designed the awkward electoral college system to avoid direct popular elections, because they lacked faith in the common people's ability to choose the best candidate. Few aspects of the Constitution have been so roundly condemned as the electoral college, because it can deny the will of the people—and has, in four elections.

In the early years of the republic, each state selected its electors by a method of its own choosing (such as popular vote or appointment by state legislature), and the number of electors equaled the sum of a state's U.S. representatives and senators, ensuring at least three electors for each state. Each elector was to cast two votes for president; the candidate with the most electoral votes would win, while the runner-up would be vice president. There was no campaign ticket with a pair of running-mates; since the Founding Fathers envisioned a political system without parties, the presidential and vice presidential candidates would have no partisan affiliations and would not need to campaign as a team against another party's candidates. Yet political parties immediately emerged, and the system they had created suffered growing pains and awkward adjustments.

For almost a century and a half, the franchise in the United States was restricted to adult white males. Women, African Americans, and American Indians could not vote. Until the 1820s, no reliable records were kept of the direct popular vote for president. The average voter had no measurable effect on the outcome unless he lived in a state where the electors were chosen by popular vote. When men voted, they did so by voice or at open tables; the secret ballot was unknown. So was a single national election day; states held elections to choose electors on various days in October and November, and in most states a voter had several days during which he could vote. (Only in 1845 did Congress designate the Tuesday following the first Monday in November as Election Day.)

In the nation's early years, presidential candidates behaved differently from the way they do today. Among the many precedents that George Washington set was that a candidate should not appear too eager to win the office or actively seek it. Rather, as the adage of the day went, "The office should seek the man." Active campaigning and making promises to the people seemed undignified, even vulgar. The more seemly behavior for a presidential candidate was to remain at home, mute. This pattern continued for more than a hundred years, and was broken only at the beginning of the twentieth century. The traditional stricture against open campaigning undoubtedly helped many early candidates who would have found speech-making torturous. George Washington wore dentures and had difficulty pronouncing certain words; John Adams, who lacked teeth but refused dentures, also had trouble speaking; Thomas Jefferson shied away from large audiences; James Madison had a weak voice.

Since early presidential candidates said nothing on their own behalf, they relied on party surrogates to speak for them. State and local party committees sponsored orators to give speeches promoting the party's nominee. For example, in 1844

Abraham Lincoln gave speeches in Illinois to endorse Henry Clay, the silent Whig candidate for president; but in 1860, as the Republican nominee, Lincoln remained in Springfield and said nothing. Newspapers, which were blatantly partisan, were also a widely used forum for promoting a candidate. Historian Keith Malden has written that in this era, "A man's politics could be readily identified by the paper he read." By the 1820s, new techniques for rallying partisan supporters and advertising presidential candidates emerged, such as national nominating conventions, nicknames and symbols for candidates, and mass electioneering events such as rallies, parades, and barbecues.

As electioneering practices changed, so did the nation. The country acquired vast expanses of land, and settlers forged westward, creating new states. Whereas America was once a provincial country where citizens felt that their first loyalty was to their home state, during the early 1800s the growth of a national party system fostered a national character. As the country grew and political parties evolved, distinct voting patterns emerged. In the early 1800s, the Federalists dominated the Northeast and New England, while the Democratic Republicans were popular in the South and West. As the eventual successors to the Federalists, the Whigs were more national in scope, with supporters in all regions of the country. In the 1850s, the Republicans began as a northern party, and were locked out of the South for nearly a century after the Civil War.

More transformations came during the twentieth century. While electioneering gimmickry such as parades began to fade, candidates began actively seeking votes. They crisscrossed the country in trains, cars, and, by midcentury, airplanes. Improved communications enabled candidates to reach voters more directly, through radio, television, and, by the end of the century, the Internet. Campaigns became more grueling, not only because of the energy it took to travel and communicate, but also because the election process itself grew more protracted and demanding, with an increasing number of state primaries and a greater need to use every weapon in a candidate's political arsenal, from "spin doctors" and saturation advertising to nationally televised debates.

Amid all the dynamism of American presidential elections, imperfections remain. Party loyalty continues to decline, as does voter participation, with turnout sometimes sinking below 50 percent of registered voters. The electoral college is still anathema to those who believe that direct vote should determine the presidential winner. Despite the problems, elections continue to be an important reflection of America's distinct geographic regions and socioeconomic groups. And while a candidate's personality has always been crucial, his personal life and image—family, fidelity, integrity—have received increasing attention, sometimes from voters and almost always from an expanding news media. Perhaps above all, elections express the popularity of candidates and their ideas. During the last half of the twentieth century in particular, elections have allowed popular presidents to serve two full terms in office, while they have repudiated other incumbents, especially for poor economic stewardship. Presidential elections will continue to shape this country's history and destiny, and their character will certainly undergo more changes.

The Elections of 1789 and 1792

George Washington
1732–1799
Washington struggled
to remain above
partisan bickering, but
in the end he adhered
to the Federalist
philosophy. The
resulting Democratic
Republicans' criticism
prompted him to retire
after two terms.

In the election of 1789, George Washington was the obvious choice for president. A Revolutionary War hero, he was idolized by the American people and had been unanimously elected president of the Constitutional Convention in 1787, where he had been a quiet but enormously prestigious presence. Indeed, at that convention the Founding Fathers designed the office of the presidency with Washington in mind. Although fearful of strong executive authority, they had created a powerful presidency by reposing their fears in the knowledge that Washington would occupy the post. But as 1789 began, Washington was 56 years old and had retired to Mount Vernon for what he anticipated would be his tranquil twilight years. He wanted nothing more than to live out these years tending his estate.

Washington viewed the presidency with a reluctance that would startle today's eager, ambitious candidates. Yet, while he dreaded the prospect of being elected and felt unequal to the new responsibilities, he felt obligated to preside personally over the executive branch to ensure the early success of the new government. With heavy resignation, he awaited word of the first presidential election.

In this election and in those of the early nineteenth century, there was no popular vote for president—only an electoral vote. On February 4, 1789, when the 69 presidential electors met in New York City, Washington received one vote from every one of them; he still holds the distinction as the only president ever to be unanimously elected. Since Washington did not indicate any special preference for a vice president, considerable speculation developed around who should fill this position. In order to balance Washington's Virginia roots, the electors felt that a northerner was desir-

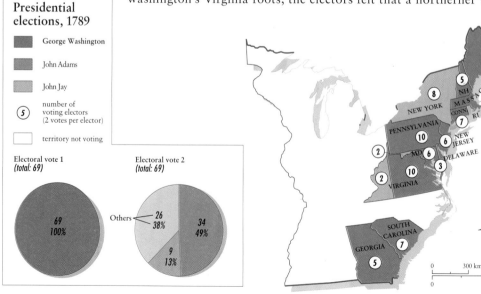

Presidential elections, 1789

- George Washington
- John Adams
- John Jay
- ⑤ number of voting electors (2 votes per elector)
- territory not voting

Electoral vote 1
(total: 69)

69
100%

Electoral vote 2
(total: 69)

Others — 26
38%

34
49%

9
13%

able. They focused on the state of Massachusetts, which had a wealth of political talent that included John Hancock and Samuel Adams. The Federalists selected the most prominent statesman there, John Adams, an ardent supporter of the Constitution who had served as a delegate to the Second Continental Congress, a negotiator for the Treaty of Paris in 1783, and a minister to Great Britain.

At this time, since there was no distinction between a presidential elector's vote for president or vice president, Adams could have received 69 votes as well, tying Washington. The situation would have been politically embarrassing and inauspicious for the new nation. Thus, already in the nation's first election, some behind-the-scenes political maneuvering took place. Alexander Hamilton, who had served as an aide-de-camp to Washington during the Revolution and who, along with James Madison and John Jay, had coauthored *The Federalist Papers* to support and defend the Constitution, set to work to avoid a tie vote. Some of Hamilton's contemporaries, including Adams, suspected that he was motivated more by political ill will toward Adams than anything else. Shrewd and manipulative, Hamilton arranged for just enough electors to vote for other candidates, thus ensuring that Adams would gain the second-highest total but not nearly enough to tie with Washington. Adams won 34 votes, while the remaining electoral votes were scattered among nine different persons (the next highest total after Adams's 34 was John Jay, with 9; John Hancock won 4; 22 electoral votes were spread among other persons). Three states did not participate in the election of 1789: North Carolina and Rhode Island had not yet ratified the Constitution, and New York had failed to appoint its electors by the January 1 deadline. On April 6, the electoral votes were officially opened in Congress, and Washington became, reluctantly, the first president of the United States.

The Constitution contains no references to political parties. This was the Founding Fathers' deliberate design. Concerned with fostering national unity, they had envisioned an America without parties. They viewed parties as a corrupting, divisive force that could prevent national harmony, subordinate the public good to party politics, and destabilize the government. As a framework of government, the Constitution was designed to discourage the development of political parties, and James Madison argued in *The Federalist Papers* that one of the virtues of a new government under the Constitution would be the absence of "faction."

But already during Washington's first term, political parties began to emerge. The presence of a strong central government and forceful personalities within that government, the sharply differing economic and social interests of Americans, and the controversies surrounding Washington's domestic and foreign policies all contributed to the growth of parties.

Early partisan warfare assumed a vituperative, highly personal nature, and the two competing parties coalesced around the two strongest personalities of the day and the most important members of Washington's cabinet.

In the early sessions of Congress, political disagreement occasionally exploded into violent scenes. Here a contemporary artist shows an event on the February 15, 1798, when Federalist Roger Griswold fought Republican Matthew Lyon, much to the amusement or horror of the onlookers.

Secretary of Treasury Hamilton's followers became known as the Federalists, and Secretary of State Thomas Jefferson led the opposition, the Democratic Republicans (or simply "Republicans," generally regarded as the precursor of today's Democratic Party).

Hamilton and the Federalists envisioned a strong central government ruled by wealthy, elite Americans, with an economy based on commerce and industry. More sensitive to the needs of merchants and businessmen, the

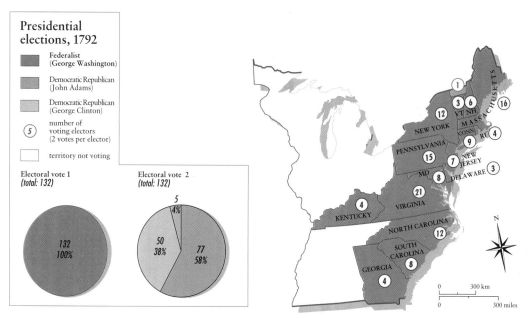

Presidential elections, 1792

- Federalist (George Washington)
- Democratic Republican (John Adams)
- Democratic Republican (George Clinton)
- ⑤ number of voting electors (2 votes per elector)
- territory not voting

Electoral vote 1
(total: 132)

132
100%

Electoral vote 2
(total: 132)

5
4%
50
38%
77
58%

Federalists lacked faith in the common man (Hamilton once referred to the common people as "a great beast") and feared excessive popular control of the government. Above all, they had an acute fear of mob rule. Jefferson and his followers, by contrast, subscribed to a pastoral ideal. Their blueprint for the nation's future involved a weak, decentralized, federal government with more power vested in the states, and an economy in which the small, inde-

While artists and designers created images like this tapestry, which eulogized the first president and his office, contemporary Republican newspapers criticized almost everything about the Federalist administration, including the president Wounded by such remarks, Washington stated, "I would rather be in my grave than in the presidency."

pendent farmer held center stage. Jefferson was particularly suspicious of urbanization and industrialization, and feared that allying America's government with the wealthy classes would lead to venality and corruption.

Foreign policy was a wedge that separated the parties even further. The guillotine and the violence of the French Revolution, which included the execution of King Louis XVI, alarmed the Federalists, who increasingly gravitated toward Great Britain, a trading partner and a source of stability and sanity in Europe. The Republicans, meanwhile, continued to champion the democratic, antiaristocratic forces that drove France to revolution. Members of each party felt that their opponents had an allegiance to France or Britain that was irresponsible, even treasonous.

America's first party system was emerging. The Federalists comprised the wealthier groups of society, such as the merchants, manufacturers, large-scale farmers, doctors, and lawyers. The Republicans attracted the old Anti-Federalists (opponents of the Constitution), small farmers, large planters, workers and artisans in urban areas, as well as immigrants such as Irish and French and religious minorities such as Baptists and Catholics. Geographically, the Federalists dominated New England, where a thriving merchant class and commercial ties to England, support for native son John Adams, and fear of revolutionary France made their party more appealing. In the mid-Atlantic states the two parties were neck and neck (although in New

A display of the United States of America prominently featuring George Washington, 1794

York the Republicans enjoyed considerable strength), while in the South the Republicans were in almost total control (the sole exception was South Carolina, where fear of the state's black majority united whites solidly under the Federalist banner).

While George Washington sought to remain statesmanlike above party conflict, his acceptance of Hamilton's financial structure and his increasing reliance on Hamilton for advice identified him with the Federalists and exposed him to partisan attack. Stung by the political sniping, by 1792 he was reluctant to seek reelection and wanted instead to retire, complaining not only about the growing antipathy of the Jeffersonians but also of his advancing age, physical infirmities, and, probably most of all, a wish to escape public life. So strong was Washington's desire to retire that he had James Madison draft a farewell address. But Madison (a fellow Virginian whose political advice and acumen Washington deeply respected), Thomas Jefferson, Alexander Hamilton, and others all implored him to stand for reelection, stressing his continued importance to the new and still precarious government.

As he said nothing in public, Washington's silence was a signal that he agreed to stand for a second term. The Republicans threw their support behind New York Governor George Clinton for the vice presidency. Knowing that Washington could not be beaten, they set their sights on an easier target, Vice President Adams.

Washington won a unanimous reelection, again winning one vote from each of the 132 electors. Adams received 77 votes, a relatively weak showing, to remain in office; George Clinton garnered 50, and two other candidates won a total of 5. Unlike in 1789, every state's electors cast ballots in this election. With the addition of Vermont and Kentucky to the Union, 15 states participated. While the Republicans failed to gain electoral votes for Clinton in any northern state except New York (12) and Pennsylvania (1), they showed their strength in the South, as Clinton won the electoral votes of Virginia, North Carolina, and Georgia. The party was poised to become a significant force in that region. Moreover, the Republicans demonstrated a New York–Virginia alliance that would serve their party well in future elections.

By today's standards, the nation's first two presidential elections were dull. They had none of the campaigns, slogans, or fanfare associated with later elections. There were no nominations, there was only one real candidate for the presidency, and there was little excitement or suspense about the election's outcome. But all of this was probably a good thing. National divisions were muted, and instead the country was able to concentrate on launching its new government. As historian Marcus Cunliffe has noted, with presidential electors unanimously supporting Washington, the political system was able to avoid a confusing array of candidates competing for the office, engendering conflict and disaffection that might have thrown the election to the House of Representatives, which would have been traumatic for the infant republic. As it was, Washington was able to portray himself as a disinterested leader who owed his election to universal support rather than to party support. The elections of 1789 and 1792 demonstrated that the new presidential election system worked, though with glitches, and thus they signaled the viability of the new political system.

The Election of 1796

John Adams
1735–1826
Adams and Jefferson,
friends during the
Revolution and the
only presidents to sign
the Declaration of
Independence, became
bitter rivals during
Adams's term.
Although in
retirement they
renewed their
friendship through
correspondence.

By 1796 partisan warfare was roiling the political waters, and this election became the first contested race in American history. The Constitution set no limit on the number of terms a president may serve, and supporters urged George Washington to seek a third term. He declined, in so doing establishing the two-term precedent. Washington delayed promulgating his decision until he released his Farewell Address in mid-September 1796, thus putting the Republicans at a disadvantage by leaving them less time to organize.

Although at this time there were no party conventions or caucuses to choose nominees, Thomas Jefferson stood as the Republican candidate for president, with Aaron Burr, a senator from New York and one of the state's foremost politicians, as his running mate. For the Federalists, the logical and expected successor to Washington was John Adams, who had loyally served two terms as vice president. In order to attract southern support, the Federalists offered as their vice presidential candidate Thomas Pinckney of South Carolina, who in 1795 had negotiated the Treaty of San Lorenzo (also known as Pinckney's Treaty) with Spain, which helped western farmers by gaining free navigation of the Mississippi River and the right to deposit export goods at New Orleans.

Without Washington to fuse the opposing factions, the campaign became a fierce fight over contending policies and clashing ideals. The Republicans railed against the recent Jay's Treaty and branded the Federalists as "monocrats" determined to establish a monarchy in America; the Federalists labeled their opponents as "Jacobins" sympathetic to mob rule. Although Adams and Jefferson had different political orientations, they had been friends for years, serving as delegates to the wartime Continental Congress and working in Washington's administration.

Thus, while the 1796 contest was strident, Adams and Jefferson preserved their friendship and refused to bloody their noses in partisan warfare. They remained at home and made no speeches. Instead, the thrust and parry of political campaign warfare took place in newspapers, pamphlets, and letters. (Aaron Burr tried a more direct approach to influence presidential electors, going to some New England states and speaking directly to potential electors.)

Although the Federalists were still the country's stronger party, they were increasingly rent by dis-

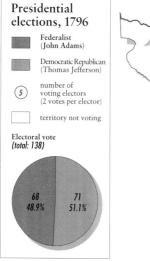

Presidential elections, 1796

- Federalist (John Adams)
- Democratic Republican (Thomas Jefferson)
- (5) number of voting electors (2 votes per elector)
- territory not voting

Electoral vote (total: 138)

68 — 48.9%
71 — 51.1%

sension. The most prominent Federalist was not their presidential candidate but rather Alexander Hamilton. Although he was too polarizing and controversial a personality to nominate, Hamilton would not sit idle. He disliked both Adams and Jefferson (the feelings were mutual) and, unable to abide either man as president, he schemed to throw the presidency to Pinckney. By influencing some Federalist electors to cast their ballots for Jefferson instead of Adams, Hamilton hoped to siphon enough votes from Adams to allow Pinckney to gain more votes than any other candidate. The ruse backfired. New England electors, insulted that Hamilton was trying to rob Adams of the presidency, manifested their outrage by throwing away some of their votes for Pinckney.

In November 1796, the 16 states selected their electors, and their ballots were counted the following February. Adams, who feared he would be defeated, was able to gain 71 votes, which represented a slim majority of the electoral votes (51.1 percent), ensuring him the presidency. With 68 votes, Jefferson received more votes than Pinckney, and was elected vice president. Pinckney gained 59 votes, and Burr won 30. Adams's support came exclusively from New England and the northern states, while Jefferson swept the South and won most of Pennsylvania's and Maryland's electoral votes.

With a president and vice president of different parties, Hamilton commented, "The Lion and the Lamb are to lie down together." The only election to produce such an anomalous situation, the contest of 1796 demonstrated the unforeseen complexities of an emerging political party system. To Adams fell the burden of working with a vice president who led the opposition, an awkward situation that poisoned their political relationship as well as their friendship. By the next election Jefferson had become an outcast in the Adams administration, and the two men were not even on speaking terms.

Despite the infelicitous relationship between the president and vice president, the young country had passed a crucial test, for presidential power shifted smoothly from the very man for whom the office was designed to another, less popular leader. But the outcome boded ill for Adams and the Federalists. Adams's three-vote victory gave him a weak mandate, and enemies gleefully reminded him of it by calling him "a president of three votes." The shaky mandate was underscored by Adams's weakness within his own party, in which he refused to take an enthusiastic role and in which Hamilton cast the longer shadow. Adams's cabinet also contained many holdovers from the Washington administration, who owed their first allegiance to Hamilton. The influence of this cabinet was all the greater because Adams was frequently absent from the capital (he would repair to his home in Massachusetts).

The election testified not only to the Federalists' internal divisions but also to the growing strength of the opposition, especially in the South. The Republicans were growing in numbers and in resources and, in an era when politicians deemed partisan opposition unnecessary and unhealthy, were committed to annihilate the Federalists. In fact, the election of 1796 proved to be the Federalists' last victory.

The Elections of 1800 and 1804

Thomas Jefferson
1743–1826
Despite a shaky
electoral mandate,
Jefferson became an
effective chief
executive, reducing the
national debt,
purchasing the
Louisiana Territory,
and sending warships
to the Mediterranean
to protect American
shipping.

The election of 1800 marked the introduction of the congressional nominating caucus, "King Caucus," whereby a group of congressmen representing a political party met to select a presidential nominee. The use of the caucus testified to the formal organization of the political parties, and the Republicans used the caucus as their standard nominating instrument until 1824.

As in 1796, John Adams and Thomas Jefferson were the contestants. This time they faced each other as president and vice president, and while Jefferson's running mate was once again Aaron Burr, Adams ran with Charles Cotesworth Pinckney of South Carolina, older brother of his 1796 running mate.

America had a choice not just between two men but between two political parties, Federalist and Republican, and between two competing visions for America. The contest was one of the most squalid in American history. Each man perceived the other as an agent of corruption, disorder, and foreign subversion. Federalists warned that Jefferson would reverse Federalist initiatives, destroy Hamilton's fiscal system, ruin the economy, and cripple federal strength by remanding authority to the states. They called him a "Jacobin" (with all the intimations of the Parisian mob rule and terror) and charged that he was a radical who would promote social bedlam in America, bringing the same havoc to this country that the French Revolution had brought to France. Some of the Federalist attacks were venomously personal: they portrayed

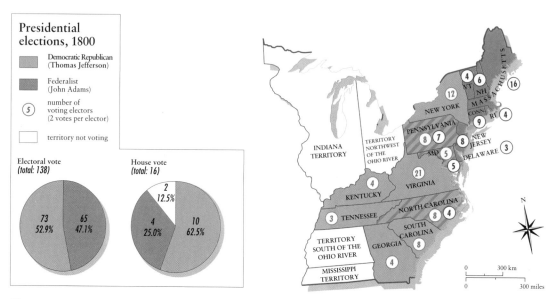

Presidential elections, 1800

- Democratic Republican (Thomas Jefferson)
- Federalist (John Adams)
- ⑤ number of voting electors (2 votes per elector)
- territory not voting

Electoral vote
(total: 138)

73 52.9%   65 47.1%

House vote
(total: 16)

2 12.5%
4 25.0%   10 62.5%

Jefferson as an atheist, drunkard, and adulterer, and unleashed the rumor that Jefferson was having an affair with one of his slaves, Sally Hemings. (This last charge has recently been supported by DNA evidence.)

Republicans fired off salvos of their own. They blasted Adams's policies such as the Alien and Sedition Acts of 1798, which stifled domestic opposition to Federalist policies and aimed to destroy the Republican Party. They charged that Adams was plotting to turn himself into a king, and started a rumor that he planned to marry one of his sons to a daughter of King George III, thereby reuniting America with England. Although Jefferson did not author any of the strictures against Adams, he encouraged friends to write them, helped to distribute pamphlets, and gave financial support to Republican newspapers.

The High Federalists, a more radical wing of the party, wanted to declare war against France, and Alexander Hamilton published a scathing pamphlet attacking Adams's conduct and character. (Aaron Burr obtained a copy of the pamphlet and distributed it to the Republican press, which joyfully used it as campaign ammunition.) Fiercely independent and aloof, Adams did nothing to mend fences with the High Federalists. The Federalists also disdained popular campaigning; by contrast, in one of the earliest examples of grassroots campaigning in U.S. history, the Republicans skillfully stumped at local levels, which had allowed them to gain both party cohesion and congressional seats in the 1798 elections.

Federalist weaknesses helped to ensure a Republican victory. Although Adams won all the electoral votes of New England, New Jersey, and Delaware, Jefferson won every electoral vote of the southern states (except for North Carolina, where he won 8 of 12 electoral votes) plus all of New York's hotly contested 12 votes, which both sides had regarded as critical. One or more of the Republican electors was supposed to discard or divert a vote for Burr, enabling him to come in second and allow Jefferson to be elected president. However, perhaps because the Republican Party organization was so effective, or perhaps because of a simple oversight, the electors cast each of their two votes for Jefferson and for Burr. The result was a tie. Each man received 73 votes; Adams finished with 65, while Pinckney got 64. Burr was clearly understood to be the vice presidential candidate, yet he refused to step aside for Jefferson. (Jefferson had felt uncomfortable with Burr's overarching ambition, and Burr's refusal to yield only confirmed his fears.) The Constitution specified that in the event of a tie, the House of Representatives would decide the election, with each state getting one vote. Although the Republicans had just won control of both houses of Congress, it was the outgoing lame-duck House, with a Federalist majority, that would decide the next president.

On February 11, 1801, voting in the House began. Needing a majority of 9 state votes out of 16 to win, Jefferson pulled up 1 vote short, polling 8, with Burr receiving 6 votes; two states were undecided. The voting became protracted and arduous: the House cast 35 ballots, but each one resulted in a deadlock. It was Hamilton's sideline influence that finally helped to decide the outcome. Hamilton regarded Jefferson as his political archnemesis, but he deeply distrusted Burr. He felt that Burr was dangerous to the country, a man unencumbered by moral scruples; he feared Burr's "extreme and irregular ambition" and declared him the "most unfit man in the United States for the office of the president." House Federalists were sufficiently persuaded by Hamilton's warnings to decide that Jefferson was the more palatable candidate. On February 17 they broke the deadlock to elect him on the thirty-sixth ballot; thus the election of 1800 was not decided until 1801, less than three weeks before the inauguration. (In the final vote, Jefferson won 10 states, Burr won 4, and 2 states had blank ballots.)

Jefferson's election marked the end of an era. Federalist rule was over forever. The Republicans now enjoyed a majority in both houses of Congress and also held the presidency; the judiciary was left as the sole bastion of Federalist power in the federal government. Jefferson tried to capture the significance of the election by later describing it as the "Revolution of 1800."

In truth, there was no revolution. In his inaugural address, Jefferson downplayed the differences between the two parties. "We are all republicans; we are all federalists," he declared. But behind this conciliatory sentence was Jefferson's goal of unchallenged Republican dominance. To that end, he functioned as both president and party chief, and adroitly

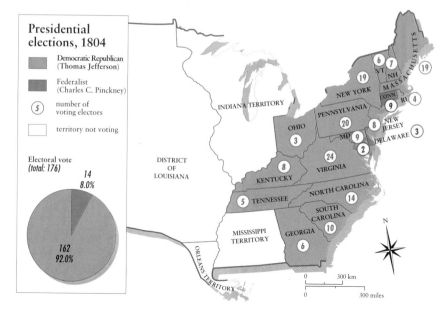

used his powers of patronage to appoint Republicans almost exclusively.

The election of 1804 occurred under an innovation, the Twelfth Amendment, which stipulated that presidential electors must cast one vote for president and another, separate vote for vice president. The amendment not only forced parties to designate their presidential and vice presidential candidates, but tacitly confirmed the existence of parties in the American political system.

On February 25, 1804, more than one hundred Republican congressmen met in an open caucus (as opposed to the secret one in 1800) and renominated Jefferson for president and, under terms of the Twelfth Amendment, designated a vice presidential candidate, George Clinton, dumping Vice President Burr, who had not only riled Republicans with his behavior during the 1800 election but had also defected from the Republicans to run unsuccessfully as a Federalist gubernatorial candidate in New York. In July 1804 Burr dueled and killed Alexander Hamilton, who had opposed Burr's gubernatorial bid, assuring an early end to his political career.

Federalist strength was ebbing, and the party did not hold a nominating caucus, instead recommending as their candidate Charles Cotesworth Pinckney, Adams's running mate in 1800. Pinckney's running mate was Rufus King, a former senator from New York.

The Federalists faced a redoubtable opponent in Jefferson, who had grown increasingly popular during his first term. His style appealed to those who knew him: a shy, lanky man, Jefferson dressed plainly and had an informal manner. He pursued his vision of a "wise and frugal" government and presided over a dramatic decrease in government expenditures and internal taxes, as well as a reduction in the public debt. These developments were set against a backdrop of relatively peaceful relations with Great Britain and France. The capstone of Jefferson's first term and of his entire presidency was the Louisiana Purchase of 1803, an achievement that virtually guaranteed his reelection and, additionally, bolstered his party's strength in the western states. The Federalists were left with few issues on which to assail the president.

The result was a Jefferson landslide. He won 162 electoral votes, while Pinckney's total of 14 was embarrassingly low (the total having been reduced by the Twelfth Amendment). Only Connecticut, Delaware, and two Maryland electors voted for Pinckney; even New England went for Jefferson. The Republicans also picked up more seats in both the House and Senate. After a narrow victory in 1800, the Republicans had trounced the Federalists just four years later. Jefferson could scarcely contain his joy, as his dream of a harmonious, one-party political system appeared within reach. He wrote to a French friend, "The two parties which prevailed with so much violence when you were here are almost wholly melted into one."

The Elections of 1808 and 1812

In January 1808 the Republicans met in a congressional caucus and nominated James Madison, Thomas Jefferson's close friend and handpicked successor, as their presidential candidate. A quiet, unassuming man of stunning erudition, Madison was the architect of the U.S. Constitution and had served loyally as Jefferson's secretary of state and principal adviser for eight years. Vice President George Clinton, at 69 years old listless and unfit for the rigors of the presidency, remained the vice presidential candidate (he later died in office). In September the Federalists met and chose their 1804 candidates, Charles Cotesworth Pinckney and Rufus King.

Foreign policy was a fulcrum upon which this election swung. Federalists charged that Secretary of State Madison had failed to protect American commercial interests on the high seas. Jefferson

James Madison
1751–1836
Before becoming
president, Madison
served for eight years
as Jefferson's secretary
of state, thus
beginning an early
nineteenth-century
pattern whereby the
secretary of state
frequently was elected
president.

cleverly released many of Madison's diplomatic correspondences, and the record indicated that these charges were baseless. In fact, the contrary was true. Madison had protested against both French and British impressment and had worked to protect American commerce.

The presidential electors voted on December 7, and Congress announced the results in February. Madison received 122 votes, while Pinckney got 47 ballots. Pinckney's total was 33 more than four years earlier, largely because New Englanders who were disgruntled with Jefferson's Embargo Act threw their support to him; Pinckney won all five New England states except Vermont. The Republicans also lost seats to the Federalists in both houses of Congress, although they still maintained their majorities. Madison's victory marked the beginning of a political pattern where the secretary of state ascended to the presidency, which reflected the importance of foreign policy as well as the high visibility of this cabinet post.

The election results ultimately said more about the state of party politics than about the candidates or the issues. The Republicans triumphed decisively even though the Embargo Act had devastated the economy; moreover, Madison was a principal architect of the ruinous policy. His victory in the face of these political handicaps testified to the Federalists' weakness.

The election of 1812 occurred under the shadow of a war that America was unprepared for and that divided the country. Although no single event or reason thrust the U.S. into war, a multitude of causes had been at work for years, the

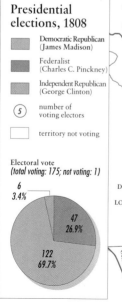

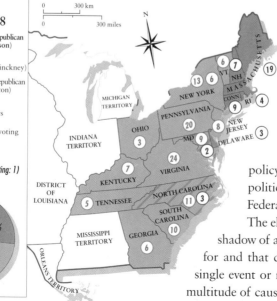

Presidential elections, 1808

- Democratic Republican (James Madison)
- Federalist (Charles C. Pinckney)
- Independent Republican (George Clinton)
- (5) number of voting electors
- territory not voting

Electoral vote
(total voting: 175; not voting: 1)

6
3.4%

47
26.9%

122
69.7%

most salient being the British practice of impressment. The U.S., with its growing merchant fleet, was angered at British violations of neutral rights, which caused economic loss as well as political and personal anguish. A new generation of young, strident congressmen dubbed "War Hawks," primarily from western and southern states, urged war against Great Britain, eyeing as a benefit of war an aggressive national expansion and the acquisition of Canada, which would eliminate British influence in North America. The War Hawks included rising political stars such as House Speaker Henry Clay of Kentucky and Representative John C. Calhoun of South Carolina. Although reluctant to fight Britain, Madison succumbed to the anti-British mood of Congress and in June 1812 asked for a declaration of war, which Congress promptly provided.

In May 1812 a Republican congressional caucus voted Madison as its candidate. His running mate this time was Elbridge Gerry, governor of Massachusetts and a signer of the Declaration of Independence. Not all Republicans supported the president. Some New York Republicans who favored peace proposed DeWitt Clinton; the nephew of George Clinton and lieutenant governor of New York, he would later be known as the father of the Erie Canal for spearheading that project. When the Federalists met in September, they nominated Clinton for president and Jared Ingersoll, a prominent Philadelphia lawyer, for vice president. Clinton did not openly portray himself as an antiwar candidate for fear of repulsing those regions of the country that supported the war. Instead, he simply opposed the administration, hoping to build a coalition of Federalists and disaffected Republicans.

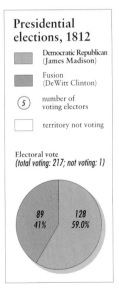

Presidential elections, 1812

- Democratic Republican (James Madison)
- Fusion (DeWitt Clinton)
- ⑤ number of voting electors
- territory not voting

Electoral vote
(total voting: 217; not voting: 1)

89 41%   128 59.0%

When the electors from the 18 states cast their ballots in 1812, Madison defeated Clinton, 128 to 89. Madison's relatively narrow victory showed how the war had cleaved public opinion in America. Clinton's support came from New England (just as in 1808, every New England state but Vermont voted against Madison) and the Mid-Atlantic states, such as New York and New Jersey, where opposition to the war was strong because it disrupted America's maritime trade, and where voters ached to rid the White House of the "Virginia Dynasty": Washington, Jefferson, and Madison. In the Northeast Madison won only Pennsylvania and Vermont; had he lost Pennsylvania's 25 votes, the election would have gone to Clinton. But in this highly sectional election, Clinton failed to receive any votes south of Maryland. With Federalist strength increasingly confined to New England, the party continued to waste away. Thus Madison owed his victory to Federalist weakness and to Republican strength in the South and West. In the South he prevailed because of his popularity and Virginia roots, and in the West farmers and frontiersmen supported the war because of the British blockade and suspected British aid to the Indians.

The Elections of 1816 and 1820

James Monroe
1758–1831

Although he lacked
the brilliance or talent
of his predecessors,
Monroe served two
tranquil terms and
enjoyed a national
political unity that no
previous president had
experienced.

Since the turn of the century, the Federalist Party had been enfeebled by many different blows. George Washington's death in 1799 seemed at once to symbolize and prefigure the Federalists' decline from power. With Alexander Hamilton's death in 1804, the Federalists lost their most pre-possessing intellect. The addition of new western states plumped the Republican ranks and made the Federalists' narrow eastern bias seem increasingly irrelevant. The Republicans also crowded the Federalists off the political platform by adopting many of their nationalistic programs that called for a strong central government and economic development. The Republicans embraced a new Bank of the United States, a protective tariff to encourage industry, and internal transportation improvements. By the time of James Madison's presidency, a new breed of Republican downplayed states' rights ideals and instead pursued national interests. The Republicans were beating the Federalists at their own game.

But it was the War of 1812 that struck down the Federalists forever. From the outset, the Federalists in New England had opposed what they derisively called "Mr. Madison's War." They deliberately hindered the American war effort by withholding state militia troops from the federal government and by spurning federal requests for money. Some Federalists openly predicted British victory, while others even rejoiced at British triumphs. Some extreme Federalists carried their thoughts one step further and murmured about secession, as during the Hartford Convention, when Federalists met in Hartford, Connecticut, to protest the war. Shortly after the convention adjourned, news came that the American negotiators in Ghent, Belgium, had successfully forged a peace treaty with Britain. The Federalists were embarrassed and discredited, and news of General Andrew Jackson's lopsided American victory at New Orleans in January —which occurred, unbeknownst to the combatants, after the Treaty of Ghent had already been signed—further blackened the Federalist name. In the end,

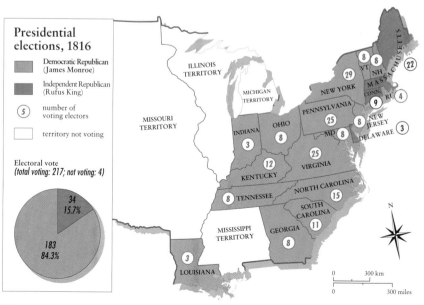

Presidential elections, 1816

- Democratic Republican (James Monroe)
- Independent Republican (Rufus King)
- (5) number of voting electors
- territory not voting

Electoral vote
(total voting: 217; not voting: 4)

34
15.7%

183
84.3%

ILLINOIS TERRITORY

MICHIGAN TERRITORY

MISSOURI TERRITORY

NEW YORK 29

VT 8 NH 8

MASSACHUSETTS 22

CONN. 9 RI 4

PENNSYLVANIA 25

NEW JERSEY 8

DELAWARE 3

MD 8

OHIO 8

INDIANA 3

KENTUCKY 12

VIRGINIA 25

TENNESSEE 8

NORTH CAROLINA 15

SOUTH CAROLINA 11

MISSISSIPPI TERRITORY

GEORGIA 8

LOUISIANA 3

0   300 km
0   300 miles

N

the war that the Federalists had so bitterly criticized had stimulated patriotism, and Americans hailed it as their "second war of independence." Although Madison was a poor commander in chief and a far less capable president than Jefferson, the successful denouement of the war allowed him to leave office riding a wave of nationalism and unity, which only enhanced the Republican Party's reputation. Meanwhile, the stigma over the Federalists' selfish, disloyal actions during the War of 1812 meant that the party had dug its own plot in the political graveyard.

By 1816 the Federalists could not even officially field a nominee. The Republicans held a congressional caucus in March 1816 and almost nominated William Crawford, a former U.S. senator from Georgia who was serving as Madison's treasury secretary. Many Republicans believed the popular Crawford was more capable than the other prospective nominee, Secretary of State James Monroe. At 60 years of age, Monroe had an extensive record of public service: Revolutionary War veteran, U.S. senator, minister to both France and Britain, twice governor of Virginia, secretary of war, and secretary of state. Despite his resumé, he was stodgy and uninspiring. Still, President Madison supported his fellow Virginian, and the Republicans settled on him as their nominee and named New York Governor Daniel Tompkins as his running mate, resulting in a Virginia–New York ticket similar to that of the Jefferson and Madison administrations.

On December 4, 1816, when the presidential electors met, some Federalists decided to cast their votes symbolically but hopelessly for Rufus King, the Federalist vice presidential candidate from 1808 and 1812, and John Howard of Maryland as vice president. Thus King became the last Federalist candidate ever to win any electoral votes for president. He received 34 votes from Connecticut, Delaware, and Massachusetts, compared to Monroe's 183 votes. Monroe's election continued the Virginia monopoly on the presidency (although he became the last of the Virginia dynasty).

The nation's fifth president was a throwback to an earlier age. The last Revolutionary War veteran to serve as president, Monroe still wore powdered wigs and knee breeches. Although he was not quite their intellectual peer, Monroe's contemporaries were the Founding Fathers, and like them he dreamed of the day when factional strife would no longer mar the American political landscape. That day seemed finally to have arrived, as Monroe's easy, practically uncontested election seemed to augur an end to partisan warfare in America. In his inaugural address Monroe declared, "Discord does not belong to our system." To illustrate the national unity and absence of political conflict, Monroe began his presidency with a goodwill tour of New England, former bastion of Federalist power, where he was greeted by adoring crowds. In what used to be the enemy's lair, erstwhile foes heaped praise on the new

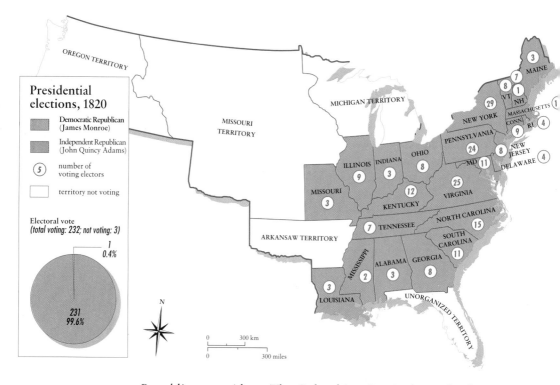

Presidential elections, 1820

Democratic Republican (James Monroe)

Independent Republican (John Quincy Adams)

5 number of voting electors

territory not voting

Electoral vote (total voting: 232; not voting: 3)

1 0.4%

231 99.6%

Republican president. The *Columbian Centinel*, a Federalist newspaper in Boston, noted the national harmony and proclaimed that an "Era of Good Feelings" had dawned in America, a term that became a popular label for Monroe's presidency. In a gesture of conciliation to New England Federalists, Monroe named as his secretary of state John Quincy Adams of Massachusetts, son of a Federalist president and a former Federalist himself.

Monroe's reelection in 1820 was as devoid of drama as his election in 1816. The Federalists had no candidate, and the Republicans did not even have to hold a congressional caucus. Monroe breezed to an easy victory, winning 231 out of 232 electoral votes; only one presidential elector voted against him. William Plumer of New Hampshire believed Monroe to be a feckless president, and cast his ballot instead for Secretary of State Adams.

The tranquility of the "Era of Good Feelings" was more apparent than real, for beneath the calm political surface fault lines began to open that soon led to the formation of a new political party system in America. (Among the divisions was the country's first sectional crisis over slavery in 1820, temporarily allayed by the Missouri Compromise, which admitted Maine as a free state and Missouri as a slave state, while banning slavery above the 36°30' line.) Monroe was at an unnatural pinnacle. The security of partyless government that he enjoyed was abnormal for a dynamic, open political system.

The Election of 1824

Since 1796 congressional caucuses had nominated presidential candidates, but during the election of 1824 the "King Caucus" system came under heavy criticism. The caucus seemed to allow a handful of politicians to subvert the will of the people. By this time an increasing awareness of democracy and popular participation in politics was sweeping the nation, with a new emphasis on giving the common man a greater role in selecting the president. (For example, the 1824 election was the first in which a majority of states selected their presidential electors by popular vote, rather than by appointment by state legislatures or other methods.) Amid these anti-caucus sentiments, more than two-thirds of the Republicans in Congress chose to sit out their party's February 1824 caucus in Washington. Those present at this caucus selected Treasury Secretary William Crawford, but the imprimatur of the caucus became more of a liability than an asset to him. The election of 1824 marked the last time a caucus nominated a party's candidate.

Irresistibly popular among his political colleagues, Crawford enjoyed the backing of former presidents Jefferson and Madison, and had an impressive record of public service in the U.S. Senate and in Monroe's cabinet. He seemed destined to become the nation's sixth president. But his hopes of reaching the White House were dealt a crushing blow in September 1823 when he suffered an incapacitating stroke, which left him half-paralyzed and almost blind.

The remaining Republican hopefuls each represented various interests in the party. Although John C. Calhoun of South Carolina, Monroe's secretary of war, was an early contender for the White House, he was just 41 years old, and in March 1824, deciding that he was young enough to try later for the presidency, he bowed out of the race. Henry Clay, who like Calhoun had been a "War Hawk" before the War of 1812, was Speaker of the House, an adroit legislator who exuded charm and enjoyed considerable popularity.

The real contest in 1824 was between John Quincy Adams of Massachusetts and Andrew Jackson of Tennessee. Like his father, the second president, Adams was crusty and uncongenial; like Henry Clay, he favored a nationalistic program of economic development. Adams was also a brilliant diplomat. His achievements as Monroe's secretary of state won him recognition as perhaps the most talented man to hold that position. Adams also gained considerable political leverage by serving as secretary of state, the post that often led to the presidency. Since the caucus was being repudiated, Adams received nominations instead from the legislatures of most New England states.

Jackson, who represented Tennessee in the U.S. Senate, was the hero of the War of 1812 and the favorite of most Americans, who admired his rise from the backwoods of the Carolinas to prominence as a well-to-do planter, general, and politician. Although he was wealthy, many Americans saw Jackson as a champion of the common man. The Tennessee legislature nominated their state's hero, as did many other local conventions in the South and West. Jackson and Crawford both represented the older, Jeffersonian wing of the Republican Party,

John Quincy Adams 1767–1848
Having a weak electoral mandate and facing combative Jackson supporters in Congress, Adams lacked the political capital and skill to promote his ambitious plans for transportation improvements, a national university, and an astronomical observatory.

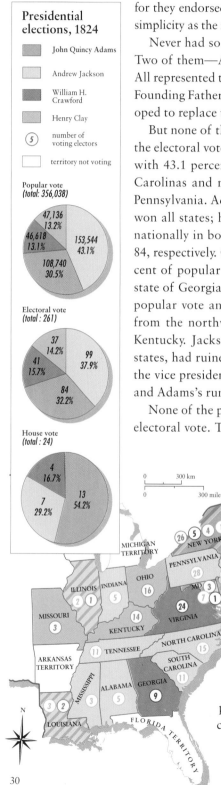

Presidential elections, 1824

John Quincy Adams

Andrew Jackson

William H. Crawford

Henry Clay

(5) number of voting electors

territory not voting

Popular vote
(total: 356,038)

47,136
13.2%

46,618
13.1%

153,544
43.1%

108,740
30.5%

Electoral vote
(total : 261)

37
14.2%

41
15.7%

99
37.9%

84
32.2%

House vote
(total : 24)

4
16.7%

7
29.2%

13
54.2%

for they endorsed states' rights, a limited central government, and an agrarian simplicity as the nation's economic bedrock.

Never had so many contestants vied for the presidency in one campaign. Two of them—Adams and Crawford—were members of Monroe's cabinet. All represented the generation of politicians that had emerged to succeed the Founding Fathers. All were Republicans, too, as no political party had developed to replace the Federalists and oppose the Jeffersonian Republicans.

But none of them was able to win a majority of either the popular vote or the electoral vote. Jackson won the election since he won a plurality of both, with 43.1 percent of the popular vote and 99 electoral votes; he won the Carolinas and most of the western states, as well as one northern state, Pennsylvania. Adams's appeal was largely limited to New England, where he won all states; he had enough popularity in other regions to place second nationally in both popular votes and electoral votes, with 30.5 percent and 84, respectively. Crawford and Clay ran nearly even. Crawford won 13.1 percent of popular votes and 41 electoral votes; he won two states, his home state of Georgia and his native state, Virginia. Clay won 13.2 percent of the popular vote and 37 electoral votes, with the bulk of his support coming from the northwestern states of Ohio, Missouri, and his home state of Kentucky. Jackson, in cutting a swath through the southern and western states, had ruined any chance of Clay becoming president. The contest for the vice presidency was not nearly so close. Calhoun ran as both Jackson's and Adams's running mate and handily won.

None of the presidential candidates had won more than 50 percent of the electoral vote. The Twelfth Amendment specified that under these circumstances, the election should be thrown to the House of Representatives, which would chose from among the top three electoral vote leaders (Jackson, Adams, and Crawford), with each state casting one vote. Although Clay was now out of the race, as House Speaker he pulled heavy oar in that chamber and could exert considerable influence on the election's outcome. With Crawford too ill for serious contention, the contest boiled down to Jackson and Adams.

Having achieved fame and glory at the Battle of New Orleans, Jackson was popular but had many liabilities. Although he had served briefly as a congressman and then a senator, he had left no legislative footprint, and his political views were still undeveloped. Many congressmen thought his qualifications for the presidency slim. Some congressmen could not abide the thought of this hot-tempered, uncouth, and uneducated man in the

White House. He had a history of gambling, dueling, and brawling, and his military exploits—such as a foray into Florida to chase Seminole Indians—had often been impulsive. Indeed, most political observers, even Jackson himself, were surprised that he had won as much support as he had. (When supporters first approached Jackson about running for president, his response was, "Do they think that I am such a damned fool as to think myself fit for president of the United States?") Henry Clay took a dim view of Jackson and had practical reasons not to support him, for doing so would boost the fortunes of a rival politician from the West. Not surprisingly, Clay threw his support to Adams.

On February 9, 1825, on the House's first ballot, Adams won 13 states and was elected the nation's sixth president. (Adams won Connecticut, Maine, Massachusetts, New Hampshire, New York, Rhode Island, Vermont, Illinois, Kentucky, Louisiana, Maryland, Missouri, and Ohio. Jackson won 7 states: Alabama, Indiana, Mississippi, New Jersey, Pennsylvania, South Carolina, and Tennessee; Crawford won Delaware, Georgia, North Carolina, and Virginia.) The first minority president, Adams also had the distinction of being the president elected with the smallest percentage of popular votes.

Jackson' supporters were crestfallen. The candidate who had won the most popular votes had been denied victory; the election of 1824 stands as one of four elections in American history (along with those of 1876, 1888, and 2000) in which the candidate with the most popular votes lost the election. Jackson accepted the House's verdict with equanimity, and even greeted Adams cordially at a reception held the night of the House vote. But three days after his victory, Adams made an announcement that made Jackson and his supporters roar with rage: the president-elect appointed Henry Clay as his secretary of state. Angry cries of "bargain and corruption" filled the air and expressed the suspicion that Adams and Clay had forged a secret deal to exchange Clay's support for a promise of the coveted cabinet post, which likely would allow Clay to succeed Adams as president.

No evidence has ever surfaced to indicate a deal between Adams and Clay. In all likelihood, none occurred. But the appearance of a deal was politically damaging to both men, and Adams began his term with the legitimacy of his presidency in question. For the next four years a dark cloud of suspicion hung over both men.

The election results shocked Americans. Theirs was a nation that prided itself on its experiment in republican government, yet they had just witnessed the will of the people being subverted. While no one urged revising the Constitution or scrapping the electoral college system, Jackson's supporters wasted no time in formulating a response to the betrayal of their candidate and their political will. The following October, the Tennessee legislature nominated Jackson as an 1828 presidential candidate. He promptly resigned his Senate seat and returned to his home in Tennessee. The campaign of 1828 had begun.

The Election of 1828

Andrew Jackson
1767–1845
Bolstered by the
greatest electoral
victories in the
nineteenth century,
Jackson became the
strongest chief
executive of his age,
opposing South
Carolina during the
Nullification Crisis,
destroying the
national bank, and
removing eastern
Indian tribes to the
interior.

By the 1820s, great changes were convulsing the country. New factories emerged, especially in New England, and stimulated the growth of an urban working class, pulling workers away from rural settings and installing them in cities, an environment of greater economic, political, and social ferment. A transportation revolution promoted new canals, roads, and later, railroads; restless Americans began to migrate to pursue economic opportunities, and their geographic movement was paralleled by an upward social mobility. A widespread reform movement in the country helped to improve education, which enabled the common man to better understand political issues. Also an economic panic in 1819 convinced many Americans of the critical interplay between public policy and economics. Thus they felt that they should actively support political leaders whose policies would promote prosperity.

This new atmosphere championed the common man and trusted his wisdom, and he became not only a more active voter but also a policymaker. A new breed of politician emerged in response. Often he came from modest or even impoverished circumstances and used politics as a means to surmount his background. Instead of dabbling in politics as an avocation, he devoted his life's work to it; he was a professional.

During the 1820s, too, more men became eligible to vote, so the electorate expanded. New states such as Ohio adopted constitutions that extended the vote to all white adult males. Extension of the franchise still had far to go, since women, slaves, and most free blacks were excluded, but the nation was gradually approaching universal white male suffrage.

The new emphasis on democracy and the common man's participation in the political process had a visible effect on presidential elections. More states made the process of selecting presidential electors more democratic by allowing them to be chosen by popular vote, dispensing with the old process where state legislatures selected them; by 1828, South Carolina was the only state whose legislators still picked presidential electors. Even more noticeable was the increased participation in presidential elections. Before the 1820s, voter turnout was low, generally estimated at less than 30 percent; in the election of 1824, only 27 percent of eligible voters went to the polls. (The election of 1824 is the first election for which there are reliable records of popular vote tallies.) Just four years later, 56 percent of the electorate cast ballots, beginning a sharp upward trend in voter participation that in 1840 witnessed a remarkable 80 percent of the electorate vote.

The increased democratic spirit was related to the emergence of a new, more competitive party system. Viewed as ruinous a generation earlier, parties now appeared constructive. The new party system was better organized at all levels—national, state, and local—and featured entertainment and popular techniques to arouse support, such as parades, picnics, and rallies. Politics became festive, even fun, and campaigns and elections were celebrations of democracy.

Andrew Jackson embodied the new democratic spirit. As a successful politician, general, and Tennessee planter (who lived in a mansion near Nashville and owned more than a hundred slaves), Jackson was wealthy and eminent. Yet he was also a rugged man whose humble origins kept him from truly belonging to the elite. Born in a log cabin in the Carolinas to Irish immigrant parents, Jackson received little formal schooling; he frequently misspelled or mispronounced words, and had primitive notions about the world around him. According to one of his relatives, he even believed that the earth was flat. But whatever he lacked in erudition Jackson made up for in intuition and common sense; his rise to the top was aided by these qualities rather than by birthright. Instead, he defended and promoted the common man, and his position brought him a surge of popular support.

Against this idealistic, promising background of growing democracy, the campaign of 1828 proved sordid, as politics still centered around a candidate's character and reputation. Both parties sidestepped the major issues and instead skewered the candidates. President John Quincy Adams, whose supporters became known as the National Republicans, ran with his treasury secretary, Richard Rush. Adams's supporters did their best to smear Jackson, whom they denounced as uneducated and unfit for the presidency. They pointed to his explosive temper and history of dueling as dangerous character defects. The nastiest charge of the campaign was directed against both Jackson and his beloved wife, Rachel. When the two had married in 1791, neither was aware that Rachel's divorce from her first husband was not yet legally complete. Adams's supporters pounced on the couple's oversight and labeled them as adulterers and bigamists. The charges gouged a deep wound in Jackson.

Yet Jackson floated upon the democratic tide. Scions of Thomas Jefferson's party, the Democratic Republicans shortened their name simply to "Democrats." In their party organization the Democrats exemplified the new political age. In contrast to their more staid opponents, the Democrats displayed remarkable sophistication and ingenuity in rallying Americans behind their banner, and in so doing introduced color and pageantry into American politics. In addition to raising money and distributing pamphlets and broadsides, the Democrats held torchlight parades and barbecues to mobilize support. In an early instance of saturation advertising, they promoted Jackson using symbols such as hickory canes, hickory sticks, and hickory brooms (Jackson's troops had called him "Old Hickory" for his toughness, and the nickname stuck). They invented songs to honor their candidate, such as "Hickory Wood" and "The Battle of New Orleans." These devices distilled the candidate's essence into tangible objects that the public could see and celebrate.

The Democrats also comprised a heterogeneous coalition of groups that included urban workers and artisans, farmers and planters, Jackson's long-standing supporters in the South and West, and new supporters, such as Senator Martin Van Buren of New York, who managed a disciplined political organization in that state, the Albany Regency, which helped to build up the Democratic Party. Like Adams, Jackson did not deign to campaign personally, but he encouraged supporters to build up what became the most formidable campaign organization to date, one that boasted a Jackson organization in every major city in the country.

But the Democrats' best asset was their candidate. The election of 1828 was the

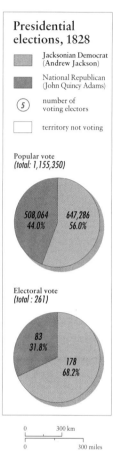

Presidential elections, 1828

Jacksonian Democrat (Andrew Jackson)

National Republican (John Quincy Adams)

(5) number of voting electors

territory not voting

Popular vote (total: 1,155,350)

508,064 44.0%
647,286 56.0%

Electoral vote (total : 261)

83 31.8%
178 68.2%

0   300 km
0   300 miles

MAINE 8 1
VT 7 8
NH (15)
MICHIGAN TERRITORY
NEW YORK 20 16
MASSACHUSETTS (15)
CONN. 8
RI (4)
UNORGANIZED TERRITORY
PENNSYLVANIA 28
NEW JERSEY 8
DELAWARE (3)
ILLINOIS 3 INDIANA 5 OHIO 16
MD 6
5
MISSOURI 3
KENTUCKY 14
VIRGINIA 24
ARKANSAS TERRITORY
TENNESSEE 11
NORTH CAROLINA 15
SOUTH CAROLINA 11
MISSISSIPPI 3 ALABAMA 5 GEORGIA 9
LOUISIANA 5
FLORIDA TERRITORY
N

first in which a candidate's image, embellished to appeal to the electorate, played a decisive role in generating victory. In Jackson the Democrats could point to a true product of the American system. Jackson himself understood the ethos of the era, whereby the ordinary man was exalted, and he capitalized on it by promising to fight special privilege, remove incompetent officeholders, and make government more responsive to the will of the people. Jackson also proved to be circumspect and shrewd, declining to discuss his specific stands on major issues, even muting his fervent distrust of the national bank. His deliberate vagueness put Adams at a disadvantage, since the latter's record as president clearly displayed his belief in nationalistic programs such as the Bank of the United States, transportation improvements, and a protective tariff to nurture industry.

Jackson supporters also depicted Adams as a creature of privilege, providing an effective contrast with Jackson. They portrayed the Harvard-educated Adams as a befuddled intellectual who had accomplished little as president, a record that wilted next to Jackson's chronicles of conquest and activity. Jacksonians said that the contest pitted "a man who can write" against "a man who can fight."

Jackson's enormous popularity and superb campaign organization won him a smashing victory. Like his father a generation earlier, John Quincy Adams was turned out of the White House after just one term. Jackson captured 56 percent of the popular tally, compared to 44 percent for Adams. In the electoral college, Jackson's total was more than twice that of Adams, 178 to 83. Jackson's victory was the product of the Democratic Party's superior organization and Jackson's popular image.

Jackson's triumph also reflected the enduring sectional divisions in America. Adams swept the old Federalist strongholds of New England and carried some of the mid-Atlantic states, such as New Jersey and Delaware. Adams also won 16 of New York's 36 electoral votes, 6 of Maryland's, and 8 of Maine's 9. (All three states awarded electoral votes in proportion to the candidate's popular vote; most of the other states awarded electoral votes on a winner-takes-all basis.) But Jackson dominated the South and West (as well as Pennsylvania), which swept him to victory and gave the country its first president from a state other than Virginia or Massachusetts, and the first president from genuinely humble origins. The election had a tragic postscript. Just weeks after her husband was elected, Rachel Jackson died of a heart attack. Jackson was devastated. He wept openly at her funeral and, believing that she had been driven to her grave by the scurrilous attacks on their marriage, he blamed his political opponents for her death and called them murderers. He was by nature combative toward his political opponents, but his wife's death made him even more so.

The Election of 1832

During Andrew Jackson's first term, a political crisis occurred that had powerful political reverberations. Bridling under the onerous 1828 Tariff of Abominations that Congress had passed in Adams's term, the state of South Carolina struck back at the national government by issuing the Nullification Proclamation, which proclaimed a state's right to reject federal laws. Jackson, who would brook no such defiance of national laws, threatened military action against South Carolina. In the end, the state backed down and rescinded its Nullification Proclamation.

A key actor in the drama was Vice President John C. Calhoun, who had also served as vice president for John Quincy Adams. A South Carolina native, Calhoun supported a state's right to nullify national laws. As the president and South Carolina squared off, in 1832 Calhoun resigned as vice president, becoming the first vice president ever to vacate the office. (Calhoun left to become a U.S. senator from South Carolina and, with help from Senator Henry Clay, ironed out a compromise to defuse the nullification crisis.) Calhoun's open break with the popular and powerful Jackson killed his presidential hopes, and his departure left Jackson without a vice president.

With the nullification crisis as a backdrop, during the election of 1832 the major issue was the Second Bank of the United States. Its twenty-year charter was due to expire in 1836, but Senators Henry Clay and Daniel Webster persuaded Bank president Nicholas Biddle to apply for a new charter in 1832. The senators wanted to set this process in motion before the 1832 election. They expected President Jackson to veto the Bank recharter bill, and hoped to turn the veto against him as an election issue.

Jackson viewed the Bank—the "monster," as he called it—as an unconstitutional, monopolistic tool of the rich and privileged. As anticipated, in July 1832 he rejected the Bank recharter bill and issued a stinging veto message. His words fomented partisan emotions and set the stage for the 1832 campaign. Jackson proved more in tune with the pulse of the public, for his veto message captured the imagination of most Americans, who saw him as their defender.

The central issue in the election was Jackson's Bank veto, but America's first-ever third political party, the Anti-Masonic Party, tried to inject another issue. The Society of Freemasons—or the Masons, as they were more commonly known—was a secret, all-male group whose members had included George Washington and Ben Franklin. The Masons had an elaborate ritual of secret passwords, handshakes, and oaths, and members rose through various levels in the organization to achieve greater rank. It was an elitist society that drew from the upper class of Americans, and many Masons held public office or were prominent business leaders and professionals. Opponents nursed deep suspicions of Masons and alleged that they were conspiratorial and undemocratic.

Although they were shrouded in secrecy, the Masons seemed innocuous enough until a disgruntled former member, William Morgan of Batavia, New York, announced that he would publish an exposé of the organization's secrets. One night Morgan was abducted, never to be seen again. Just as disturbing as Morgan's apparent murder was the conspiracy of silence that followed, as

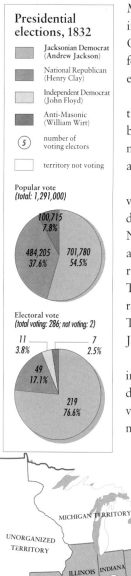

Presidential elections, 1832

Jacksonian Democrat (Andrew Jackson)

National Republican (Henry Clay)

Independent Democrat (John Floyd)

Anti-Masonic (William Wirt)

⑤ number of voting electors

territory not voting

Popular vote
(total: 1,291,000)

100,715
7.8%

484,205
37.6%

701,780
54.5%

Electoral vote
(total voting: 286; not voting: 2)

11
3.8%

7
2.5%

49
17.1%

219
76.6%

Masons in western New York State used their power and influence to block the investigation of Morgan's disappearance and to protect those responsible. Opponents of the Masons parlayed their anger and frustration into a political force by forming the Anti-Masonic Party, which was built on a single issue: the elimination of all secret societies, especially the Masons.

The Anti-Masonic Party held the first presidential nominating convention in the nation's history. The convention was designed not only to select a candidate but also to foster unity and strength in the new party. In September 1831 they nominated William Wirt of Maryland, who had served as President Monroe's attorney general. The Anti-Masons also adopted the first party platform.

The other two political parties followed the Anti-Masons' lead and held conventions of their own. At these gatherings, the practice began whereby delegates decided upon the nominee's running mate. Meeting in December 1831, the National Republicans nominated Henry Clay, who had won election to the Senate after serving as Adams's secretary of state, as their presidential candidate. Clay's running mate was John Sergeant of Pennsylvania, a friend of Nicholas Biddle's. The Democrats met in May 1832 and nominated Jackson, an action that merely ratified the work of numerous state conventions that had already nominated him. The delegates at the convention selected Martin Van Buren of New York, a loyal Jackson protégé and former secretary of state, as their vice presidential candidate.

While the Bank veto dominated the political campaign, Jackson's overarching popularity was the decisive factor. He swept to an easy victory, thoroughly dominating Clay in the electoral college with more than four times as many votes, 219 to 49. William Wirt, who drew votes away from both candidates but mostly from Clay, managed to win one state, Vermont, and its 7 electoral votes. Virginia Governor John Floyd received votes from all 11 South Carolina electors, who were appointed by the legislature of that state, which was locked in the bitter nullification crisis against Jackson and federal law. With this victory Jackson exacted a measure of revenge against Clay, whom he believed had conspired, along with John Quincy Adams, to steal the presidency from him in 1824. Compared to 1828, Jackson had won 40,000 more popular votes, and his share of the popular vote was 54.5 percent, down just 1 percent. It was to be the last truly lopsided presidential victory of the nineteenth century, and it was a ringing endorsement of Jackson's presidency and of his Bank veto. During his second term Jackson tried to resolve both the nullification and the Bank crises, composing peace with South Carolina by signing a compromise tariff bill and removing federal deposits from the Bank of the United States, which helped to speed the Bank's destruction.

MICHIGAN TERRITORY

UNORGANIZED TERRITORY

0   300 km
0   300 miles

MAINE 10

VT 7 NH 7
NEW YORK 42 MASSACHUSETTS 14
CONN. 8 RI 4
PENNSYLVANIA 30 NEW JERSEY 8
OHIO 21 MD 5 DELAWARE 3
ILLINOIS 5 INDIANA 9
VIRGINIA 23
MISSOURI 4 KENTUCKY 15
TENNESSEE 15 NORTH CAROLINA 15
ARKANSAS TERRITORY SOUTH CAROLINA 11
MISSISSIPPI ALABAMA 7 GEORGIA 11
LOUISIANA 5
FLORIDA TERRITORY

N

The Election of 1836

In a sense, the election of 1836 served as a midwife to America's second party system. Throughout American history, the appearance of a third party often portends or paves the way for a significant shift in the electorate. Frequently one of the two larger parties co-opts the ideas or programs of the third party and thus attracts members of the maverick party, which would be too weak to survive as a permanent political party. In the mid-1830s, the Anti-Masonic Party, America's first third party, was absorbed by a new party, which soon became an effective political opposition to the Democrats.

*Martin Van Buren
1782–1862
Although Van Buren
promised economic
prosperity in his
inaugural address, for
most of his term the
nation was mired in
economic depression,
leaving him
exasperated and
politically wounded.*

Perhaps the most signal testimony to how intense emotions were against Andrew Jackson was that a national political party grew specifically to oppose him. Fueled by their anti-Jackson passions, the National Republicans were able to crystallize into a new force. They objected to what they claimed was Jackson's tyrannical use of executive power, starkly exhibited by his veto of the Bank recharter. Harkening back to the eighteenth-century politicians of England who had tried to circumscribe the king's power, Jackson's opponents called themselves "Whigs" and portrayed the president as the high-handed "King Andrew." Yet the Whigs also favored a strong federal government in which Congress, rather than the president, held the reins of power and had a greater ability to promote economic growth. Whigs built support from the same constituency as the old Federalists, the merchants and manufacturers of the Northeast and wealthier, aristocratic Americans, as well as from the members of the Anti-Masonic Party, who had distrusted Jackson. The Democrats, by contrast, glorified the common man, exalted Jeffersonian ideals, and drew from the traditional Democratic constituency.

As vice president, Martin Van Buren had a formidable advantage at the outset of the presidential race. For his running mate the Democrats selected Colonel Richard Johnson of Kentucky, whom they advertised as a military hero, a logical tactic in light of General Jackson's political success. It was Johnson, Democrats claimed, who had killed the legendary Indian warrior Tecumseh during the War of 1812's Battle of Thames. Whether Johnson had really slain the Indian was uncertain, but the legend made him popular in the West. Moreover, as a westerner, Johnson gave geographical balance to the ticket. But he had a skeleton in his closet: he had lived with a mulatto woman and had two daughters with her.

The Whigs were too new and disjointed to mount a unified national opposition. They could not even back a single candidate or hold a nominating convention. Instead they offered three candidates, each representing a section of the country. Senator Daniel Webster of Massachusetts would attract the New England vote; Senator Hugh Lawson White of Tennessee would appeal to the South; and General William Henry Harrison of Ohio would capture votes in the West. The Whigs knew that they could not win outright. Their strategy was to win enough electoral votes to prevent Van Buren from winning. The contest would then be thrown to the House, where the Whigs could unite behind one candidate and perhaps prevail.

While politically urbane and an efficient organizer and administrator for the Democratic Party (so much so that his nickname was the "Little Magician"), Van

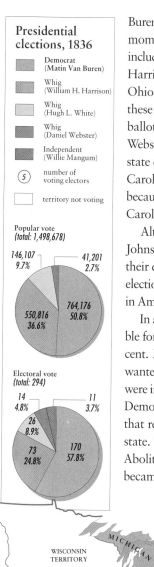

Presidential elections, 1836

Democrat (Matin Van Buren)

Whig (William H. Harrison)

Whig (Hugh L. White)

Whig (Daniel Webster)

Independent (Willie Mangum)

⑤ number of voting electors

territory not voting

Popular vote (total: 1,498,678)

146,107 9.7%
41,201 2.7%
764,176 50.8%
550,816 36.6%

Electoral vote (total: 294)

14 4.8%
11 3.7%
26 8.9%
73 24.8%
170 57.8%

Buren lacked the stature and charisma of Jackson. But in the end, Van Buren rode the momentum of Jackson's popularity to an easy win. He claimed 15 of 26 states, including the key states of New York, Pennsylvania, and Virginia. Among the Whigs, Harrison appeared on the ballot in 15 states, and he won in 7: Indiana, Kentucky, and Ohio in the West, plus Vermont, Maryland, Delaware, and New Jersey in the East; these states brought him 73 electoral votes. White, whose name appeared on the ballot in 10 states, almost all in the South, won 2 states and 21 electoral votes. Webster, appearing on the ballot exclusively in New England, won only his home state of Massachusetts and its 14 electoral votes. As in the election of 1832, South Carolina was defiant, refusing to support the Whigs' southern candidate, White, because he had backed Jackson during the nullification crisis. Instead, the 11 South Carolina electors cast their votes for Senator Willie Mangum of North Carolina.

Although Van Buren prevailed, his running mate did not fare as well. To protest Johnson's relationship with a mulatto woman, Virginia Democrats refused to cast their electoral votes for him, which denied him the majority he needed to win. The election was thrown to the Senate, where senators elected him, marking the first time in American history that the Senate had to confirm a vice presidential candidate.

In an ironic way, Van Buren's victory offered hope to the Whigs and spelled trouble for the Democrats. Van Buren's majority of the popular vote was just 50.8 percent. Moreover, the spirit of secularism was splitting the country, and the Whigs wanted to exploit the growing division. Most of the 15 states that Van Buren won were in the North, his native region. In the South the Whigs ran almost even with the Democrats, a far cry from the runaway victories that Andrew Jackson had scored in that region. The Whigs had even managed to capture Tennessee, Jackson's home state. The Whigs owed part of their strength in the South to the issue of slavery. Abolitionist agitation increased dramatically during the 1830s, and southerners became increasingly defensive of their "peculiar institution." Many southerners feared Van Buren, a northerner, and distrusted Johnson for his relationship with a mulatto woman. The Whigs tried to capitalize on these feelings by portraying Van Buren as an antislavery man, even though in reality he was no friend of the abolitionists and had no plans to interfere with slavery.

While their southern strength was particularly notable, the Whigs picked up states in every region of the country. Their strong showing shattered the solidarity that had characterized party politics since 1800, when the Democrats began to dominate—even obliterate—the opposition. In place of this solidarity was a vibrant two-party system, national in scope and competitive everywhere in the country. This second two-party system was to prevail until the mid-1850s.

The Election of 1840

In 1840 the Democrats renominated President Martin Van Buren, but did not renominate Richard Johnson for vice president (because of objections to his personal life), opting instead to have the states pick a candidate for vice president, the only time that a major party candidate was nominated without a running mate. At their convention the Democrats also adopted the first national party platform.

William Henry Harrison 1773–1841 The new, loosely knit Whig Party never revealed Harrison's stands on controversial issues, such as slavery and protective tariffs, choosing instead to exploit his military record and his common-man imagery.

Economic issues loomed large in this campaign. Many Americans held President "Van Ruin" accountable for failing to alleviate the depression following the Panic of 1837, though Van Buren's reluctance to use federal resources to correct economic downturns was customary for presidents during the era. This election marked the first in which Americans blamed a president for their economic woes and vented their frustrations at the polls.

Van Buren was hurt even more by a clever Whig campaign. The Whigs rejected their most eminent spokesmen, Henry Clay and Daniel Webster, and instead settled on the safe and noncontroversial General William Henry Harrison of Ohio. Harrison was the victor against the Shawnee Indians during the Battle of Tippecanoe in 1811, and he had garnered the most popular and electoral votes among Whig candidates in the 1836 election. Harrison's political views were unknown, and the Whigs were determined to keep them that way; his public pronouncements were deliberately vague, so much so that Democrats ridiculed him as "General Mum." The Whigs did not adopt a party platform, and they studiously refrained from addressing controversial issues such as the national bank and the abolition of slavery. The Whigs sought to demonstrate the party's geographical diversity by naming John Tyler of Virginia as Harrison's running mate. Tyler had been a Democrat until he broke with Jackson over the Bank veto, which Tyler viewed as a heavy-handed use of federal power and an assault on states' rights. By selecting Tyler, the Whigs hoped to attract other Democrats disenchanted with Jackson's presidential behavior.

In 1840 the Whigs parroted the campaign techniques that had worked so effectively for the Democrats when Andrew Jackson had run for president. In "Old Tippecanoe" the Whigs championed a military hero and man of the people, like "Old Hickory." But although Jackson could have truthfully said that he had been born in poverty and lacked a formal education, Harrison could not. He came from an affluent background; his father, Benjamin, was a signer of the Declaration of Independence, and William had attended Hampden-Sydney College in Virginia. Yet the Whigs still painted a rustic image of Harrison. Although Harrison owned a large farm in Ohio, the Whigs claimed that he lived in a log cabin and drank hard cider. These two items became symbols of Harrison's campaign. The Whigs developed a number of campaign newspapers, including Horace Greeley's highly successful *Log Cabin* in New York, and *The Hard Cider Press* in Chicago. At campaign rallies Whigs liberally dispensed cider and even paraded log cabins on horse-drawn floats. Whigs also celebrated Harrison with "cabin raisings," in which they erected a log cabin and then used it as a local campaign headquarters.

The Whigs portrayed Van Buren as a haughty aristocrat. They charged that while Old Tippecanoe tippled cider, Van Buren drank expensive foreign wines, ate off gold plates, and used fancy colognes. The charges were spurious, but their effect on Van Buren's image was devastating. The Whigs created the impression of an aloof, insensitive dandy who lived the good life while so many Americans were unemployed and were going hungry.

Historians often trace the origins of the modern political campaign to 1840. In this race Harrison campaigned in person, delivering 23 speeches in Ohio, marking the first time that a presidential candidate took to the stump on his own behalf (he even drank hard cider while campaigning). More important, during this contest the standard features of modern political campaigns were on display: two competitive parties, both organized on a national basis, used popular techniques to appeal to the hoi polloi, stimulating voter turnout to exceed 50 percent. In this race the Whigs expanded the Jacksonians' arsenal of electioneering tactics, all of which subsequent political campaigns adopted: barbecues, torchlight parades, and mass meetings. These events often attracted

A Whig campaign flag bears one of the symbols of Harrison's campaign.

thousands of spectators. The Whigs used symbols, songs, and slogans such as "Tippecanoe and Tyler, Too." Liquor was a good way to win voter loyalty, and a Philadelphia distiller named Edmund Booz marketed hard liquor in bottles shaped like log cabins, enabling "booze" to enter the American lexicon as a word for liquor. These tactics allowed the Whigs to eviscerate substantive issues from the campaign and replace them with symbols and imagery.

Voter participation in the election was astounding. More than 80 percent of eligible voters cast ballots, making this the election with the heaviest voter turnout in American history. It was also the first race in which the two major candidates each won more than one million votes.

In the end, the combination of a sluggish economy and an exuberant Whig campaign proved too much for Van Buren, who won only 7 states to Harrison's 19. Van Buren even lost his native New York, and won only one state in New England: New Hampshire. Van Buren's only bright spots were in the South, where he won Virginia, Alabama, Arkansas, and Missouri—all of which he had won in 1836—and South Carolina, which had refused to support him four years earlier. Harrison coasted to an easy victory in the electoral college, with 234 votes versus 60 for Van Buren. The popular vote totals were much closer, with Harrison winning by 150,000 out of 2.4 million votes. The Whig Party also captured both houses of Congress.

The Whigs had capitalized on the Jacksonian Democrats' campaign techniques, so much so that the *Democratic Review* ruefully noted, "We have taught them how to conquer us." But the Whig victory was short-lived. On March 4, 1841, the 68-year-old Harrison was inaugurated. In the bitter winter cold of Washington he stood with neither coat nor hat and delivered the longest presidential inaugural address in history, lasting more than two hours. Afterward he fell ill with pneumonia, and he died on April 4, 1841. He had served exactly one month as president, the shortest tenure ever.

John Tyler 1790–1862 The Whig Party ousted Tyler, a former Democrat, while he was president because he renounced its principles and vetoed its legislation. Tyler's peripatetic politics later included election to the Confederate Congress.

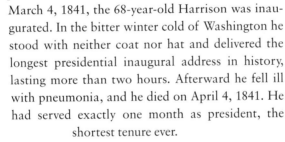

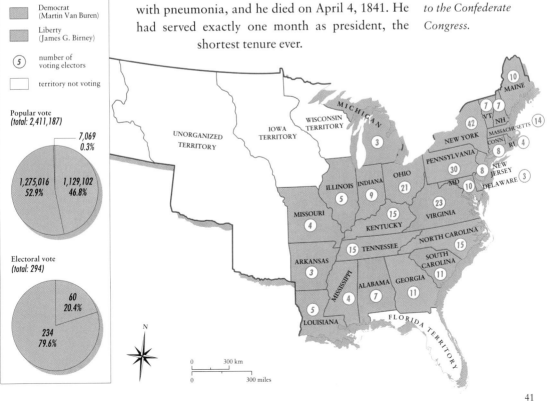

Presidential elections, 1840

- Whig (William H. Harrison)
- Democrat (Martin Van Buren)
- Liberty (James G. Birney)
- ⑤ number of voting electors
- territory not voting

Popular vote (total: 2,411,187)
7,069 0.3%
1,275,016 52.9%
1,129,102 46.8%

Electoral vote (total: 294)
60 20.4%
234 79.6%

The Election of 1844

*James K. Polk
1795–1849
Democrats promoted
Polk, an expansionist,
with the slogan "Fifty-
four Forty or Fight,"
demanding that the
U.S. occupy the
Oregon territory up to
that latitude. Once
president, Polk
compromised,
accepting the 49th
parallel.*

John Tyler became the first vice president ever to succeed a fallen president. For the Whigs, Tyler's rise to power only compounded the tragedy of William Henry Harrison's death. Outward appearances gave the impression that Tyler was easygoing, but beneath the surface lay a complete inability to compromise. Tyler, deeply suspicious of federal power and a rigid, unyielding advocate of states' rights, rejected key Whig proposals for federal aid for internal improvements and a new Bank of the United States. After Tyler's second Bank veto, Henry Clay, his most conspicuous opponent on Capitol Hill, resigned his Senate seat in March 1842 to make another run for the White House.

While the election of 1840 had focused on the depressed economy, in 1844 the key issue was continental expansion, especially the annexation of Texas. Thousands of Americans poured westward to create new lives for themselves and to fulfill the national ambition to own the continent. Texas, an independent republic since its successful rebellion against Mexico in 1836, was a prime target of expansionists. However, inextricably intertwined with the acquisition of new territory was the thorny problem of slavery: would any new states allow slavery or prohibit it?

Since the Whigs had literally banished Tyler from their party and since the Democrats regarded him as an apostate as well, he became a man without a political party. In 1844 neither side selected him as its nominee. As the campaign approached, the front-runners for each party were clear: Henry Clay for the Whigs, and Martin Van Buren for the Democrats. Neither man was enthusiastic about acquiring Texas (both feared a war with Mexico would result), so after conferring privately with each other, both tried to neutralize Texas as an issue by issuing independent statements declaring their opposition to annexation.

Expansionist sentiment was stronger among Democrats than among Whigs, and southern Democrats in particular wanted the U.S. to acquire Texas so as to gain more cotton-growing land as well as another slave state. To them, Van Buren's stand was unacceptable. When the party held its convention in Baltimore on May 27, the Democrats instead nominated James K. Polk, a Tennessee slaveholder and ardent expansionist. George Dallas of Pennsylvania, another expansionist, became his running mate.

Polk was a "dark horse," a candidate who emerged out of relative obscurity to beat out the rest of the pack, the first ever to win the nomination of a major national party. (The nomination of a dark horse was possible during an era before state primaries, when national conventions sometimes met without a clear idea of a favored nominee.) After word of Polk's nomination spread by means of a new invention, the telegraph, the Whigs poked fun at Polk's relative anonymity with the campaign slogan, "Who is James K. Polk?" Yet Polk was more experienced than the slogan suggested. A successful Tennessee lawyer, he had been a congressman for

14 years, four of them as House Speaker, and was elected governor of Tennessee in 1839. Just 49 years old and nicknamed "Young Hickory," Polk was a loyal follower of Andrew Jackson, who strongly supported his candidacy. Most important, Polk advocated expansion, and the Democratic platform called for the "reannexation" of Texas, implying that the United States would be reclaiming what rightfully belonged to it.

The Whigs nominated their aging leader, the 67-year-old Clay, with Theodore Freylinghuysen of New Jersey, the mayor of Newark, as his running mate. With Clay, one of the country's most eminent politicians, the Whigs looked forward to an easy victory over the relatively obscure James Polk.

Paradoxically, Clay was a slave owner who disapproved of slavery. The ambiguity of his position was reflected in his stand on Texas annexation. He recognized that the national sentiment favored expansion, especially in the South, where Whigs wanted him to declare all-out in favor of Texas annexation. Clay decided to modify his earlier position, stating that he would support expansion under the right circumstances. Although he was shilly-shallying, Clay believed that he could retain his antislavery support in the North while attracting new support among southern expansionists. He badly miscalculated. His waffling failed to win him new adherents in the South, while disgusted northern Whigs defected and cast their lot with the abolitionist Liberty Party, the only party to take a firm stand against slavery.

Ultimately, it may have been the presence of this third political party that propelled Polk to victory in a tight race. James G. Birney of New York, a former Kentucky slaveholder turned abolitionist, had run four years earlier as the candidate of the Liberty Party. Amid the hoopla of the 1840 campaign he had attracted little attention and won only 7000 votes. In 1844 Birney tried again and managed a more impressive showing with 62,000 votes. Birney's strength in New York State was especially significant; there he polled almost 16,000 votes, winning ballots from antislavery voters who were disgusted by Clay's equivocation on annexation. Clay consequently lost the state and its 36 electoral votes; had he received them he would have won with electoral votes. The presence of the Liberty Party plus the strength that Clay had inadvertently given it by fudging the Texas issue may have cost him the presidency in his third and final run for the White House. Abraham Lincoln, an Illinois Whig congressman who regarded Clay as a political role model and who had campaigned hard for him, lamented, "If the Whig abolitionists of New York had voted with us ... Mr. Clay would now be president."

Polk's triumph in popular votes was narrow: he won by a margin of only 38,000 of the 2.7 million ballots cast. Both candidates showed even

"This is the house that Polk built." This cartoon from 1846 reflects on president Polk's difficult position in balancing the many issues facing his administration.

strength in all regions of the country (Clay even managed to beat Polk in his home state of Tennessee).

The election showed that the two major parties were competitive in national political power (although the Democratic organization was superior at the local level). Beginning with this election, no candidate was able to win a majority of the popular vote until the election of 1864. Polk's victory also showed the strength of expansionist sentiment. Although far less distinguished than Clay, Polk had beaten his celebrated opponent because he favored expansion.

Illustration of Polk's inauguration from the Illustrated London News, *1845*

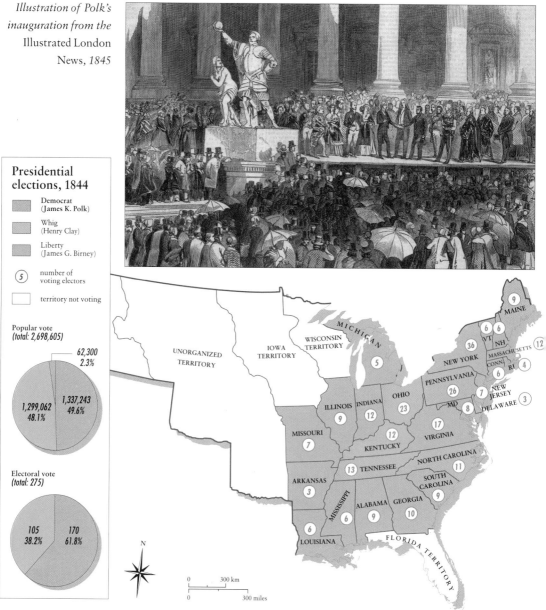

Presidential elections, 1844

- Democrat (James K. Polk)
- Whig (Henry Clay)
- Liberty (James G. Birney)
- (5) number of voting electors
- territory not voting

Popular vote (total: 2,698,605)

- 62,300 / 2.3%
- 1,337,243 / 49.6%
- 1,299,062 / 48.1%

Electoral vote (total: 275)

- 105 / 38.2%
- 170 / 61.8%

UNORGANIZED TERRITORY

IOWA TERRITORY

WISCONSIN TERRITORY

MICHIGAN (5)

MAINE (9)

VT (6)

NH (6)

NEW YORK (36)

MASSACHUSETTS (12)

CONN. (6)

RI (4)

PENNSYLVANIA (26)

NEW JERSEY (7)

DELAWARE (3)

MD (8)

ILLINOIS (9)

INDIANA (12)

OHIO (23)

MISSOURI (7)

KENTUCKY (12)

VIRGINIA (17)

TENNESSEE (13)

NORTH CAROLINA (11)

ARKANSAS (3)

SOUTH CAROLINA (9)

MISSISSIPPI (6)

ALABAMA (9)

GEORGIA (10)

LOUISIANA (6)

FLORIDA TERRITORY

N

0   300 km
0   300 miles

The Election of 1848

During the Mexican-American War, the United States won a decisive victory and in 1848, Mexico ceded California and New Mexico, increasing America's territory by 20 percent. But not all Americans applauded the gains. Abolitionists denounced the war as a plot to extend the country's slave territory. The question of whether slavery should be allowed in the federal territories threatened to imperil national unity, so in the election of 1848 both major parties trod softly around the issue, preferring the safety of silence.

Although Polk lacked charisma, a sense of humor, and broad popularity, he was an efficient chief executive. But to preserve party unity, he had pledged not to run for a second term. (A hard-driven, furious worker throughout his presidency, Polk died just three months after leaving office.) The Democrats turned to the bland Senator Lewis Cass of Michigan. Cass had previously served as territorial governor of Michigan and was the first Democratic nominee from the Northwest. He had also been a foremost proponent of popular sovereignty, which held that the people of a territory, expressing their will through their territorial legislature, would decide whether the territory should permit slavery. General William Butler of Kentucky, a veteran of the War of 1812, was selected as Cass's running mate.

Zachary Taylor 1784–1850 Taylor's election marked the first time that the U.S. had a single national Election Day, taking place on Tuesday, 7 November.

The Whigs repaired to the same strategy that had brought victory for them in 1840 by nominating a military man, General Zachary Taylor of Louisiana, hero of the Mexican-American War. One of Taylor's most celebrated achievements came in February 1847 at the Battle of Buena Vista where, despite being outnumbered, he had repulsed General Santa Anna and his troops. Although not a brilliant general, Taylor retained a common touch that enhanced his popularity among troops, who affectionately called him "Old Rough and Ready."

All his life Taylor had been a professional soldier. He had never held public office, was ignorant of the issues, and had never even voted before. For the Whigs, the apolitical Taylor was the ideal candidate. The Whigs gave him no platform to run on, so as to keep him above political controversy. Moreover, since Taylor was a slaveholder from a southern state (he owned three hundred slaves), his presence on the ticket would reassure southern Whigs who were uneasy with the antislavery Whigs of the North. The Whig ticket found geographical balance with a running mate from New York, Millard Fillmore, the comptroller for that state who had begun his political career in the Anti-Masonic Party, had served as a New York congressman, and had never opposed slavery.

Antislavery elements in both parties were unhappy with their respective nominees. Northern antislavery Democrats were known as "Barnburners" because they would burn down the barn (the Democratic Party) to get rid of the rats (advocates of slavery). The Barnburners opposed Cass's concept of popular sovereignty because it allowed the extension of slavery into the new territories. Meanwhile, antislavery "Conscience" Whigs resented Taylor because he owned slaves. These two groups combined with Liberty Party members to form a new third party, the Free Soil Party, and presented former president Martin Van Buren as their candidate, with Charles Francis Adams of Massachusetts as his running mate. Hunger

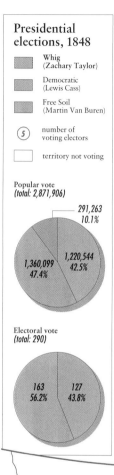

Presidential elections, 1848

Whig
(Zachary Taylor)

Democratic
(Lewis Cass)

Free Soil
(Martin Van Buren)

(5) number of voting electors

territory not voting

Popular vote
(total: 2,871,906)

291,263
10.1%

1,360,099
47.4%

1,220,544
42.5%

Electoral vote
(total: 290)

163
56.2%

127
43.8%

for vengeance, rather than antislavery convictions, was probably the chief factor that led Van Buren to accept the nomination; he relished the opportunity to strike back at the southern Democrats who had denied him the nomination four years earlier. Adams's antislavery credentials were strong, and were bolstered by his pedigree. He was the son of John Quincy Adams, who had died in 1848 after 17 distinguished postpresidential years in the House as a champion of the abolitionist cause.

The Free Soil Party drew members of the now-defunct Liberty Party and was the only contender in 1848 that took a clear stand on slavery: it was unalterably opposed to extending slavery into federal territories. (In order to attract more voters into its already diverse coalition, the Free Soil Party advocated only the containment of slavery, rather than its abolition.) Indicative of its stance was the slogan "Free Soil, Free Speech, Free Labor, Free Men." The party represented the first stage in the breakup of the existing party system and was a precursor of the Republican Party.

As in 1844, the third party again played a decisive role in the election. Van Buren registered an impressive showing, polling 10 percent of the national vote. Although he won no states outright, he placed second behind Taylor in Massachusetts, Vermont, and his native New York. By forcing Cass into third place in those states, Van Buren helped to deny the Democrats a victory. As it was, both Taylor and Cass won the same number of states, 15. Cass fared well in his native Northwest, where Whigs had performed poorly since their 1836 genesis as a party. Taylor ran much stronger in the southern states than Clay had four years earlier. He won a slim plurality in popular votes nationwide, 47.4 percent to 42.5 percent, and his 36-point lead in the electoral college was relatively narrow. For the Union the nature of his victory seemed to augur well, because his triumph cut across sectional lines and appeared national in character, since he had won 9 free states and 6 slave states (of the 30 states in the Union, 15 were slave and 15 were free).

But the second Whig ever elected president had an early end to his tenure, just like his Whig predecessor, William Henry Harrison. On July 4, 1850, in the sweltering summer heat of Washington, Taylor was stricken with gastroenteritis at a ceremony, and he died five days later.

UNORGANIZED
TERRITORY

MICHIGAN

WISCONSIN
4

5

MAINE
9

VT
6
NH
6

MASSACHUSETTS
12

CONN
6
RI
4

NEW YORK
36

PENNSYLVANIA
26

NEW JERSEY
7

MD
8

DELAWARE
3

IOWA
4

ILLINOIS
9

INDIANA
12

OHIO
23

MISSOURI
7

KENTUCKY
12

VIRGINIA
17

CALIFORNIA

ARKANSAS
3

TENNESSEE
13

NORTH CAROLINA
11

SOUTH CAROLINA
9

MISSISSIPPI

ALABAMA
9

GEORGIA
10

TEXAS
4

LOUISIANA
6

FLORIDA
3

N

0   300 km

0   300 miles

The Election of 1852

In 1850, the country weathered a political storm over the expansion of slavery when Congress passed the Compromise of 1850. By 1852, both parties were eager to prevent slavery from destroying them or the Union. Thus they played it safe, and the election was dull, with few major issues to debate and widespread voter apathy. The two major candidates, both uninspiring, contributed to voter disenchantment.

At the Democratic convention four men vied for the nomination: James Buchanan, Lewis Cass, Stephen Douglas, and William Marcy. The Democrats went through 49 arduous ballots and finally selected a dark horse, Franklin Pierce, a lawyer from Concord, New Hampshire. A brigadier general during the Mexican-American War, Pierce was a recovered alcoholic who had served as both a congressman and a senator from the Granite State. His wife opposed his candidacy because she feared that once in public office again, he would succumb to the bottle. Yet he seemed a promising find for the Democrats. Young and handsome, Pierce was an inoffensive compromise figure who could appeal to both sections of the country because he was a "doughface," a northerner with southern sympathies. The Democrats balanced Pierce with a running mate from Alabama, Senator William King.

Franklin Pierce 1804–1869 By signing the Kansas-Nebraska Act in 1854, Pierce did irreparable political damage to himself, and two years later he failed to win renomination from his party.

Luckily for Pierce, the Democrats were more united than in 1848. Party brethren who had joined the Free Soilers in 1848 returned to the fold; indeed, even the 1848 Free Soil candidate, Martin Van Buren, supported Pierce. New Irish and German voters also bolstered the party's strength, and the Democrats published pamphlets in foreign languages to appeal to immigrants. The Democrats also formed local "Granite Clubs" and held mass meetings to rally support for Pierce, whom they called "Young Hickory of the Granite Hills," to evoke the still-popular Jacksonian imagery. Although the Whigs also tried to woo the immigrant vote and held local meetings, the Democrats were more organized and effective in these tactics.

The Whigs, in fact, were disintegrating. Their most venerable statesmen, Henry Clay and Daniel Webster, died in 1852, leaving the party without effective national leadership. More ominously, the Whigs' sectional split widened. The northern Conscience Whigs were troubled by proslavery southerners in the party, while southern Cotton Whigs so distrusted northern antislavery Whigs that some of them defected to the Democratic Party. The party's nomination of Winfield Scott of Virginia, with Secretary of the Navy William Graham of New York as his running mate, made southern Whigs even more uneasy, for they regarded Scott and Graham as mere hacks for the most influential Whig, antislavery Senator William Seward of New York. Scott, a general, had led a brilliant campaign that culminated in the successful capture of Mexico City during the Mexican-American War. Standing 6 feet 5 inches tall, Scott struck an imposing figure, but his political skills were feeble, which only added to the lukewarm feelings that many Whigs had for his candidacy.

Whig dissension and Democratic unity produced a smashing victory for Pierce, who at 48 became the youngest man ever elected president. Pierce's victory was especially notable because it was national in character, attracting votes from both the North and South. In terms of states won and lost, Scott suffered the worst defeat ever for the Whig Party, taking only four: Massachusetts, Vermont, Kentucky, and Tennessee. The Free Soil Party candidate, Senator John Hale of New Hampshire, failed to win a single state and won an even smaller percentage of popular votes than Van Buren had in the previous election, a result that reflected a nationwide desire for calm instead of sectional strife. But Pierce's victory was less decisive when measured by popular votes. He had failed to win a majority and had garnered only 45,000 more votes than the combined totals of Scott and Hale.

The Whigs were moribund, and this humiliating defeat marked the last election in which they were a national force. With their passing and with increasing sectional strife, the Democratic Party remained the last remaining political cord binding the two sections of the country together.

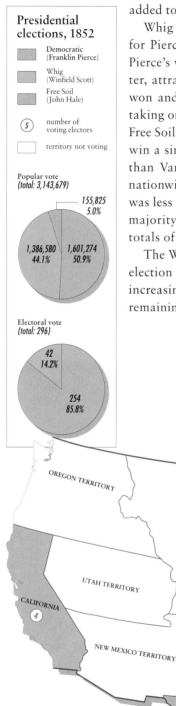

Presidential elections, 1852

- Democratic (Franklin Pierce)
- Whig (Winfield Scott)
- Free Soil (John Hale)
- ⑤ number of voting electors
- territory not voting

Popular vote
(total: 3,143,679)

155,825
5.0%

1,386,580
44.1%

1,601,274
50.9%

Electoral vote
(total: 296)

42
14.2%

254
85.8%

The Election of 1856

The demise of the Whigs was hastened by one of the most misbegotten pieces of legislation in American history, the Kansas-Nebraska Act of 1854. Senator Stephen Douglas of Illinois, seeking to organize a huge territory west of his state, presented a bill that created two territories, Kansas and Nebraska. In order to win southern support, Douglas's bill allowed popular sovereignty to decide the fate of slavery in these new territories, and repealed the section of the Missouri Compromise that prohibited slavery above the 36° 30' line.

Northerners were infuriated. By opening the possibility of slavery in an area where it had been prohibited since 1820, the Kansas-Nebraska Act vitiated a compromise that had maintained sectional peace for a generation. The act seemed solid proof that southerners were conspiring to extend slavery. It also split the Whig Party. Northern Conscience Whigs opposed it, while southern Cotton Whigs supported it, and many of the latter were becoming Democrats. As southerners came to dominate the Democratic Party, northern Democrats abandoned it in protest. The Kansas-Nebraska Act thus left many northern Whigs and northern Democrats politically adrift, searching for a new political identity.

James Buchanan 1791–1868 Buchanan, who pledged to serve only one term, did little to prevent the country's drift toward civil war. By 1860 he was relieved that his presidency was ending, and supported vice president John Breckinridge as his successor.

Against this backdrop of increasing sectional tensions, the election of 1856 witnessed the emergence of two new political parties. One was the American Party. During the 1840s, 1.7 million immigrants streamed into the country, most notably Irish, who fled their native land to escape the devastating potato famine. The presence of these new arrivals disturbed many Americans and aroused nativist passions and fears that often approached hysteria. The nativists formed the American Party, which by 1853 had become second-largest political party and seemed likely to step into the breach left when the Whigs collapsed. Promulgating the slogan "Americans should rule America," the American Party especially sought to curtail the voting privileges of immigrants to reduce their political influence. The party nominated former president Millard Fillmore as its candidate.

The second new party that appeared in the 1856 election, the Republican Party, was to prove far more important and enduring. In the wake of the Kansas-Nebraska Act, its critics from both parties—known as anti-Nebraska Democrats and anti-Nebraska Whigs—staged protests and held meetings throughout the North, especially in the states of the Northwest. (Historians often pinpoint the founding of the new party to one anti-Nebraska meeting held on March 1, 1854, in Ripon, Wisconsin, while the name "Republican" came from a July meeting at Jackson, Michigan.) As a party, the Republicans at first focused on one issue, the containment of slavery. They accepted slavery where it existed in the South but wanted to prevent its expansion into Western territories. Allowing slavery into the territories, Republicans feared, would ruin the chances for free men there to advance economically and socially through free labor. While the party was not an abolitionist party (that is, it was not dedicated to the outright elimination of slavery), most abolitionists began to vote Republican. Moreover, the party wisely widened its appeal by embracing additional issues, especially federal support for manufacturing and internal improvements. Thus the Republican Party comprised mostly former Whigs and Free Soil Party members, but it also absorbed northern antislavery Democrats as well

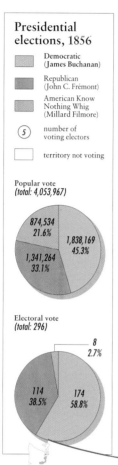

Presidential elections, 1856

Democratic (James Buchanan)

Republican (John C. Frémont)

American Know Nothing Whig (Millard Filmore)

⑤ number of voting electors

☐ territory not voting

Popular vote (total: 4,053,967)

874,534
21.6%

1,838,169
45.3%

1,341,264
33.1%

Electoral vote (total: 296)

8
2.7%

114
38.5%

174
58.8%

as the northern adherents of the American Party. Above all, the Republicans were an exclusively northern party, but this would suffice. If their candidate captured the northern states, populous and rich in electoral votes, he would take 176 electoral votes, 27 more than was needed to win. The South had only 120 electoral votes.

The Republicans held their first-ever national convention in Philadelphia. They, too, selected a war hero with little political experience and obscure views on the controversial issues of the day. Their nominee, John C. Frémont of Missouri, was a brash, adventurous soldier celebrated for exploring and mapping the West (his nickname was "The Pathfinder") and for helping to win California early in the Mexican-American War. Frémont was young—43 years old—and his exposure to political office was a brief stint as a U.S. senator from California. His running mate was Senator William Dayton of New Jersey, who had opposed the Compromise of 1850. The defining plank of the Republican platform was the party's opposition to the extension of slavery, and the party's slogan in the election was "Free Soil, Free Speech, and Frémont." Like the party he represented, Frémont exuded youthfulness and energy.

The Democrats met in Cincinnati. Largely because of the Kansas-Nebraska Act, control of the Democratic Party had shifted to the South. Pierce indulged the unrealistic hope that he could run again, but he had been a feckless president, and his approval of the Kansas-Nebraska Act irreparably damaged him. The party settled on James Buchanan of Pennsylvania, who had a reputation as a doughface. Buchanan was a lifelong bachelor and a man of mediocre talents. He had extensive political experience, including service as a U.S. congressman, senator, and secretary of state under James Polk, but his preeminent qualification for winning the nomination was that he had been out of the country in 1854, serving as American minister to Great Britain, and thus had kept clean of the mess surrounding the Kansas-Nebraska Act. Buchanan's running mate was a southerner, John Breckinridge of Kentucky, a former congressman just 35 years old.

The Republicans ran a more aggressive, energetic campaign than the Democrats did, and they were quick to contrast their youthful nominee with the 63-year-old Buchanan. Chanting "We shall overcome" and promising to prevail over their more established political opponents, the Republicans held rallies, picnics, and torchlight parades. They pressed into service their most celebrated party members: Senators Salmon Chase and Charles Sumner and *New York Tribune* founder Horace Greeley all gave speeches for Frémont.

In addition to dismissing Frémont as young and inexperienced, Democrats condemned the Republicans as a band of radicals, and some Democratic newspapers predicted that the Union would dissolve if the Republicans won the election. Many southerners took this prophecy to heart. Buchanan remarked, "This race ought to be run on the question of Union or disunion." Indeed, Republican remarks did nothing to dispel this notion, as some demanded "the speedy, peaceful and equitable dissolution of the existing union."

Buchanan had a lock on the South. The battleground was in the North, and campaigners concentrated on a handful of swing states that would determine the election: Illinois, Indiana, Maryland, New Jersey, and Pennsylvania. Buchanan won all of these states except Maryland and managed a narrow victory. But he won only 45 percent of the popular vote nationwide. Even though it had been weakened by northern defections after the Kansas-Nebraska Act, the Democratic Party was still the strongest political party in the nation.

With this election, America's third party system had arrived. Unlike the two earlier party systems, this one was divided along sectional lines. In the North, the Republican Party's showing was impressive, but in the South the Republicans won nothing. Frémont's name did not even appear on the ballot in 11 southern states, yet he almost won the election. Of the 16 free states, Frémont won 11; if he had won the key swing states of Pennsylvania and Illinois, he would have had enough electoral votes to be president. For the South, this was a startling, insulting possibility, especially for a region that had furnished so many presidents during the country's first half-century. For a party that was less than two years old and drew its strength entirely from the North, the Republican Party's national performance struck fear in white southern hearts.

The American Party was especially strong in the border states, and former President Fillmore's victory in Maryland gave him 8 electoral votes, marking the first time a third-party candidate had ever won electoral votes. With 21.6 percent of the popular vote, the former president achieved the best showing of any third-party candidate in the nineteenth century. But the American Party faded quickly after the 1856 election. It lacked professional leadership, and its secrecy aroused suspicions that undermined its credibility.

The country also grew more absorbed with the extension or containment of slavery. Unlike the American Party, the new Republican Party was stocked with political veterans, and it proposed to gain control of the presidency and then impose decisions adverse to slavery upon the South. With such a party rapidly gaining strength in the North, the South's future in the Union rested upon the outcome of the next presidential election.

The Election of 1860

Abraham Lincoln
1809–1865
One of the most
celebrated Lincoln
images in the 1860
campaign was that of
"The Rail Candidate
for President," which
emphasized how the
hard physical labor of
rail-splitting had
enabled Lincoln to rise
from humble origins.

James Buchanan was a weak, indecisive president who did little to prevent the drift toward civil war. The Supreme Court contributed to the sectional crisis with its decision in *Dred Scott* v. *Sanford* (1857), which incensed northerners by declaring the Missouri Compromise unconstitutional and guaranteeing that the Constitution protected the right to own slaves. By permitting slavery in the territories unconditionally, the decision destroyed the principle of popular sovereignty: a territory had no constitutional right to prohibit slavery. The election of 1860 brought all the conflicting emotions to a terrible climax.

In April 1860 the Democratic Party met in Charleston, South Carolina. The party had been traumatized by an open split between its two leading figures, President Buchanan and Senator Stephen Douglas. The main issue was the admission of Kansas, which had adopted a proslavery constitution in a tainted vote. Buchanan favored admitting Kansas, while Douglas opposed it. Compounding the weakened condition of the party was the meeting site of the convention. South Carolina stood out as one of the most radical proslavery states in the Union. Within the Democratic Party the two sections, North and South, immediately clashed. The southern delegates wanted a strong proslavery platform, guaranteeing federal protection for slavery, while the northern delegates supported popular sovereignty, which the Dred Scott decision had invalidated. The convention adopted a platform favoring the latter, and the southern delegates walked out. The remaining northern delegates tried to nominate their favorite son, Stephen Douglas, but, with the southern delegates absent, they lacked the requisite two-thirds majority and adjourned.

The party met again in Baltimore in June, but the two sides immediately locked horns, and the southern delegates again left. The northern wing of the party remained in Baltimore and nominated Douglas on a platform of popular sovereignty, with Herschel Johnson, the former governor of Georgia, as his running mate. The southern delegates returned to Charleston, where they adopted a platform calling for federal protection of slavery in the territories and named the current vice president, John Breckinridge of Kentucky, as their presidential candidate. The delegates picked Senator Joseph Lane of Oregon to run with him. The 39-year-old Breckinridge had the backing not only of President Buchanan but also of former presidents John Tyler and Franklin Pierce. The Democratic Party—the only national party in 1860—had cleaved itself into sections, dashing one of the last hopes for the Union to remain intact.

Earlier, in May, the Republican Party had met in Chicago. The choice of this midwestern city as a host was of great moment, for it reflected the country's growing emphasis on westward expansion. The party assumed a moderate tone in its platform so as to broaden its appeal and counteract Democratic charges that it was a group of antislavery radicals. Rather than advocating abolition, the Republicans opposed the extension of slavery into the territories, allowing slavery to exist where it currently did. In order to attract former Whigs, the party also endorsed the Whig program of nationalistic economic development, supporting measures such as a high tariff (especially attractive to Pennsylvania, a swing state that the Republicans had lost in 1856), a homestead act giving free land to settlers in exchange for their promise to farm it, and internal improvements such as federal help for a transcontinental railroad. The most eminent Republican was Senator William Seward of New York, and his supporters were so sure of his nomination that they erected a cannon in front of his home in Auburn, New York, to be fired when news came of his victory. But the Republicans were wary of nominating Seward because his unyielding antislavery views were too well known and had created many enemies. Moreover, he had openly opposed the nativists, a group that the Republicans had to win over, especially in Pennsylvania.

Abraham Lincoln emerged as the leading challenger to Seward. Though he had served only one term in the House (1847–49), he had become the most eminent lawyer in Illinois, well known for his eloquent yet humorous and self-effacing addresses to jurors. In 1858, he attracted national attention when he ran unsuccessfully for Stephen Douglas's Senate seat. That contest featured seven debates between the two candidates, held in cities throughout Illinois. To everyone's surprise, the self-educated, small-town lawyer performed skillfully against the energetic, intimidating, and nationally renowned senator. The debates gave Lincoln a national name, yet he was still obscure enough not to have cultivated the enemies that Seward had. Lincoln deprecated the nativists, but unlike Seward, he had not been vocal. All the more attractive was Lincoln's moderation on the issue of slavery; although he personally despised the institution, he was no abolitionist. He was also a walking advertisement for the Republican Party's ideal of free labor. His rise from humble roots was inspirational and demonstrated the virtues of free labor, mobility, and opportunity—as opposed to the degradation by slavery—in a fluid American society.

Lincoln's drive for the nomination was also aided by the site of the party convention, in his home state of Illinois, a battleground state that the Republicans had lost in 1856. Lincoln's floor managers at the convention printed extra admission tickets to pack the meeting place with his supporters and, much to his chagrin, haggled for his nomination, promising cabinet posts in exchange for support. Seward led Lincoln on the first ballot; Lincoln almost pulled even on the second and won the nomination on the third. Lincoln's running mate was Senator Hannibal Hamlin of Maine, a former Democrat who had abandoned that party because of its failure to oppose the spread of slavery.

A fourth political party—the Constitutional Union—entered the fray, making the field the most crowded since 1836 and illustrating the instability of the political system in 1860. Comprising former Whigs from the South as well as former American Party members from the border states, the Constitutional Union Party expressed concern over the prospect of secession and disunion. Meeting in Baltimore, it settled on John Bell of Tennessee, a former Whig and former House Speaker. The party's platform ignored the slavery question and instead only pledged support for the Constitution and the Union.

The 1860 election saw the Republican Party strategy for winning the presidency come to fruition. In reality, the election was composed of two contests. Lincoln and Douglas contended in the North, where Breckinridge and Bell had no hope. In the South, where Douglas had only a small following and where Lincoln's name did not even appear on the ballot in 10 states, it was Breckinridge versus Bell. Lincoln won 18 states in the North, capturing every one except New Jersey, where he won 4 of that

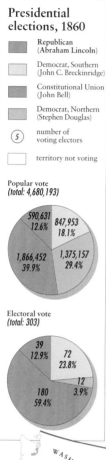

Presidential elections, 1860

- Republican (Abraham Lincoln)
- Democrat, Southern (John C. Breckinridge)
- Constitutional Union (John Bell)
- Democrat, Northern (Stephen Douglas)
- (5) number of voting electors
- territory not voting

Popular vote
(total: 4,680,193)

- 590,631 — 12.6%
- 847,953 — 18.1%
- 1,866,452 — 39.9%
- 1,375,157 — 29.4%

Electoral vote
(total: 303)

- 39 — 12.9%
- 72 — 23.8%
- 180 — 59.4%
- 12 — 3.9%

state's 7 electoral votes. Significantly, Lincoln won the critical swing states of Illinois, Indiana, and Pennsylvania, all of which John Frémont had lost four years earlier. Breckinridge easily won every state in the Deep South, plus 2 border states, Delaware and Maryland. Bell won 3 states in the Upper South, Virginia, Kentucky, and Tennessee. Ironically, Douglas—by far the best-known of the four candidates—won only one state outright, Missouri, plus 3 of New Jersey's electoral votes. His failure to win any states in the North came despite an energetic campaign in which Douglas became the first presidential candidate to crisscross the nation personally. Lincoln bowed to political tradition and remained at home throughout the campaign, keeping silent on the explosive issues of the day.

Lincoln was running against the vice president, a former House Speaker, and the most eminent senator in the country. Though Lincoln had the slimmest political resumé of the four candidates, he won the election. He gained a clear majority in the electoral college, 180 versus 123 for all of his opponents combined (157 votes were needed to win), and he won a plurality of popular votes. But Lincoln would be a minority president. He had garnered only 39.9 percent of the popular vote, and he had been elected without any support from the South. Only John Quincy Adams in 1824 had been elected with a smaller percentage of the popular vote (30.5 percent). Lincoln's mandate was one of the weakest ever.

Now that Lincoln was president-elect, what little remained of southerners' sense of security was shattered. For South Carolina, Lincoln's election was the last straw. On December 20, 1860, the state seceded. Within the next month and a half, 6 more southern states joined the Palmetto State, and the 7 seceded states formed the Confederate States of America. History will always remember the election of 1860 as the one that triggered secession and hence civil war.

The Election of 1864

The first two years of the Civil War brought little good news for the North. In the East, the Union suffered stalemate and setback, beginning with the first major clash, the Battle of Bull Run in July 1861, where northern troops panicked and retreated. The Union's only bright spots were in the war's western theater, where Union forces captured New Orleans and brought large sections of the Mississippi River under their control. On January 1, 1863, President Abraham Lincoln made history by signing the Emancipation Proclamation, which freed all the slaves in rebelling states and endowed the Union cause with increased fervor. During the Battle of Gettysburg in July 1863, the North finally achieved a major victory in the East. In 1864, Union forces in the East were stalemated again, as General Ulysses S. Grant's troops were locked in a long siege of Petersburg, Virginia.

Doubts flourished over the upcoming presidential contest. The doubts were not just about who would win, but also whether the election would take place at all. During the middle of a wrenching war, no government enjoys the prospect of an election, for the chance of being unseated is great. So it was for the Lincoln administration, which for much of the year expected to lose the election. Nonetheless, when faced with suggestions to postpone the election until the war was over, Lincoln refused. "We cannot have free government without elections; and if rebellion could force us to forgo, or postpone a national election, it might fairly claim to have already conquered and ruined us," he declared.

The Democrats hoped to capitalize on the war weariness of the North to turn Lincoln out of office, but their party was still badly divided. Some Democrats, the so-called War Democrats, supported the Union war effort, while many others, called Peace Democrats or "Copperheads," opposed it. The Democrats, holding their national convention in Chicago for the first time, adopted a Copperhead platform that criticized the Lincoln administration's handling of the war and called for a cease-fire and immediate negotiations with the South.

The Democrats nominated General George McClellan of New Jersey, the former commander of the Army of the Potomac, with George Pendleton, a congressman from Ohio, as his running mate. A self-assured, brash officer, McClellan assumed command of the Army of the Potomac in late 1861 but showed little inclination for action. He chronically postponed attacking the Confederate army, overestimating the enemy's troop strength and demanding more reinforcements from Washington, which he bitterly blamed for his own timidity. Lincoln, frustrated by what he called McClellan's "slows," removed him from command in July 1862 but out of desperation restored him later that month, dismissing him for good in November 1862. McClellan had often shown a brazen disrespect for his commander in chief, referring to Lincoln as "an idiot" and "a well-meaning baboon." By running for president, McClellan hoped to exact a measure of vengeance. (A Democratic saying in this campaign was "Old Abe Removed McClellan, We'll Remove Old Abe.")

Lyrics from a Democratic Party campaign song, 1864

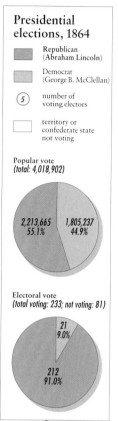

Presidential elections, 1864

Republican (Abraham Lincoln)

Democrat (George B. McClellan)

(5) number of voting electors

territory or confederate state not voting

Popular vote
(total: 4,018,902)

2,213,665 55.1%

1,805,237 44.9%

Electoral vote
(total voting: 233; not voting: 81)

21 9.0%

212 91.0%

In a move designed to placate War Democrats, McClellan backed away from the Democratic platform by declaring that the one and only immutable condition of an armistice with the South would be the restoration of the Union. McClellan was harshly critical of Lincoln's Emancipation Proclamation. He maintained that emancipation should not be a war goal, and Democrats played on racist sentiments in the North by charging that the tyrant leader "Abraham Africanus the First" favored intermarriage between blacks and whites, calling the Emancipation Proclamation the "Miscegenation Proclamation." Privately, to ensure their return to the Union, McClellan wanted to guarantee returning southern states their constitutional rights, including the right to slavery.

At the Republican convention in Baltimore, Lincoln secured his renomination and the delegates picked as his running mate Andrew Johnson. Johnson was not a Republican; he was a War Democrat who had been a U.S. senator from Tennessee and the only senator from a Confederate state to remain loyal to the Union. In 1862 Lincoln appointed him the military governor of Tennessee. Since 1861 the Republican Party had been known as the "National Union" party to emphasize its commitment to preserving the Union and to attract Unionist Democrats of the same stamp as Johnson. The party's platform demanded the South's unconditional surrender and also called for a constitutional amendment to end slavery.

Lincoln was in deep political trouble. Recent history boded ill for him, as no sitting president had won two terms since Andrew Jackson. The war had dragged on for three years, with appalling casualties and no immediate end in sight. Northern morale had sunk to a nadir, and many Americans doubted Lincoln's stewardship. Given the war's slaughter,

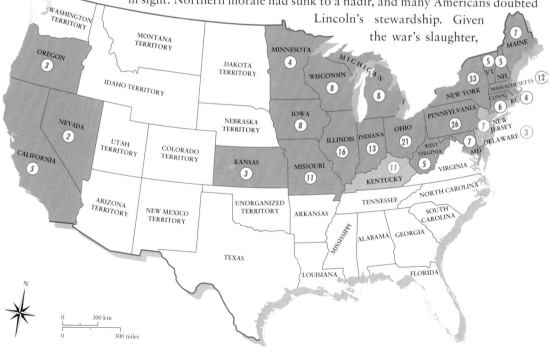

Democrats labeled him "Abe the Widow-maker," and even Republicans were ready to abandon him. He had scant support in Congress, and the Radical Republicans, a wing of the party that favored civil rights for blacks and harsh peace terms for the South, wanted to dump Lincoln and nominate instead his treasury secretary, Salmon Chase. In the summer of 1864, after having won the nomination, Lincoln dolefully predicted, "I'm going to be beaten, and unless some great changes take place, badly beaten." As historian James McPherson has written, "If the election had been held in August 1864 instead of November, [Lincoln] would have lost. He would have thus gone down in history as a loser, a failure unequal to the challenge of the greatest crisis in the American experience."

*Andrew Johnson
1808–1875
Although Johnson left
office in 1869 after a
tumultuous tenure as
president, in 1874 he
won election to the
Senate, but died only a
few months after his
term began.*

But late in the summer two smashing military successes caused a dramatic change of Lincoln's political prospects. On September 1, Union General William Tecumseh Sherman captured Atlanta, a crown city of the lower South, paving the way for his devastating "March to the Sea" to Savannah. General Philip Sheridan added to the carnage on southern soil by conducting a merciless campaign of total war through Virginia's Shenandoah Valley. Ulysses Grant's instructions to Sheridan were to transform the region into "a barren waste … so that crows flying over it … will have to carry their [supplies] with them." Sheridan inflicted utter destruction on a region that Confederate General Robert E. Lee was counting on to supply his troops.

The tide of the war was clearly turning in the Union's favor, and the victories of Sherman and Sheridan boosted northern morale enough to ensure Lincoln's reelection. Also helpful to Lincoln was the entry of Nevada, another free state, to the Union, plus the vote of Union soldiers, many of whom were granted temporary furloughs so that they could return home to cast ballots; estimates were that Lincoln won 80 percent of the soldier vote.

Only the northern states voted in the election of 1864. The 11 states that had seceded and proclaimed themselves a new nation did not participate. Lincoln won every state in the Union except for Kentucky, Delaware, and McClellan's home state of New Jersey. He crushed McClellan in the electoral college, 212 votes to 21. This time Lincoln won a comfortable majority of popular votes, 55 percent to McClellan's 45 percent. *Harper's Weekly* ran what became a famous cartoon showing the tall, lanky chief executive with unusually long legs. "Long Abraham Lincoln A Little Longer," the caption read.

One of the most important results of this election was that it paved the way for emancipation. The Emancipation Proclamation had no legal standing and did not apply to the rebelling states. Had McClellan won, he would have repudiated it. After winning reelection, Lincoln led the drive for a constitutional amendment outlawing slavery. He got to see Congress pass the amendment on January 31, 1865, but its ratification was completed in December, eight months after his death.

The Election of 1868

*Ulysses S. Grant
1822–1885
Grant, who had
once owned slaves,
benefited from the
support of newly
enfranchised African
Americans in the
South. As president,
he tried to protect
southern blacks by
opposing the Ku Klux
Klan.*

The Civil War came to a close on April 9, 1865, when Robert E. Lee surrendered to Ulysses S. Grant at Appomattox Court House in Virginia. Five days later Abraham Lincoln was assassinated. Vice President Andrew Johnson had succeeded Lincoln, and at first Republicans, who controlled both houses of Congress, expected an amiable relationship with the new president, even though he had been a Democrat. Instead, what followed was the most tumultuous struggle between a president and Congress in the nation's history, as the two sides immediately clashed over plans for readmitting the Confederate states to the Union. Johnson, an inveterate racist as well as a fervent states' rights advocate, opposed civil rights for the freed slaves, which the Radical Republicans sought. He stubbornly vetoed congressional Reconstruction bills, and for the first time in history Congress overrode presidential vetoes, and did so with astonishing regularity. Congress sought an opportunity to remove Johnson from office, and when he attempted to fire his secretary of war, Congress charged him with violating the Tenure of Office Act. In February 1868 the House impeached Johnson, making him the first of only two presidents ever to be impeached. In the Senate trial that followed, Johnson was acquitted by just one vote. He served out the balance of his term politically impotent, and the nation looked for new leadership as the election of 1868 approached.

Of all the northern heroes to emerge from the Civil War, Ulysses S. Grant was the most popular. Early in the war, when the Confederates were pummeling Union forces in the East, Grant provided some of the few bright spots for the Union with his 1862 victories in Tennessee. In 1864 Lincoln appointed Grant commander of the Union forces, and he led a successful campaign in Virginia that resulted in the fall of Richmond, the Confederate capital.

After the war Grant found himself in the curious position of being mentioned as a possible presidential contender. The general had no political experience and little interest in politics. He had voted only once before, in the 1856 election, when he cast his ballot for James Buchanan. But Grant was enjoying his postwar fame, and at the age of 46, he worried about fading into oblivion if he did not advance his career somehow. Moreover, he believed that he had a duty to begin a new role as a political leader. Grant gravitated toward the Republican Party, and in May 1868, just days after President Johnson's Senate trial ended, the former Democrat Grant accepted the Republican nomination for president, on a ticket with House Speaker Schuyler Colfax of Indiana. In a letter accepting his nomination, Grant used the simple phrase "Let us have peace." The phrase became his campaign slogan, and after his death these four words were carved in stone atop his majestic Manhattan tomb.

Meeting in Chicago, the Democrats nominated Horatio Seymour, who had been governor of New York during the war, along with Frank Blair of Maryland, a former Union general whose father had been a close adviser to Andrew Jackson. Seymour, dispirited about his chances against Grant, had clearly told the convention, "When I said here at an early day, that honor forbade my accepting a nomination by this convention, I meant it … your candidate I cannot be." Yet convention delegates were determined to draft him, and he accepted the nomination only under coercion. His reluctance earned him the nickname of the "Great Decliner."

The Democratic platform, designed to appeal to the South, lashed out against the Radical Republicans for "unparalleled oppression and tyranny" for subjecting ten former Confederate states to "military despotism and negro supremacy" after the Civil War. During the campaign, Democrats criticized congressional Reconstruction, which the Republicans defended while branding Democrats as disloyal to the Union, "the party of treason." A favorite Republican saw was, "Not every Democrat was a rebel, but every rebel was a Democrat." Republicans engaged in a tactic known as "waving the bloody shirt," reminding voters of Republican sacrifice and courage and Democratic Copperhead perfidy during the war. Wealthy Americans such as the Vanderbilt family contributed mightily to the Republican campaign fund.

Although he was not enthusiastic about being the Democratic nominee, Seymour broke with campaign convention and launched a speaking tour in various northern states. Grant stuck to custom and remained aloof from campaigning. After receiving some visitors at his home in Galena, Illinois, he went on vacation in the West. Back in Galena when he learned of his victory, he

A ticket from Grant's 1869 inauguration.

accepted the news with little outward enthusiasm. Grant amassed an overwhelming total in the electoral college, 214 to 80. He won 26 states compared to just 8 for Seymour. But these results were not as lopsided as they seemed. Grant was not nearly as dominant in the popular vote, with 52.7 percent compared to Seymour's 47.3 percent; he had only 310,0000 more votes. For such a well-known candidate, this margin of victory was surprisingly thin. Seymour lost several states by just a few thousand votes. The results showed that the

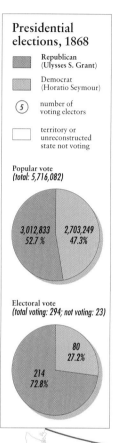

Presidential elections, 1868

■ Republican
(Ulysses S. Grant)

■ Democrat
(Horatio Seymour)

(5) number of voting electors

☐ territory or unreconstructed state not voting

Popular vote
(total: 5,716,082)

3,012,833
52.7 %

2,703,249
47.3%

Electoral vote
(total voting: 294; not voting: 23)

80
27.2%

214
72.8%

Democratic Party was still the majority party in the country. Despite the blot of alleged treason on its record and despite its mediocre candidate being pitted against a renowned war hero, the Democratic Party was still competitive and even managed to win three states in the North—New York, New Jersey, and Connecticut. (Mississippi, Texas, and Virginia had not yet been readmitted to the Union and did not participate in the election. Had citizens there voted, Grant might have lost the election.)

A critical issue in the campaign was black suffrage. Although some Democrats agreed with the principle of black suffrage, many others challenged the notion that blacks were fit to vote. Vice presidential candidate Blair proclaimed that "the white race is the only race in the world that has shown itself capable of maintaining free institutions of a free government." In this election, for the first time in American history southern black males voted in large numbers, about 410,000 in total, and almost all voted for the party of their liberation, the Republicans, thus helping Grant to win six former Confederate states: Alabama, Arkansas, Florida, North Carolina, South Carolina, and Tennessee. The strong and loyal black vote provided a powerful incentive for the Republican Congress to pass the Fifteenth Amendment, designed to protect voting rights. But in parts of the South, blacks faced threats, intimidation, and violence when they attempted to vote. These menaces decimated the Republican Party organization, which tried to offer the freed slaves protection and support when they tried to cast ballots. In Georgia and Louisiana, the violence directed at blacks and the Republican Party was so severe that the Republicans abandoned their political campaign there. Not surprisingly, Seymour won both states.

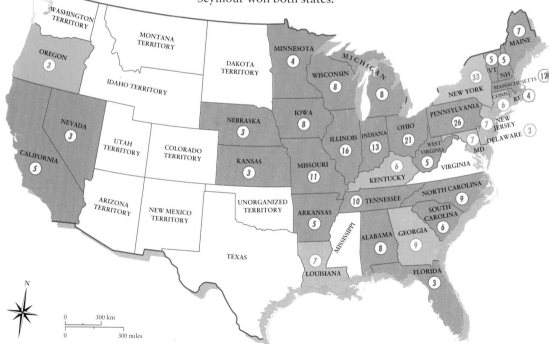

The Election of 1872

Throughout his adult life, Ulysses S. Grant had been dogged by failure. Before finally achieving success as a Civil War general, he had been dismissed from the army in 1854 for heavy drinking, and then had failed as a farmer, real-estate agent, and bill collector. As president, Grant's record of failure persisted. His administration was pockmarked by scandals involving Vice President Schuyler Colfax and high-ranking cabinet officers. Although Grant was not personally implicated in any of the scandals, his political naïveté was painfully obvious, as he had selected a wretched group to help him run the executive branch. Still, when the Republicans held their 1872 convention in Philadelphia, they renominated the general. Senator Henry Wilson of Massachusetts, a former cobbler, replaced Colfax, who had irritated Grant with intimations that he was interested in succeeding him. The Republicans tried to invoke some common-man imagery by advertising "the tanner and the cobbler" on their ticket, a reference to the long-ago vocations of Grant and Wilson.

A large contingent of Republicans was disillusioned with the Grant scandals and the president's failure to promote civil service reform. These disgruntled "Liberal Republicans" were high-minded, erudite men who wanted reform and believed that government deserved better men than Grant and his ilk. Decrying "Grantism," a term that became synonymous with graft and corruption, they broke away from the party and nominated their own candidate, Horace Greeley, the editor and publisher of the *New York Tribune*. As Greeley's running mate they advanced Governor Benjamin Gratz Brown of Missouri, the birthplace of the Liberal Republican movement.

After years of internal strife and eclipse from national power, the Democrats had no viable candidate and met in a brief, cheerless convention in Baltimore. To increase their chances of beating "Useless" Grant, the Democrats expediently joined forces with the Liberal Republicans and simply endorsed the Greeley-Brown ticket and adopted the Liberal Republicans' platform. The endorsement of Greeley was an incongruous and unenthusiastic one for the Democrats, since he was a Republican who had for many years poured invective onto the Democratic "rascals" (as he called them) in his newspaper.

Greeley was one of the oddest nominees of any major party. A querulous man whose flowing white hair and beard made him a caricaturist's delight, he espoused an eclectic range of causes, including spiritualism, socialism, prohibition, and vegetarianism. He even wanted to change America's name to "Columbia." Greeley's political experience consisted of serving as a U.S. congressman for just three months, a short tenure during which his eccentricities and tactlessness created so many enemies that his House colleagues considered censuring or expelling him. In picking Greeley, the Liberal Republicans had made a bizarre, unfortunate choice. New York diarist George Templeton Strong commented, "This is the most preposterous and ludicrous nomination to the Presidency ever made on this continent."

Greeley attacked the Reconstruction governments and advocated local "self-government"—really, white rule—in the South and an end to federal protection for southern blacks. The Democrats also stood for lower tariffs and civil service reform. Serious reformers doubted Greeley's own capacity to implement substantive reform.

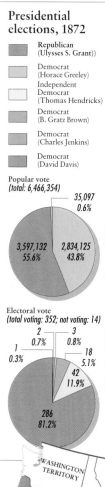

In truth, his nomination reflected the dearth of qualified candidates from which the Liberal Republicans could choose.

Bowing to tradition and to his limited speaking skills, Grant remained silent in the campaign. But Greeley hit the campaign trail, giving more than two hundred speeches during an 11-day stretch. Speaking extemporaneously and intemperately, he managed to offend many who came to hear him.

Grant, who called for federal protection of black rights, won a resounding victory, which sounded an immediate death knell for the Liberal Republican movement. He nearly doubled his margin of victory from 1868, beating Greeley by 800,000 popular votes. Grant received 55.6 percent of the popular vote, a majority that no candidate had approached since Andrew Jackson's 55 percent in 1832. Of 37 states, Grant won 31; Greeley failed to carry any states in the North. Greeley's low of 66 electoral votes was not to be matched until Herbert Hoover won just 59 in 1932. Grant also ran strongly in the Midwest, where many Democrats broke ranks to vote Republican. Grant interpreted the results as a personal victory, but many Republicans were simply voting against Greeley, and many Democrats refused to vote for him.

Greeley was crushed and humiliated. After the election he was immediately committed to a mental hospital. Three weeks later he died.

Since Greeley's death occurred before the presidential electors met to count their votes, a voting anomaly occurred. With Greeley gone, the Democratic electors could vote for anyone else as president. Thus Greeley's 66 electoral votes ended up scattered among four men: Thomas Hendricks, the Democratic governor-elect of Indiana, received 42; Democratic vice presidential candidate Benjamin Gratz Brown got 18; Charles Jenkins received 2; and Supreme Court Justice David Davis received 1. Three presidential electors voted for Greeley, but Congress did not officially count these votes.

The Election of 1876

The election of 1876 turned out to be the most drawn-out in American history and was also one of four elections in which the popular-vote winner was not elected. Ulysses S. Grant, the first president to serve two full terms since Andrew Jackson, wanted to run for a third term, but the Republicans would not hear of it. Both parties were clamoring for civil service reform, and Grant's sorry record of scandals would have made him a liability for the Republicans. What they needed was a man of unimpeachable integrity. Meeting in Cincinnati, the Republicans settled on Rutherford B. Hayes, a Civil War veteran who had achieved the rank of major general during the war. With a degree from Harvard Law School, he was the first presidential nominee with a graduate degree, had served as a U.S. congressman, and was a three-term governor of Ohio, a key swing state. Second place on the Republican ticket went to Representative William Wheeler of New York. Neither man was especially prepossessing. Hayes had a dull personality, and his political career was undistinguished; writer Henry Adams called him a "third-rate nonentity." Wheeler was so afflicted by stage fright that he avoided public speaking. Neither trait was offensive, though, and both men, if bland, appeared honest.

Rutherford B. Hayes 1822–1893
Once president, Hayes attempted to implement civil service reform, and his actions included dismissing Chester Arthur, collector of customs for New York and a future president.

At their convention in St. Louis, the Democrats turned to a well-respected foe of corruption, Samuel Tilden, a millionaire corporate lawyer and one of the richest men in the country. While a district attorney for the state of New York, he had helped send to jail William Marcy Tweed and other members of the corrupt Tammany Hall political machine, which had raided millions from New York City coffers. Tilden's honest reputation won him election as governor of New York in 1874. His running mate was Thomas Hendricks of Indiana, his main rival for the nomination.

The Democrats smelled victory. The country was offended by the corruption of the Grant administration, weary of Republican Reconstruction, and mired in an economic depression that had begun in 1873, which the Democrats blamed on the Republicans. It was time, the Democrats chanted, to "Turn the Rascals Out!" The Democrats' capture of the House in the 1874 midterm elections seemed to presage their presidential victory in two years. The party was resurgent, and southern Democrats yearned to be free of the Reconstruction governments in the South.

When the results of the popular vote came in after the election, the Democrats thought they had indeed won, and many newspapers trumpeted their victory. In his diary, Hayes privately conceded defeat. During the last quarter of the nineteenth century the strategy of the Democrats was to sweep the South and add to this base New York plus one other swing state, such as Connecticut, Illinois, Indiana, New Jersey, or Ohio. Tilden did just that, winning his home state of New York plus Connecticut, Indiana, and New Jersey. He won a slim majority of the popular vote, 51 percent, while Hayes garnered 47.9 percent. But in the electoral college Tilden had 184 votes, just one shy of the number needed to win; Hayes had 165. Twenty electoral votes were disputed, and 19 of them were from the three southern states that the Republicans still controlled, supported by federal troops: Florida, Louisiana, and South Carolina (the remaining electoral vote was from Oregon).

With the election's outcome hanging fire, the nation was tense. Democrats demanded that Tilden be declared the winner. Some Democratic newspapers

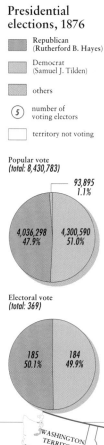

Presidential elections, 1876

- Republican (Rutherford B. Hayes)
- Democrat (Samuel J. Tilden)
- others
- ⑤ number of voting electors
- territory not voting

Popular vote (total: 8,430,783)

- 93,895 — 1.1%
- 4,036,298 — 47.9%
- 4,300,590 — 51.0%

Electoral vote (total: 369)

- 185 — 50.1%
- 184 — 49.9%

thundered, "Tilden or War," while nervous freedmen in the South feared that a Democratic victory would result in the reestablishment of slavery. As the threat of more civil strife hovered over the nation, in late January 1877 Congress assembled a 15-man committee, comprising ten members of Congress and five Supreme Court justices, to resolve the issue of the disputed electoral votes. The commission was originally established with an even balance of Republicans and Democrats, plus one independent, but the independent withdrew and was replaced by a Republican, giving the commission a makeup of eight Republicans and seven Democrats. The commission voted along party lines to award all 20 contested votes to Hayes, which would make him the nineteenth president. In the House, Democrats threatened a filibuster to protest these results.

Republicans and southern Democrats in Congress, who had been meeting in secret for weeks, negotiated a compromise. The Democrats promised to accept Hayes's claim to all 20 electoral votes and therefore to the presidency; in exchange, once in office, Hayes would withdraw the remaining federal troops from the South, support internal improvements in the region, and appoint at least one southerner to a cabinet post.

The arrangement became known as the "Compromise of 1877." With this deal in place, the announcement came at 4:10 A.M. on March 2, 1877, just two days before the scheduled inauguration: Hayes was officially elected president with 185 electoral votes. The president-elect rushed by train from Ohio to be sworn in. He began his presidency in the maw of controversy, his claim to the office in doubt; Democrats called him "Rutherfraud B. Hayes." One sad legacy of the compromise was that it allowed southern whites to institute "home rule," under which they systematically denied civil and political rights to African Americans. It would be almost a century before African Americans in the South won the right to vote.

The Election of 1880

The presidential elections of the "Gilded Age," the last quarter of the nineteenth century, were marked by a rough equilibrium between the two parties. Although besmirched by allegations of disloyalty during the Civil War, the Democrats staged a remarkable comeback to level the political playing field. Each party claimed approximately the same proportion of the electorate, and presidential contests were consistently close. In fact, in the elections of 1880, 1884, and 1888, the difference in popular votes separating the two major candidates was less than 1 percent. With the competitors so evenly matched and the contests decided by razor-thin margins, no candidate wanted to stick his neck out. Each presidential contender played it safe during campaigns, avoiding controversial issues and falling back on platitudes.

James Abram Garfield 1831–1881
An Ohio congressman for 17 years, Garfield was elected to the Senate in 1880 but never took his seat because of his election to the presidency the same year.

Despite the dull rhetoric, voter turnout was impressively high, averaging around 78 percent for the presidential elections from 1876 to 1896, which reflected a sturdy allegiance to party as well as the festive nature of presidential contests. Campaigns featured parades and paraphernalia such as songs, buttons, and posters. Politics was one of the main forms of popular entertainment, and politicians were celebrities. Election Day was consecrated to the ritual of voting. In cities, businesses shuttered up for the day; in the countryside, farmers abandoned their farms for hours and drove to town to cast ballots. However, women still could not vote, despite efforts to gain a constitutional amendment for their suffrage. And in the South, white southerners stripped blacks of the political gains the latter had made during Reconstruction, denying them the right to vote through techniques such as poll taxes and literacy tests. As a result, black voting declined rapidly throughout the period.

During this time each party retained the allegiance of particular sections of the country. The Republicans controlled the North, the Midwest, and the Pacific Coast states but were virtually nonexistent as a political force in many areas of the South, which became known as the "Solid South" for its Democratic loyalty. Although the Republicans had broader national appeal, the Democrats' thorough domination of the South and of urban areas of the Northeast allowed them to be a viable national force. Only a handful of states were of uncertain political allegiance: New York, Connecticut, New Jersey, Ohio, Illinois, and Indiana. These so-called "doubtful states" often determined close elections, and both parties devoted considerable time and attention to win them over, especially New York, which had the largest number of electoral votes, and Ohio, which had the fourth-largest. In total, the six doubtful states accounted for about one-quarter of the nation's electoral votes.

Not surprisingly, the doubtful states produced a disproportionate number of presidential and vice presidential candidates. The Republicans frequently nominated a presidential candidate from Ohio or Indiana and balanced the ticket with a vice presidential nominee from New York; the Democrats often picked a presidential candidate from New York and selected a vice presidential candidate from Ohio, Illinois, or Indiana. Of the nine different presidential candidates between 1876 and 1900, only three (Winfield Scott Hancock in 1880, James G. Blaine in 1884, and William Jennings Bryan in 1896) did not come from New York, Ohio, or Indiana. All three men lost their elections.

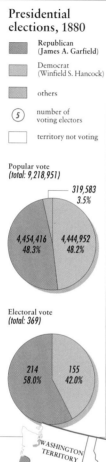

Presidential elections, 1880

■ Republican
(James A. Garfield)

□ Democrat
(Winfield S. Hancock)

▨ others

(5) number of voting electors

□ territory not voting

Popular vote
(total: 9,218,951)

319,583
3.5%

4,454,416
48.3%

4,444,952
48.2%

Electoral vote
(total: 369)

214
58.0%

155
42.0%

As a general rule, during the Gilded Age the Republican Party held the presidency (winning all but two elections from 1860 to 1908) and the Senate. The Democrats usually controlled the House. The president typically faced a Congress with at least one house belonging to the opposite party, and partly because of this divided government, the presidents of this period accomplished little of historical note. Congress dominated the national agenda, a political situation portended by congressional dominance during Reconstruction and by Congress's impeachment and trial of President Andrew Johnson, which clipped the wings for a generation of presidencies. Business titans such as Andrew Carnegie and John D. Rockefeller often provided the most visible national leadership. The president did not promulgate any national vision or objective and sponsored precious few legislative programs. On many major issues the parties' positions were practically indistinguishable. Ultimately the tariff became the only national issue on which the two parties clashed. The Republicans were protectionist and wanted a high tariff, while the Democrats favored a low tariff.

During the Gilded Age, Republican Party unity was threatened by a serious division, as the party was split into two camps, the Stalwarts and the Half-Breeds. The Stalwarts, led by powerful New York Senator Roscoe Conkling, were blatant in their pursuit of patronage and looked to build Republican strength and black suffrage in the South. The Half-Breeds, led by Maine Senator James G. Blaine, were less disposed toward unabashed patronage and less loyal to Radical Republican principles, as their name suggested. Perhaps the greatest wedge dividing the two factions was not any substantive issue or belief but the personal enmity between Blaine and Conkling.

At the Republican Party's June 1880 convention in Chicago, the two sides vied to nominate one of their own. (Hayes declined to run for a second term and neither Republican faction wanted to touch him anyway, because he had openly opposed the spoils system and because he had withdrawn the remaining federal troops from the South, effectively

ending hopes of Republican political growth in that region.) The Stalwarts wanted to run Ulysses S. Grant for a third term, while the Half-Breeds advanced Blaine. Neither side could get its way, and on the thirty-sixth ballot a dark horse emerged, Senator-elect James Abram Garfield from Ohio, a brigadier general during the Civil War who had also served nine terms as a congressman. Garfield was a Half-Breed, and in a move to conciliate the Stalwarts, the convention nominated as his running-mate Chester A. Arthur of New York, a prominent Stalwart in that state and an unerringly loyal Conkling protégé. The Republicans had picked a young ticket; Garfield was just 48 and Arthur was 49.

The Democrats wanted Samuel Tilden to run again for the presidency to avenge his loss in 1876 but, stricken with ill health and opposed by New York City political bosses, he bowed out. So the party, meeting in Cincinnati, turned to General Winfield Scott Hancock of Pennsylvania, a Civil War veteran who had fought at the Battle of Gettysburg and whose only political experience was a tenure as military governor of Louisiana. His running mate was William English of Indiana, a banker and former congressman.

Chester Arthur 1829–1886 Although Arthur liked to socialize and held lavish White House dinners, he guarded his privacy, even burning his private papers. Without a favorable public image, loyal following, or party support, he failed to win nomination for a full term.

Garfield came from a simple, pastoral background. Born in a log cabin in Ohio, he had worked on the Ohio Canal as a mule driver, which earned him the nickname "Boatman Jim." The Republicans capitalized on his humble roots with the slogan "From the towpath to the White House." But as a congressman, Garfield had accepted $329 in stock dividends from the Crédit Mobilier, which collapsed in scandal during the Grant administration. Democrats used chalk to blanket landmarks in various cities—sidewalks, buildings, fences—with the number "329," a not-so-subtle reminder of Garfield's alleged corruptibility. The decisive factors in the election all favored the Republican Party: the economic recovery after the depression of 1873–79, the party's superior financial backing (especially from business), and the enhanced reputation that it owed to President Hayes's civil service reform. Garfield boosted his prospects by giving talks to hundreds of visitors who trooped to his home in Mentor, Ohio. This "front-porch" campaign set a pattern for later candidates to follow and marked a move away from the tradition of silent presidential aspirants.

Garfield won the two sections of the country where the Republicans were dominant. In the North, he won all states except New Jersey; in the West, he won everything but Nevada. The Solid South went uniformly for Hancock. Garfield won the important swing state of New York by just 20,000 votes. The state's 35 electoral votes determined the election. (Interestingly, this election marked the only time in the nineteenth or twentieth centuries that the Republican Party won the presidency without the help of California.) Nationwide, Garfield managed to edge Hancock narrowly in popular votes by a margin of just 9,464 out of more than nine million votes cast.

On July 2, 1881, as Garfield walked toward a train to embark on a New England vacation, he was shot in the back by Charles Guiteau, a mentally unbalanced Stalwart who was angered that the president had not awarded him a job. Garfield lingered for less than three months, dying on September 19, 1881. He had served only half a year in office, the second-shortest presidency in history. Vice president Chester A. Arthur succeeded Garfield as president.

The Election of 1884

Grover Cleveland
1837–1908
Despite the
political liabilities of
having avoided service
in the Civil War and
fathering an
illegitimate child,
Cleveland beat a more
experienced, better-
known opponent in
1884.

After James Abram Garfield's assassination by a demented office seeker, cries for civil service reform grew louder, and President Chester Arthur responded by showing fair-mindedness and a commitment to reform, evinced by his signing the Pendleton Civil Service Act in 1883, which established a system of competitive exams for federal office seekers. But when the election of 1884 came, the Republican Stalwarts felt that Arthur had betrayed them by pursuing civil service reform instead of richly rewarding fellow Stalwarts with jobs. At the same time, the Half-Breeds could not overlook his Stalwart past. To both Stalwarts and Half-Breeds, Arthur could not be trusted, and neither wing wanted to nominate him as the presidential candidate. (Arthur, who was ill with Bright's disease, probably would not have been able to run, anyway. He died just one year after leaving office.)

Meeting in Chicago, the Republicans turned to the most popular, magnetic party leader of the Gilded Age, James G. Blaine of Maine. Blaine had plenty of political assets: charisma, wit, a steel-trap memory, and good looks. He had a long record of service in Congress, having won election to the House in 1863. President Lincoln had observed the new congressman and called him "one of the brightest men" in the House; within a few years Blaine was House Speaker. He also served briefly as secretary of state for Garfield. The leader of the Half-Breeds, Blaine was the arch foe of the Stalwarts, and in 1880 their opposition had turned his presidential aspirations to ashes. But in 1884 his charm and popularity proved insuperable. Blaine finally nabbed the nomination, and the Republicans nominated Senator John Logan of Illinois, a Stalwart, as his vice presidential candidate. The Stalwarts grumbled at Blaine's nomination, and the fractiousness of the party hurt them in the election. When Republicans asked Blaine's intraparty rival, Roscoe Conkling, to support the nominee, he shot back a withering reply: "I do not engage in criminal practice."

The Democrats also met in Chicago and nominated the reform governor of New York, Grover Cleveland. His rise had been meteoric. A native of western New York, the hardworking Cleveland was elected mayor of Buffalo in 1881; the following year he won the governorship of New York; just two years later he became his party's presidential nominee. In sharp contrast to Blaine, the 47-year-old Cleveland lacked both charisma and extensive political experience; he had never even visited Washington before. But the party trusted this rising star because he was honest and a reform leader. Democrats called him "Grover the Good" and placed its hopes for national victory on his burly shoulders (he weighed 260 pounds). Second place on the ticket went to Senator Thomas Hendricks of Indiana, who had been Samuel Tilden's running mate in 1876. The Democrats were aided by a group of Republicans, the Mugwumps (from the Algonquin Indian word for "Chief") who sided with the Democrats in this election. The Mugwumps were an elite group comprising many socially prominent

Americans; their ranks included such former Liberal Republicans as Senator Carl Schurz of Missouri as well as intellectuals like Mark Twain. The Mugwumps denounced patronage and corruption in politics and could not stomach Blaine, whom they charged was tainted by scandal.

As was usual for Gilded Age politics, the parties differed little on substantive issues, but the campaign tactics of the two nominees provided some contrast. Cleveland remained in Albany and tended to his duties as New York governor. Toward the end of the race, James Blaine hit the campaign trail and gave four hundred short speeches throughout the country, urging the protective tariff as an instrument to help boost wages. Because few concrete issues distinguished the parties, the two sides turned to personal scandal to gain political advantage. The publication of the "Mulligan Letters," which implicated Blaine in accepting bribes from the Little Rock and Fort Smith Railroads, cast doubt on his integrity. Blaine stoutly denied any wrongdoing, but his denials fell flat, and even made him seem disingenuous. The Democrats roused their ranks with the chant, "Blaine! Blaine! James G. Blaine! Continental Liar from the State of Maine!"

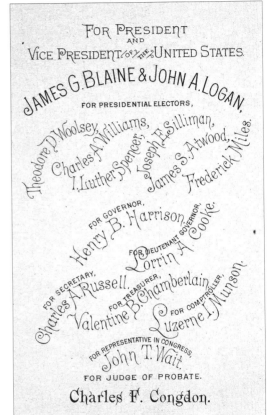

The Republicans found an even more sensational charge to pin on Cleveland. They found that he had fathered an illegitimate child with a widow in Buffalo. When worried Cleveland supporters queried the candidate about how to diffuse the charge, he simply instructed them, "Tell the truth." The Republicans mockingly chanted, "Ma! Ma! Where's my Pa?" But many voters found Cleveland's acceptance of his behavior admirable and refreshingly candid. Ironically, the scandal may have helped rather than hurt Cleveland. (When Cleveland won the election, Democrats gleefully repeated the Republican taunt with the addition, "Gone to the White House. Ha, ha, ha!")

A broadside supporting the Republican ticket.

Just as in 1880, the road to victory lay through New York. As a native of the state, Cleveland had a clear advantage over Blaine, who was better-known nationally, and his support from New York was further bolstered by an infelicitous remark from a Presbyterian minister and Blaine supporter. On October 29, in the closing days of the campaign, Protestant clergymen assembled at a pro-Blaine meeting in New York City. There, with Blaine sharing the dais, the Reverend Samuel Burchard laced into the Democratic Party, saying, "We are Republicans, and don't propose to leave our party

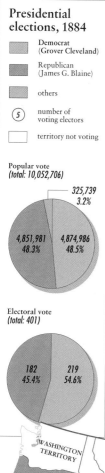

Presidential elections, 1884

Democrat (Grover Cleveland)

Republican (James G. Blaine)

others

(5) number of voting electors

territory not voting

Popular vote (total: 10,052,706)

325,739 3.2%

4,851,981 48.3%

4,874,986 48.5%

Electoral vote (total: 401)

182 45.4%

219 54.6%

and identify with a party whose antecedents have been Rum, Romanism, and Rebellion." (Burchard was attacking the Democratic Party's bonds with Roman Catholic immigrants, as well as its alleged support of southern secession.) The words smacked of bigotry and intolerance, and Democrats pounced on them. They immediately blanketed the city with reports quoting Burchard's insult and insinuating Blaine's agreement with it. Coming so close to the election, the remark blighted Blaine's hopes for the presidency. Irish-Americans were especially incensed and on Election Day turned out to vote for Cleveland.

In New York State, out of 1.1 million votes cast, Blaine lost by only 1,149. A furious rainstorm drenched the state on Election Day and kept many upstate farmers from the polls, which helped the Democrats, who were able to turn out the vote in the cities despite the elements. Nationally, Blaine won the West and most of the North, while Cleveland swept the Solid South. This time, the doubtful states came through for the Democrats, as Cleveland won not only New York but also Connecticut, Indiana, and New Jersey. Cleveland had a slim majority of the national popular vote, only 23,000 out of ten million votes cast, and beat Blaine in the electoral college by 219 to 182. Had Blaine won New York's 36 electoral votes, he would have edged out Cleveland in the electoral college and won the presidency. This election was one of the closest in history.

Cleveland was the first Democratic president to be elected since James Buchanan in 1856. Blaine blamed the weather and Burchard: "As the Lord sent upon us an ass in the shape of a preacher and a rainstorm to lessen our vote in New York, I am disposed to feel resigned to the dispensation of defeat which flowed directly from these agencies."

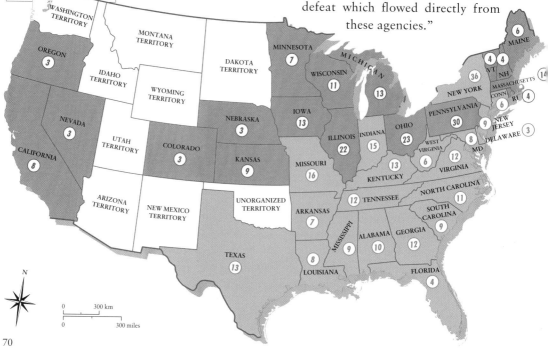

The Election of 1888

In 1888 the Democrats held their national convention in St. Louis and renominated Grover Cleveland. Vice President Thomas Hendricks had died in 1885, and the Democrats picked the ailing, 75-year-old former Senator Allen Thurman of Ohio as Cleveland's new running mate.

Cleveland devoted his December 1887 annual message to Congress entirely to the issue of the tariff, marking the first time in the Gilded Age that a party staked out a clear, unequivocal stand on a national issue, thus differentiating itself from the other party. Cleveland attacked high tariffs, calling them "vicious, inequitable, and illogical," and established the Democratic Party for the next half-century as the advocate of low tariffs. Cleveland was gambling with his political future, but he explained to people who questioned his tactics, "What is the use of being elected or reelected, unless you stand for something?"

Benjamin Harrison
1833–1901
Politics was in Harrison's blood. His father was a congressman, and his grandfather was the nation's ninth president. In the 1888 campaign, Republicans chanted, "Grandfather's hat fits Ben."

For the third straight time the Republican Party held its national convention in Chicago. Many Republicans wanted to nominate James Blaine again, but Blaine, overseas in Europe, wrote a letter emphatically declining the nomination. The party nominated former Senator Benjamin Harrison of Indiana, grandson of the ninth president, William Henry Harrison. Benjamin Harrison had been a brigadier general during the Civil War; he had served under General William Sherman in his campaign through Georgia. Harrison's only major political service had been one term as a U.S. senator. Harrison's vice presidential candidate was Levi Morton of New York, a wealthy banker and former congressman. The Republican platform's support of the tariff was emphatic: "We are uncompromisingly in favor of the American system of protection. We protest against its destruction, as proposed by the President and his party."

Reserved, aloof, and innocent of a sense of humor, Harrison had a personality so cold that colleagues called him a "human iceberg." But a number of assets offset his shortcomings. Harrison could point to his Civil War record; Cleveland, by contrast, had hired a substitute during the war. Cleveland did not campaign personally. Harrison, meanwhile, conducted an effective "front-porch" campaign: thousands of Americans visited him at his Indianapolis home, where he gave more than 80 short speeches from his front porch, promoting protectionism and calling Cleveland's wish to lower the tariff "unpatriotic." This technique of campaigning had several advantages, most notably that the candidate could attract constant newspaper attention and gain exposure to large volumes of people while remaining at home and preserving his energy.

Few Democrats stumped for Cleveland. (Many party members were angered that he had awarded jobs to Liberal Republicans rather than to Democrats.) By contrast, powerful Republicans came to Harrison's aid. Once back from Europe, Blaine campaigned effectively on Harrison's behalf, trying to whip up excitement over the otherwise bland tariff issue. (Once he became president, Harrison appointed Blaine as secretary of state.) Senator John Sherman of Ohio, brother of General William Tecumseh Sherman, hit the hustings for Harrison in the doubtful states of Connecticut, Indiana, New Jersey, and New York. Harrison's campaign chairman, Senator Matt Quay of Pennsylvania, led a well-organized, well-funded Republican political machine and reached deeply into his own pockets to help buy votes in the crucial states of New York and Indiana, both of which Harrison won. (In Indiana the corruption was especially blatant, and Harrison managed to win the state by a mere 2,348 votes.) The Republicans raised much more money than the Democrats. Businessmen—attracted especially by Republican support of high tariffs—now pitched in generously, as did organizations such as the American Iron and Steel Association and the Protective Tariff League.

The election of 1888 was the third race in American history in which the candidate who won the popular vote lost the election (the others being the elections of 1824 and 1876). Cleveland polled 100,000 more votes than Harrison, especially because he won the entire South and solidified the Democratic lead in the Deep South, winning states there by large margins. But Harrison won the preponderance of states rich in electoral votes. He swept the West Coast states and the North, winning all the doubtful states except Connecticut and New Jersey. These two states, plus Pennsylvania, were the only northern ones in Cleveland's column. (Cleveland even lost his home state, New York.) In all, Harrison won 20 states to Cleveland's 18 and beat Cleveland in the electoral college, 233 to 168. Curiously, many of the states that Harrison lost in the Northeast and the West were manufacturing states that favored protectionism, indicating that his endorsement of a high tariff had failed to resonate with voters there. Since the Republicans won not only the presidency but both houses of Congress as well, their victory was the most resounding of any in an era of close elections, and it offered an augury of the next three decades, during which the GOP was the dominant party in national politics. (The day after Harrison's victory, the *New York Tribune* congratulated the "Grand Old Party" on its victory, and the name stuck.) The Republican Congress, set to work on its mandate and in 1890 passed the McKinley Tariff Act, which raised tariffs to their highest levels in history.

Frances Cleveland, the president's wife, gave instructions to White House servants that may have seemed implausible: "Take good care of the place. We'll be back." Four years later, her words proved true.

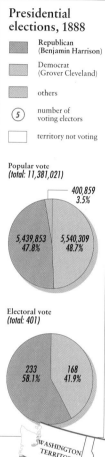

Presidential elections, 1888

- Republican (Benjamin Harrison)
- Democrat (Grover Cleveland)
- others
- ⑤ number of voting electors
- territory not voting

Popular vote
(total: 11,381,021)

400,859
3.5%

5,439,853
47.8%

5,540,309
48.7%

Electoral vote
(total: 401)

233
58.1%

168
41.9%

The Election of 1892

During the 1880s, agriculture fell on hard times. In addition to having their crops seared by droughts, farmers were burdened by low farm prices, exorbitant railroad rates, and chronic debt. To combat the deflation that was lowering crop prices, farmers wanted to reform the country's financial system. Their most vocal demand was that the government mint silver coins, abandoned in favor of gold during the early 1870s, at the old ratio of 16 ounces of silver equaling 1 ounce of gold. To farmers and other "silverites," the metal had a talismanic appeal. Farmers reasoned that an increase in the supply of money would bring higher prices and greater prosperity. Silverites believed that limiting the nation's coin to gold only crimped economic growth and caused economic distress and debt.

In February 1892, radical farmers met in St. Louis and formed the People's Party, which became the Populist Party. The party met again in Omaha, Nebraska, and nominated a presidential candidate, James B. Weaver of Iowa, who had been a Union general during the Civil War and a congressman afterward. His running mate was a former Confederate soldier, James Field of Virginia. The Populist platform called for national ownership of the railroads and the telegraph and telephone systems, a graduated income tax, and a subtreasury system whereby the government would buy surplus farm products and keep them in storage until market prices were higher. Above all, the Populists called for the free and unlimited coinage of silver.

The Democratic National Convention met in Chicago and nominated former President Grover Cleveland, a firm advocate of the gold standard. In order to balance his position, the party selected a silverite as his running mate, Congressman Adlai Stevenson of Illinois. Many Republicans were unenthusiastic about President Benjamin Harrison, but since he was president and party leader, the Republicans renominated him and tapped Whitelaw Reid, the publisher of the *New York Tribune*, to run with him. Just as in 1888, the issue distinguishing the two parties was the tariff, as the Republicans supported the high tariff while the Democrats favored lowering the tariff. This time the Democrats charged that Republican protectionism had increased prices and fueled worker discontent by encouraging trusts and monopolies, which often lowered wages. Proof seemed to come in July, when workers at Andrew Carnegie's steel plant in Homestead, Pennsylvania, went on strike and had a bloody confrontation with guards hired to protect the plant.

Grover Cleveland and Adlai Stevenson riding down Pennsylvania Avenue, Inauguration Day, 1893.

The campaign of 1892 was dull, a rematch of the 1888 contest, and neither party was enthusiastic about the nominees. Harrison's campaign was especially subdued because of the illness and subsequent death of his wife, and the Democrats toned down their campaign out of sympathy. Few Republicans campaigned enthusiastically for Harrison. Cleveland spent most of the campaign at his cottage in Massachusetts, while vice presidential candidate Stevenson went on a speaking tour of the West.

The election of 1892 was the first in which a majority of states, 33 in all, used the secret ballot. The election results indicated that the Democratic stand on the tariff issue, and Cleveland's probity and good character had given an edge to the former president. Cleveland had a comfortable plurality over the incumbent Harrison, 46.1 percent to 42.9 percent. His margin of victory, 400,000 votes, was large for Gilded Age politics, the greatest spread since Ulysses Grant beat Horace Greeley in 1872. Cleveland's margin in the electoral college was more decisive, 277 to 145. Cleveland won the entire South and several doubtful states, such as New York, Connecticut, and New Jersey. He also won the midwestern states of Illinois, Indiana, and Wisconsin, the last of which he had lost in 1888. Though Harrison was shut out in the South, he won almost all of New England and captured several states in the upper Midwest. But he had 263,745 fewer popular votes compared to 1888, and whereas he had won 19 states outright that year, he won only 13 in 1892.

Cleveland became the first president to serve two nonconsecutive terms. The Democrats now controlled the presidency and both houses of Congress for the first time in a generation, and the party had gained strength in urban areas, especially among immigrants and working-class Americans. But an economic crisis during Cleveland's term would soon wash away many of the party's gains.

The real story to emerge from this election was the Populist Party, which added life to an otherwise insipid race. Weaver, unlike Cleveland and Harrison, actively went on the campaign stump and often generated controversy, suffering abuse in the form of hecklers, rotten eggs, and tomatoes; but he became the first third-party candidate ever to break the one million mark. He captured the silver-mining states of Colorado and Nevada and the farm states of Idaho and Kansas, plus parts of Oregon and North Dakota. In all, he gained 22 electoral votes. The Populists also elected five senators and ten congressmen and showed political strength at the state level, electing three governors and 1,500 members of state legislatures. But the Populist showing, while respectable for a new party, revealed weaknesses. In southern states Weaver ran poorly, in part due to intimidation and fraud by the Democratic Party, while in northern states he failed to win urban areas or the vote of labor. The question for the next election was whether the Populists would build on their groundwork or sink into obscurity.

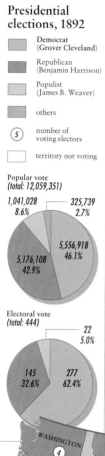

The Election of 1896

In 1893, at the start of Grover Cleveland's term, the nation fell into the worst economic depression it had thus far experienced. National unemployment hit 20 percent, and an epidemic of strikes swept across the country, the most crippling of which, the Pullman strike, paralyzed railway traffic. Cleveland blamed the depression on silver; his unremitting belief in the gold standard led him to believe that the furor for silver had weakened the confidence of American business and thereby touched off the economic slump. In 1893 he lobbied for and obtained the repeal of the Sherman Silver Purchase Act, which officially severed the government's relationship with silver. But the act contracted the currency, worsened the economic downturn, and alienated many Democrats in the South and West from Cleveland's administration, which had no other plan for reversing the slide. As the election approached, a mood of political, social, and economic crisis hung over the nation.

William McKinley 1843–1901 McKinley's home in Canton, Ohio, took a beating during his 1896 "front-porch" campaign, as crowds trampled on his lawn, wore down his porch, and removed portions of his fence as souvenirs.

A beleaguered Democratic Party assembled in Chicago. In the 1894 congressional elections the Democrats had suffered terrible setbacks, losing control of both the House and Senate (they lost 113 seats in the House, a defeat unparalleled in American history). The party was rent between two factions. The southern and western silverite sections of the party comprised many farmers who were dissatisfied with Cleveland's adherence to the gold standard and wanted to return to bimetallism. The eastern, Cleveland wing of the party represented the financial interests and preferred the stability of the gold standard. The silverites dominated the convention and presided over the adoption of a free-silver platform, and when a silverite gave one of the most famous speeches in American history, he became an instant national celebrity, as well as the party's nominee.

William Jennings Bryan was a former congressman from Nebraska. Young, handsome, and articulate, he had a booming voice and a gift for oratory. Bryan was not a deep thinker and was something of a Johnny-come-lately to the cause of free silver; as a congressman he had once proclaimed, "The people of Nebraska are for free silver and I am for free silver. I'll look up the reasons later." His early ignorance of the issue and unquestioning faith in the people notwithstanding, Bryan took to supporting free silver with a missionary zeal. In the closing days of the convention, he delivered what became known as the "Cross of Gold" speech. The audience of Democrats sat at rapt attention, utterly enthralled by Bryan's words. He extolled the virtues of silver, and closed with a peroration rich with allusions to Christ: "You [supporters of the gold standard] shall not press down upon the brow of labor this crown of thorns, you shall not crucify mankind upon a cross of gold." After a moment of stunned silence, the delegates erupted in wild cheers. The next day they nominated Bryan.

The Democratic Party's nomination of Bryan and adoption of a prosilver platform posed a quandary for the Populist Party. They could remain as an independent third party and nominate their own candidate, but in so doing, they would siphon votes away from Bryan and thereby almost ensure a Republican victory. Alternatively, they could fuse with the Democrats and support Bryan, in which case they risked losing their identity and independence. Meeting in St. Louis, the

Populists decided to take the pragmatic approach and support Bryan. But in a move designed to preserve a degree of independence, the Populists nominated their own vice presidential candidate, Tom Watson of Iowa. The Democrats ignored the gesture and instead stuck to their original vice presidential nominee, shipbuilder Arthur Sewell of Maine, a silverite.

William McKinley, Ohio's affable governor, won the Republican nomination at the party's St. Louis convention, largely with the financial help of wealthy industrialist Marcus Hanna, chairman of the Republican National Committee and boss of the political machine in Cleveland. McKinley and Hanna formed one of the most effective political partnerships in American history. Hanna's advertising campaign billed McKinley as "the Advance Agent of Prosperity," a handle that appealed to jobless Americans, and Hanna poured out money unstintingly. McKinley's running mate was corporate lawyer Garret Hobart of New Jersey, selected to help win that state, which frequently voted Democratic. Hobart was also a favorite of McKinley and Hanna, who both urged delegates to pick him.

Unlike earlier elections during the Gilded Age, the parties staked out clear differences on two important issues. The Republicans supported high protective tariffs, best exemplified by their nominee, who as a congressman had sponsored the McKinley Tariff of 1890. More important, the Republican platform favored the gold standard and opposed the coinage of silver (except by international agreement). McKinley warned against the "silver menace," and his followers often wore gold bug pins, gold neckties, and gold headbands as symbols of support. The election of 1896 became known as "the battle of the standards," as the Republicans advanced gold while the Democrats supported both silver and gold, or bimetallism.

William J. Bryan's "Cross of Gold" speech so enraptured his audience that it won him the Democratic nomination. Byran is seen here in a political cartoon from 1896.

Bryan and McKinley were a study in contrasts. McKinley was 53 years old and had an extensive record of public service. A Civil War veteran who had fought at the Battles of Antietam and Gettysburg, he was elected to the House of Representatives in 1876, served six terms there, and was elected governor of Ohio in 1891. By contrast, Bryan was just one year old when the Civil War broke out. At the age of 36, he was the youngest presidential nominee of any major party in American history. His national political experience consisted of only two terms in the House. "The Great Commoner," as Bryan was known, was a good representative of the middle-class Americans of the Midwest, the "work-worn" and the "dust-begrimed" people, as he once called them.

One of the greatest contrasts between the two men was in their campaign styles. Energetic and flamboyant, Bryan crisscrossed the country, traveling 18,000 miles and giving spellbinding speeches in the most thorough, ambitious, and grueling campaign ever waged by a presidential candidate up to that time. Visiting hamlets as well as large cities, Bryan gave up to 20 speeches a day, often from the back of a railroad train, making more than 600 speeches in all. His efforts were all the more remarkable considering that he relied solely on his unamplified voice to reach large crowds.

McKinley knew that he could not match Bryan's eloquence or energy. "I might just as well put up a trapeze on my front lawn and compete with some professional athlete as go out speaking against Bryan," he commented. Repairing to the winning formula of Benjamin Harrison, he conducted a "front-porch" campaign from his home in Canton, Ohio. With Hanna paying for pilgrimages by groups from all over the country, the events were carefully controlled and choreographed. Crowds assembled outside the McKinley residence, drank refreshments generously provided, and heard the candidate field questions—which he had received and prepared for in advance—and give short talks that extolled the Republican Party as an agent of economic prosperity. In what became a famous campaign slogan, McKinley promised a "full dinner pail" for jobless Americans. Hanna also sent thousands of speakers to various parts of America to stump for McKinley, and underwrote a massive advertising campaign that inundated the country with 250 million pieces of literature (the electorate was just fifteen million). While Hanna had $3.5 million at his disposal, the Democrats had a meager $650,000 to spend on the campaign. The Republicans ran one of the most well-funded, well-organized campaigns in history.

But the election of 1896 represented more than just a choice between two men or two political parties. It involved two competing visions for America's future, rival sections of the country, and different interests. Bryan equated silver with the common people, and charged that the gold standard represented the privileged interests of the Northeast, home of America's elite, whose interests were inimical to those of the average American. He stood as the defender of the farmer and of Americans wracked by debt and economic hardship; he was the voice of the West and the South. Most important, Bryan looked to America's past as a blueprint for its future. Holding the interests of the farmer paramount, he extolled the ideals of rural America, representing an alternative to the crushing onslaught of industrialization and urbanization. McKinley and the Republicans, by contrast, stood for an American future that was oriented toward business, manufacturing, and commerce, and favored the Northeast over other sections of the country.

With 51 percent of the popular vote, McKinley won the first majority since Ulysses S. Grant in 1872. In addition to gaining the White House, Republicans retained control of both houses of Congress. The results showed that Bryan's vision for America's future failed to ignite support in America's most populous areas. McKinley had won only one more state than Bryan, 23 to 22, but he had won the large states with the bulk of the electoral votes. The election signaled the end of the American farmer as a dominant political force. By 1896, only one-third of the nation's workforce was still engaged in agriculture, and their support was not enough to win a national election.

Although Bryan won most states west of the Mississippi River, he failed to carry any industrial states and lost Democratic urban centers that Cleveland had won four years earlier—New York, Boston, Chicago, and Minneapolis. Every county in New England went Republican in the election, as did all but one in New York State. Almost all of the prestigious urban newspapers threw their editorial support to McKinley. In a nation that was rapidly urbanizing and industrializing, city

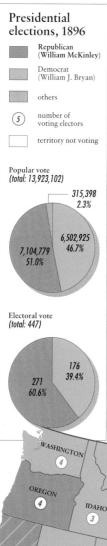

Presidential elections, 1896

- Republican (William McKinley)
- Democrat (William J. Bryan)
- others
- ⑤ number of voting electors
- territory not voting

Popular vote
(total: 13,923,102)

- 315,398 2.3%
- 6,502,925 46.7%
- 7,104,779 51.0%

Electoral vote
(total: 447)

- 176 39.4%
- 271 60.6%

workers were clearly unmoved by Bryan's message, for the silver issue had meaning only for farmers. Even among farmers, Bryan's support was disappointing. Many farmers in the Northeast, who were better off than their midwestern counterparts, voted Republican, and McKinley won some farm states in the Midwest, including Iowa, Minnesota, and North Dakota. In this election the East triumphed over the South and the West, the two sections that Bryan had hoped in vain to unite.

The election also broke the political equilibrium between the Republican and Democratic parties. Now the Republican Party successfully identified itself as the party of economic prosperity, while the Democrats were stuck with the stigma of being the party in power when the Panic of 1893 had struck. As Bryan lamented, "I have borne the sins of Grover Cleveland."

The election was rougher on the Populists. Fusion had robbed them of their identity, and defeat finished them off. The Populists had a reputation for radicalism, and their sometimes wild rhetoric hurt Bryan's campaign by lending credence to charges that he was a dangerous rabble-rouser. The *New York Tribune* labeled Bryan as "simply a demagogue, who tries to play upon the passions and prejudices of workingmen, in order to win their votes." By contrast, against a backdrop of social and economic turbulence, Republicans portrayed McKinley as a pillar of stability.

Once ensconced in power after the election, the Republicans repudiated key planks of the alleged radicals. Congress passed and McKinley signed bills that raised tariff rates to a record high and that officially converted the country to the gold standard, thus ending the silver issue once and for all. While free silver, the most prominent arrow in the Populist sling, may have missed its target, other Populist arrows later hit their mark. Ideas such as the direct election of U.S. senators and a progressive income tax later became part of mainstream American politics.

The Election of 1900

The election of 1900 was a rematch of the 1896 contest, pitting William McKinley against William Jennings Bryan. When they met in Kansas City for their national convention, the Democrats picked as their vice presidential nominee Adlai Stevenson of Illinois, a silverite who had served as vice president during Cleveland's second term. One of the great questions was who McKinley's running mate would be, since Vice President Garret Hobart had died in 1899. New York Governor Theodore Roosevelt, just 41 years old, was the front-runner. He had enjoyed a successful tenure as governor, and had earned fame during the Spanish-American War by leading his Rough Riders in the Battle of San Juan Hill. The Republican convention, held in Philadelphia, nominated a reluctant Roosevelt, who said he would be a "dignified nonentity for four years." The prospect of Roosevelt being a heartbeat away from the presidency alarmed Marcus Hanna, now a senator from Ohio. Calling Roosevelt a "madman," Hanna implored McKinley, "Your duty to the country is to live for four years from next March." Other Roosevelt detractors, especially New York political bosses who wanted the rambunctious governor out of their state, considered the vice presidency a perfect place for him, for it would keep him out of the limelight and, they hoped, relegate him to political obscurity.

Theodore Roosevelt 1858–1919 Although Roosevelt wanted to continue serving as governor of New York, the state's Republicans, exasperated by his reforms and independence, compelled him to accept the vice presidential nomination to remove him from their state.

Just as he had in 1896, Bryan energetically hit the campaign trail, delivering six hundred speeches in 24 states (out of the nation's 45 states) and concentrating especially on the swing states of New York, Illinois, Indiana, and Ohio. He tried to focus on four issues: imperialism, the coinage of silver, monopolies and trusts, and the economy. None resonated strongly with the American public. Two years earlier, the United States had fought a brief war with Spain and had acquired the Philippines, Puerto Rico, and Guam as colonies. Although he had supported the war itself and even assembled a volunteer regiment, Bryan objected to America's imperialism and reminded Americans that by governing millions of colonial subjects without their consent, America was mocking its democratic principles, not to mention its isolationist tradition. But the war had been popular, and most Americans did not share Bryan's scruples. They felt that, by divine right and moral and genetic superiority, they should rule the Western Hemisphere. Bryan himself seemed inconsistent on imperialism, for he had supported the Paris Peace Treaty that had ended the Spanish-American War and granted the United States its new colonies.

Although Bryan tried once again to invoke the magical charm of silver, by 1900 it was a dead issue. His insistence on supporting free silver divided the Democratic Party and hurt him in the East, for it drove many anti-imperialists there—who otherwise would have supported him—into McKinley's arms.

Bryan awkwardly switched focus again. He declared that trusts should be broken up and that they endangered the American worker: "My greatest objection to the trust is closing the door of opportunity against our young men and condemning the boys of this country to perpetual clerkship." But Bryan's attempt to focus on economic issues rang hollow. The nation had enjoyed prosperity under McKinley's stewardship, and Republicans promised "Four Years More of the Full Dinner Pail." Most Americans believed them. Hanna once again managed McKinley's campaign with

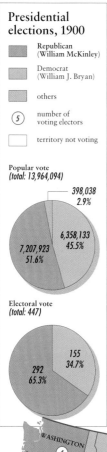

Presidential elections, 1900

Republican (William McKinley)

Democrat (William J. Bryan)

others

⑤ number of voting electors

territory not voting

Popular vote (total: 13,964,094)

398,038 — 2.9%

6,358,133 45.5%

7,207,923 51.6%

Electoral vote (total: 447)

155 34.7%

292 65.3%

smooth efficiency, accumulating a huge chest of funds, and although McKinley did little campaigning, Roosevelt's energetic efforts matched Bryan's and often allowed the vice presidential candidate to overshadow McKinley. Roosevelt, who detested the anti-imperialists, gave an especially vigorous defense of McKinley's expansionist foreign policy. Hanna also hit the campaign trail on McKinley's behalf, concentrating especially on South Dakota and Nebraska (states where Bryan was popular), and drew huge crowds of people anxious to catch a glimpse of the wealthy senator.

Bryan lost by a larger margin than he had four years earlier. He received 144,792 fewer popular votes, while McKinley gained 102,144 votes over his 1896 total and again won a majority of the popular votes, 51.6 percent. Bryan continued to have difficulty in generating appeal among urban workers, and his support was confined to agricultural states. Even there he fared worse than he had in 1896, as commercial farmers rode the wave of McKinley prosperity. Bryan lost Kansas, South Dakota, Utah, Wyoming, and even his home state of Nebraska, all of which he had won four years earlier. He did retain the support of the silver states, Colorado, Idaho, Montana, and Nevada. McKinley, by thoroughly dominating Bryan, helped further to break the South-West alliance that Bryan had tried to forge four years earlier.

McKinley became the first president since Abraham Lincoln to be elected to a second consecutive term. But on September 5, 1901, just half a year into his second term, McKinley was fatally shot by an anarchist, Leon Czolgosz, in Buffalo, New York. He succumbed to his wounds—and to poor medical care by doctors—nine days later, the third president to be assassinated. Theodore Roosevelt succeeded him and, at 42, was the youngest chief executive in the nation's history. Marcus Hanna despaired, "Now look, that damned cowboy is president of the United States!"

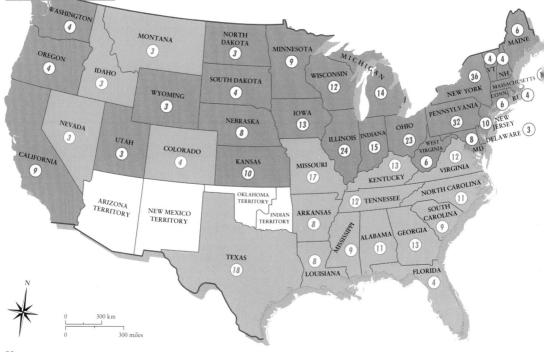

The Election of 1904

Theodore Roosevelt became an instant hit as president. One of the most popular chief executives in American history, he was especially celebrated for his impressive reservoir of energy. That was an irony, for as a boy he had been frail, nearsighted, and sickly. To compensate for his physical weaknesses, he dedicated himself to athletic development. He spent long hours in his home gym, lifting weights and working out with a punching bag, and as an undergraduate at Harvard continued to box at the school gym. An exponent of the "strenuous life," Roosevelt also became an avid out-doorsman. As president he would even leave the White House at night to run around the Washington Monument—to burn off excess energy, he explained.

Summoning his immense energy, Roosevelt threw the power and prestige of the presidency behind the progressive movement. The progressives, who cut across party lines, were reformers who wanted to alleviate the social and economic ills caused by America's rapid industrialization and urbanization. Roosevelt captured the progressive spirit by investigating dangerous trusts and successfully fighting to break up the powerful Northern Securities Corporation, which controlled many railroads in the country. He established the Department of Commerce and Labor to oversee working conditions in America.

Some of the most important progressive reforms dealt with presidential elections. Progressives felt that the process of selecting presidential nominees lay in the hands of party bosses, who often were wheeling and dealing in back rooms at the national nominating conventions. With much power and little accountability, they could frustrate the wishes of the average voter. In order to give the people more say in the nominating process, progressives promoted presidential primaries, which several states adopted in the early 1900s. In a state primary, voters could either vote for delegates to a party's national convention (a delegate selection primary) or vote directly for a presidential candidate of a party, in which case delegates would be legally bound to vote for the candidate who won the primary (a preference primary). In 1901, Florida became the first state to pass a presidential primary law. Progressives also pushed for the secret ballot, which was winning widespread adoption, especially with the introduction of automatic voting machines. The secret ballot allowed voters to cast their ballots with less fear of observation or peer pressure, which made them more independent of party bosses.

When the Republicans met in Chicago in June 1904, they nominated Roosevelt and chose Senator Charles Fairbanks of Indiana for second place on the ticket. Unlike the Republicans, the Democrats seemed disordered. In 1900 they had turned to William Jennings Bryan for a second time because there were no other Democrats of stature available. By 1904, the situation had not changed. Since his second defeat Bryan had been angling for the 1904 nomination, and his attempts to keep alive the tired issues of free silver and anti-imperialism exasperated his supporters and breached party unity. Eastern conservative Democrats who favored the gold standard—known as the "reorganizers"—gained control of the party and rejected Bryan's gospel. Casting about for a conservative nominee, the reorganizers tried to induce former President Grover Cleveland to run, but he declined. At their convention in St. Louis, Democratic reorganizers settled on Alton B. Parker, chief justice of

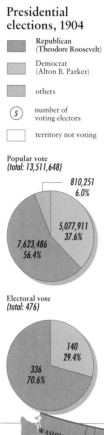

Presidential elections, 1904

Republican
(Theodore Roosevelt)

Democrat
(Alton B. Parker)

others

5 number of
voting electors

territory not voting

Popular vote
(total: 13,511,648)

810,251
6.0%

5,077,911
37.6%

7,623,486
56.4%

Electoral vote
(total: 476)

140
29.4%

336
70.6%

the New York Court of Appeals, a man with no national reputation. His running mate was Henry Davis, an 82-year-old millionaire and former senator from West Virginia. Davis became the oldest man ever nominated by a major party on a national ticket. In selecting Parker, a wealthy conservative and an advocate of the gold standard, the Democrats were trying to attract support among business interests, but it was a tough sell, for their party was still closely associated with Bryan and the populist crusade of 1896.

Roosevelt, meanwhile, won lavish support from business. He promised the country a "Square Deal," a slogan that stood as a landmark in campaign advertising by capturing his agenda in a catchy phrase. The Square Deal promised active, assertive presidential leadership and grabbed the imagination of the American electorate.

In what was a generally dull race with a foregone conclusion, neither Roosevelt nor Parker campaigned much. But Roosevelt's Square Deal had great appeal, and Roosevelt won the election with the largest share of the popular vote thus far in American history, surpassing even Andrew Jackson's 56.0 percent in the election of 1828. Parker won only 13 states, all in the South. Roosevelt also managed to chip away at southern Democratic strength by winning two border states, Missouri and West Virginia, the former of which voted Democratic just four years earlier. Roosevelt had worried that he might lose the race, and the magnitude of his victory surprised him. "I am stunned by the overwhelming victory we have won," he confided to his son Kermit.

But Roosevelt's elation overtook him. On election night he committed an egregious political blunder by issuing a statement that he would not seek reelection in 1908, consonant with his belief that a president should serve only two terms. His pledge made him an instant lame-duck president and a less formidable political leader. Roosevelt later regretted the remark so much that he once pointed to his wrist and said, "I would cut my hand off right there if I could recall that written statement!"

The Election of 1908

Theodore Roosevelt's progressive reforms did not sit well with the conservative "Old Guard" of the Republican Party. They viewed Roosevelt's actions as radical, and his increasingly strident criticism of conservatives only exacerbated his relations with them. But Roosevelt avoided a potentially divisive confrontation with the Old Guard by having pledged not to seek another term. He passed the presidential mantle to his close friend and hand-picked successor, Secretary of War William Howard Taft, an Ohio native and the first governor-general of the Philippines, who was formally nominated at the party's convention in Chicago. Taft's running mate was veteran Congressman James Sherman of New York, whom the Old Guard supported; his nomination represented a rebuke of Roosevelt.

William Howard Taft 1857–1930
A jurist rather than politician by inclination, Taft ran for president reluctantly, in his first-ever campaign for national office.

Taft was hardly an enthusiastic candidate. "I don't like politics," he once admitted. His first love was the judiciary, and he had developed a taste for this profession by serving as a federal judge in Ohio. Taft much preferred to be chief justice of the Supreme Court than president, but his wife, Helen, an ambitious, headstrong woman who dreamed of being First Lady, scotched talk of anything but the presidency. (In 1921 President Warren Harding would appoint Taft as chief justice of the Supreme Court, a position he would hold until his death in 1930.) Roosevelt was also an ardent Taft supporter once telling him, "I have always said you would be the greatest president, bar only Washington and Lincoln." Taft abhorred political stumping and predicted that the campaign would be "a kind of nightmare for me."

The Democrats met in Denver and, with the western wing of the party dominating the convention, turned once again to William Jennings Bryan, and nominated John Kern of Indiana as their vice presidential candidate. Although Bryan was a two-time loser, and former president Grover Cleveland warned Democrats that nominating him again would spell certain defeat, the crushing defeat of Alton Parker in 1904 plus the dearth of qualified Democratic prospects made the party once again pin its hopes on the Nebraskan. Calling the Republicans "plutocrats," Bryan tried to portray the Republican Party as the refuge of the wealthy and privileged. He positioned himself as more progressive a reformer than Taft, advocating tougher antitrust laws, stricter railroad supervision, a lower tariff, prolabor legislation, and the direct election of U.S. senators. "Shall the People Rule?" was Bryan's campaign mantra, expressing his belief that government had become a servile agent of corporations and big business. Bryan knew that he could not win the Northeast or the West Coast, so he counted on the South plus several midwestern and Rocky Mountain states.

Partly flushed out by Bryan's activity, Taft hit the campaign trail and gave speeches, making this one of the first campaigns in which both candidates actively traveled to stump for votes. Although pale next to Bryan's, Taft's oratory improved during the campaign. He had many advantages in his candidacy. The economy was robust again after the brief Panic of 1907. A "fatigue factor" encumbered Bryan, as even Democrats had grown tired of him.

Business leaders and most newspapers supported Taft. One of his most formidable assets was the backing of President Roosevelt, who was still immensely popular. People joked that Taft stood for "Take Advice from Theodore"; the very knowledge that Taft was Roosevelt's chosen successor was enough to win him votes. Taft gave further assurances to Roosevelt supporters by promising to carry on his policies. Of course, Bryan saw Roosevelt's shadow in a different light. Roosevelt, Bryan protested, "should let his man and me fight it out before the people." While on the campaign trail, Bryan needled Taft for living in Roosevelt's political shadow, saying that he was not sure about Taft's stand on various issues because Taft had not yet consulted with Roosevelt on them.

In his final run for the White House, Bryan suffered his worst defeat. His 6.4 million votes provided Taft had beaten Bryan decisively, with 29 states to Bryan's 16, and had lost only the South and three midwestern states (Colorado, Nebraska, Nevada, and Oklahoma). Bryan thus joined Henry Clay as the only three-time loser among major political party candidates for president.

But Bryan had adopted reform positions that moved the Democratic Party into the mainstream of American politics, and it recovered many of the votes that Alton Parker had lost in 1904. Bryan put the party in a propitious position for the next election.

On March 4, 1909, Taft was inaugurated as the nation's twenty-seventh president. The day was marked by a harsh winter blizzard, and Taft joked, "I always said it would be a cold day when I got to be president of the United States." The unusually severe snowstorm was perhaps an ill augur of Taft's presidency and his 1912 campaign for reelection.

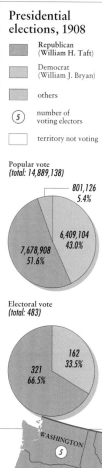

Presidential elections, 1908

- Republican (William H. Taft)
- Democrat (William J. Bryan)
- others
- ⑤ number of voting electors
- territory not voting

Popular vote
(total: 14,889,138)

- 801,126 — 5.4%
- 6,409,104 — 43.0%
- 7,678,908 — 51.6%

Electoral vote
(total: 483)

- 162 — 33.5%
- 321 — 66.5%

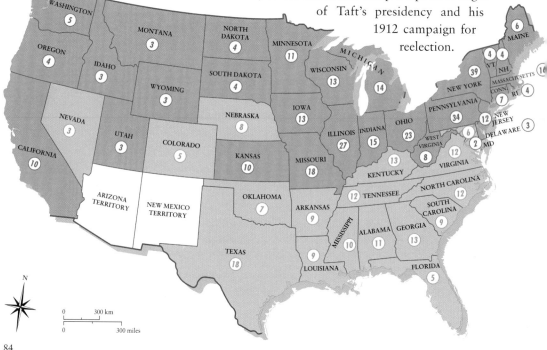

The Election of 1912

As president, William Howard Taft was miscast. Not only did he disdain the competitive arena of politics, but his personal qualities made for an unflattering contrast with Theodore Roosevelt. Roosevelt was a captivating public orator; Taft spoke in a dull, soporific style. Where Roosevelt was energetic and athletic, Taft was slow and lethargic. Roosevelt's dynamic, visionary leadership enlarged the powers of the presidency; Taft's approach to the office was disappointingly stolid and unimaginative. Having a legal cast of mind, he believed that he should scrupulously observe the limits of presidential power, and he frequently ended up deferring to Congress. Moreover, in the tightrope walk between conservatives and progressives, Roosevelt had maintained a balance for most of his presidency. Taft leaned in a conservative direction and alienated progressives, even though his record of progressive reform legislation was impressive.

Woodrow Wilson
1856–1924
A deeply religious man and son of a minister, Wilson believed that divine power helped him to win the Democratic nomination and the presidency.

After leaving the presidency, Roosevelt embarked on an African hunting safari and an extended junket in Europe. Even thousands of miles away, he heard progressives' rumblings of discontent with Taft. After getting fired by Taft, progressive ally and conservationist Gifford Pinchot went to Europe in hot haste and met with Roosevelt to complain about Taft. In 1910 Roosevelt returned to his home on Long Island. Though he said he wanted to retire, he was itching to return to politics. And he could no longer conceal his mounting dissatisfaction with Taft. He had entrusted Taft with the progressive agenda and felt that Taft had "completely twisted around the policies I advocated and acted upon." In February 1912, he declared, "My hat is in the ring."

What followed was a bitter intraparty fight. Roosevelt trounced Taft in the primaries, winning nine states compared to Taft's one (Roosevelt even won the primary in Taft's home state of Ohio). Roosevelt approached the party's national convention in Chicago confident of winning the nomination, but Taft, as president, controlled the Republican National Committee, and he was the favorite of the Old Guard. Moreover, most states selected delegates through local caucuses or conventions, where Taft supporters ran the show. So the national committee ignored the primary results, and Taft won the nomination. Infuriated, Roosevelt supporters stalked out of the convention. The Republicans continued about their business, selecting James Sherman once again to run with Taft. (Sherman died just before Election Day, on October 30; his replacement was Nicholas Murray Butler, the president of Columbia University.)

Roosevelt and his supporters immediately regrouped in Chicago and formed a third party, the Progressive Party, with the former president as their nominee and Governor Hiram Johnson of California taking second place on the ticket. The delegates gave Roosevelt a 52-minute standing ovation. "We stand at Armageddon and we battle for the Lord," he declared in his acceptance speech. The Progressive platform, embodied by Roosevelt's "New Nationalism," was ambitious and detailed. It called for an eight-hour workday and a six-day workweek; an end to child labor under the age of 16; women's suffrage, which made the party the first major national party to demand the vote for women; and many other reforms. After Roosevelt declared that he was as "strong as a Bull Moose," the Progressive Party became known as the Bull Moose Party.

The Republicans were hopelessly divided. The split between Taft and Roosevelt almost ensured the election of the Democratic nominee. Both men were likely aware of this certainty, but they were too stubborn to compromise. The Democrats, sensing a real chance to gain the White House after 16 years, met in Baltimore in June. The leading contender for the nomination was House Speaker Champ Clark of Missouri. But William Jennings Bryan declared his opposition to Clark, and the Nebraska delegation eventually supported the liberal reform governor of New Jersey, Woodrow Wilson. After 46 agonizing ballots, the convention finally nominated Wilson. (Wilson felt a sense of gratitude toward Bryan, and after his election selected the Nebraskan as his secretary of state.) The vice presidential candidate was Governor Thomas Marshall of Indiana, best known for his witticism, "What this country needs is a good five-cent cigar."

Wilson came from a background different from that of any other president. After graduating from law school, he dabbled briefly in a legal career and then studied political science at Johns Hopkins University, where he earned a doctorate, making him the first presidential candidate to have a Ph.D. He became a college professor, wrote several books, and in 1902 became president of Princeton University. Eight years later he left the university and was elected governor of New Jersey. Where most presidential candidates had come from a political or military background, Wilson had spent most of his adult life in academia.

With three distinguished candidates, the election of 1912 was an exciting contest. Most of the media focused on Wilson and Roosevelt. After a few speeches early in the campaign, Taft became listless. He was the first president ever to take to the campaign stump after winning renomination, but he expected defeat, and his heart was not in the contest.

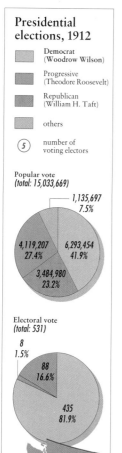

Presidential elections, 1912

- Democrat (Woodrow Wilson)
- Progressive (Theodore Roosevelt)
- Republican (William H. Taft)
- others
- (5) number of voting electors

Popular vote
(total: 15,033,669)

1,135,697
7.5%

4,119,207
27.4%

6,293,454
41.9%

3,484,980
23.2%

Electoral vote
(total: 531)

8
1.5%

88
16.6%

435
81.9%

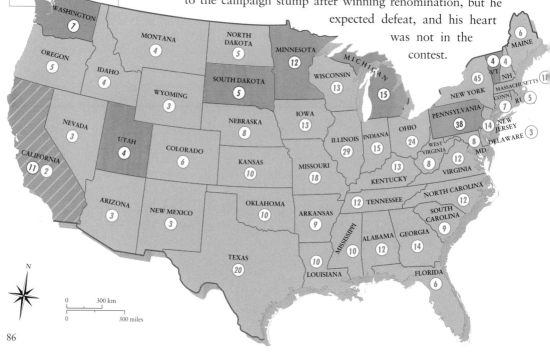

"Sometimes I think I might as well give up…. There are so many people in the country who don't like me," he wrote. Taft felt that Roosevelt had betrayed him, and he persisted in the campaign to prevent his former friend from winning.

Roosevelt and Wilson were relatively close on the issues. Wilson called his version of progressivism "New Freedom" and took an antimonopoly stance. While both men favored an activist federal government, Wilson shied away from federal government planning and programs and was more sympathetic to states' rights. Roosevelt's New Nationalism, which he had first promulgated in 1910, called for a protective tariff as well as stronger intervention by the government to control corporations and protect labor, women, and children. But the two strains of progressivism were very similar.

The most tense moment of the campaign came in its last few weeks. On October 14, in Milwaukee, Roosevelt was on his way to give a speech when a crazed gunman shot him in the chest. The bullet lodged near his heart, but its path had been slowed by a spectacle case and a folded copy of the speech that Roosevelt had in his breast pocket. Roosevelt insisted on delivering the address, and the audience gasped as he pulled out the blood-drenched text. In a typical display of vim, he spoke for an hour and a half, but he had to take two weeks off from campaigning to recuperate. Out of respect for Roosevelt, Taft and Wilson suspended their campaigns as he convalesced.

Wilson proved to be an effective campaigner—eloquent, cogent, and even witty. While he restricted his campaigning primarily to the Northeast, Bryan went on the stump for him in the West, where he made a significant contribution to Wilson's cause.

In the electoral college Wilson demolished his opponents. Roosevelt won 6states, while Taft won only Utah and Vermont. But in popular votes Wilson's victory was not nearly as impressive. He was a minority president, winning only 41.9 percent of the popular vote. His total of 6,293,454 was less than Bryan's 6,409,104 in 1908. Roosevelt came in second, a testimony to his popularity; it was the strongest showing of any third-party candidate in American history and was one of only two times that a third party won more than 20 percent of the popular vote. Taft trailed with the lowest share of the popular vote for any president seeking reelection.

The candidate of the Socialist Party, Eugene Debs of Indiana, made a respectable showing. Although he won no electoral votes, he did attract 900,000 popular votes, 6 percent of the total, the highest amount ever for a Socialist candidate and more than twice the 400,000 votes he had won in 1904 and 1908.

Although Wilson did not win a majority of popular votes, the support for himself and for Roosevelt's Progressive Party constituted a mandate to proceed with progressive reform. Taft's dreary showing, and the support received by Roosevelt and Debs, indicated that the electorate did not want conservative rule. Moreover, the Democrats won control of the Senate, so that they now ruled both houses of Congress. The way was clear for a period of reform legislation and activist presidential leadership.

The Election of 1916

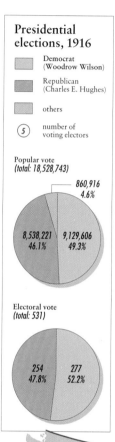

Presidential elections, 1916

- Democrat (Woodrow Wilson)
- Republican (Charles E. Hughes)
- others

(5) number of voting electors

Popular vote
(total: 18,528,743)

860,916
4.6%

8,538,221
46.1%

9,129,606
49.3%

Electoral vote
(total: 531)

254
47.8%

277
52.2%

During his first term, Woodrow Wilson fulfilled many progressive aspirations for reform and expanded presidential authority. But as the election of 1916 approached, another issue concerned the electorate even more than progressive reform. The "Great War" broke out in 1914, pitting the Allied Powers of Great Britain, France, Italy, and Russia against the Central Powers of Germany, Austria-Hungary, and the Ottoman Empire.

From the war's outset, Wilson implored Americans to remain "impartial in thought as well as in deed." While most Americans desperately wanted to avoid hostilities, true neutrality was impossible. Wilson himself was an Anglophile, and America's pro-British tropism was accentuated by the German invasion of Belgium and stories of German atrocities. Then, in February 1915, Germany began unrestricted submarine warfare around the British Isles. In May, the Germans sank the British luxury liner *Lusitania*; 1,200 persons died, including 128 Americans.

In early 1916, responding to American pressure, Germany suspended submarine warfare. As the American political conventions approached, the issue of neutrality hung thick in the air. At the Democratic National Convention in Chicago, keynote speaker Martin Glynn, the former governor of New York, extolled neutrality. He electrified the audience by citing examples of Wilson's actions that had preserved American neutrality. For each example the crowd screamed in unison, "What did we do? " ... "We didn't go to war!" Glynn shouted in response. The convention enthusiastically renominated Wilson, and the phrase "He kept us out of war" became the Democratic campaign slogan.

In June the Republicans met in Chicago. Theodore Roosevelt sought the nomination, but many party regulars, especially the Old Guard, could not forgive his 1912 campaign against William Howard Taft. The Republicans nominated Charles Evans Hughes, a former progressive governor of New York who was an associate justice of the Supreme Court and one of the country's foremost legal

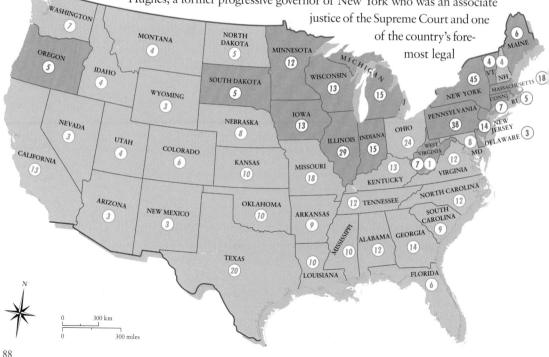

N

0   300 km

0   300 miles

scholars. Hughes's candidacy marked the first time a Supreme Court justice had run for the presidency as a major party candidate. In nominating Hughes, the Republicans hoped to attract the votes of former Progressive Party members. His running mate was Roosevelt's vice president, Charles Fairbanks. The skeletal remains of the Progressive Party wanted Roosevelt to run again, but he spurned their advances in the interest of Republican unity.

Yet many of Roosevelt's actions hurt Hughes. His support for the Republican nominee was tepid and largely symbolic; in private he had harsh words for Hughes. Moreover, Roosevelt's attitude toward the European war was much more aggressive than that of the GOP, which affirmed neutrality and denounced Wilson's foreign policy for failing to defend America's rights as a neutral nation. Roosevelt's bellicose statements startled war-wary Americans and drained support from the Republican Party. Trying to satisfy Roosevelt supporters, Hughes advocated a tough stand against Germany. The Democrats immediately branded him a warmonger. A full-page Democratic newspaper advertisement posed the haunting questions: "Wilson and Peace with Honor? or Hughes with Roosevelt and War?"

Hughes traveled and spoke extensively, but his personality was dull and his speeches even duller. Moreover, by trying to avoid getting caught between Republican conservatives and progressives, Hughes blundered. When campaigning in California, he failed to meet with Hiram Johnson, the Progressive candidate for senator and Roosevelt's running mate in 1912. It seemed like a snub of Johnson, who subsequently made no effort on Hughes's behalf. Hughes lost California by just 3,773 votes.

The loss of California proved decisive. Hughes swept the Northeast except for New Hampshire and Maryland and also won seven states in the Midwest. On election night, with the results still being counted, Wilson trudged off to bed believing that he had lost the White House. But when the news came the next day that California went for Wilson, victory slipped from Hughes's grasp. Wilson's margin was narrow, only 591,385. Just as in 1912, he failed to win a majority of the popular vote, this time gaining 49.3 percent. Like Grover Cleveland, the only other Democratic president since the Civil War to win two terms, Wilson was a minority president both times. But he became the first president since Ulysses S. Grant to serve two full consecutive terms.

While William Jennings Bryan had never managed to unite the West and South, Wilson did. Wilson carried the entire South and won all states beyond the Mississippi River except Oregon, Iowa, South Dakota, and Minnesota. In the farming states of the Midwest, Wilson's foreign policy had especially strong appeal, because these areas favored neutrality and even isolationism.

Other factors helped Wilson. His reform legislation had won the votes of many progressives who had voted for Roosevelt in 1912, as well as the votes of many Socialists. Wilson was able to sew together a coalition of traditional Democrats, including southerners, urban voters, and rural voters, and he added to them labor, women, and intellectuals. This coalition foreshadowed the groups that Franklin D. Roosevelt later was able to bring together under the Democratic umbrella. Perhaps most of all, Wilson won as the peace candidate, for his proclaimed neutrality was popular in a nation that desperately wanted to avoid getting embroiled in a European war.

Despite Roosevelt's aggressive "preparedness" campaign, Wilson came out the clear winner with his neutrality policy.

The Election of 1920

Warren G. Harding
1865–1923
Republicans picked
Harding as a
compromise candidate
whom they could
easily control.
Doubting his own
abilities to be an
effective president,
Harding once
commented, "I am a
man of limited talents
from a small town."

Despite Woodrow Wilson's 1916 campaign posture as the peace candidate, renewed unrestricted German submarine warfare forced his hand. In April 1917, at his request, Congress declared war against the Central Powers. American help secured an Allied victory, and Wilson fought to ensure that the Versailles Treaty, which dictated the terms of peace, included provisions for establishing the League of Nations to maintain world peace. But in trying to secure the treaty's ratification at home, Wilson faced stout opposition from a Republican Senate and faced a personal crisis when he was incapacitated by a stroke. In a devastating defeat for him, the Senate rejected the treaty. Wilson wanted the election of 1920 to be a referendum on the League of Nations, hoping that a Democratic victory would breathe life back into Senate consideration of the Versailles Treaty.

The ranks of both political parties were filled with mediocrities; few candidates had national stature. The Democrats met in San Francisco in June and produced a platform that supported the League. Their nominee was Ohio Governor James Cox, and his running mate was the young assistant secretary of the Navy, Franklin D. Roosevelt. Although the 38-year-old Roosevelt had little political experience, Cox had pushed for his selection, and the Democrats hoped that the magic of his last name (he was a distant cousin of Theodore) would capture votes.

The Republican National Convention produced a deadlock between General Leonard Wood, a progressive, and Governor Frank Lowden of Illinois. Warren G. Harding, an obscure senator from Ohio, emerged as the compromise candidate.

Both major candidates hailed from Ohio, and Harding's selection marked the ninth time in the 12 elections after 1872 that the Republican Party had picked an Ohio man as its nominee. The party especially wanted an Ohio man because the state had gone to Wilson in both 1912 and 1916. The Republicans could almost taste victory, and GOP senators and party regulars wanted a president of limited talent and skills, someone tractable and unassertive whom they could easily manipulate.

Harding was one of the least impressive presidential nominees in history. His vacuous mind fixed on pursuits that included adultery, late-night poker games, and liquor at a time when it was outlawed by the Eighteenth Amendment. He had few political convictions and put too much trust in his cronies—dubbed the "Ohio gang"—many of whom were unprincipled.

Yet Harding's image was appealing. With his mane of white hair, trim figure, and dapper dress, he came across as a handsome product of small-town America. Moreover, his easy affability made him a pleasant contrast to the arrogant and aloof Wilson. Harding's running mate, Calvin Coolidge, the governor of Massachusetts, also came across favorably. In 1919 Coolidge had acted forcefully to end a strike by Boston police officers. "There is no right to strike against the public safety by anybody, anywhere, anytime," he declared, a statement that enshrined him as a tough-minded defender of the people.

Harding's lack of sophistication was painfully evident in his diction. While speaking in Boston, he declared, "America's present need is not heroics but healing; not nostrums but normalcy; not revolution but restoration … not surgery, but serenity." The speech text had the word "normality," which Harding read as "normalty," and newspapers improved to the more dulcet "normalcy." The Republicans seized upon the campaign shibboleth, "Back to Normalcy," which appealed to an electorate weary of progressive reform, world war, and postwar economic dislocations. The Republican platform also pointed toward isolationism by vaguely implying that the U.S. might not take part in the League of Nations.

Harding won in a landslide, and for the first time a candidate won more than 60 percent of the popular vote, almost double Cox's share. The election confirmed the strength of the GOP, which held majorities in both houses of Congress (which they had won in 1918). Cox won the smallest share of the popular vote of any Democratic nominee since 1860, when Stephen Douglas and John Breckinridge split the Democratic vote.

The first sitting U.S. senator to win the presidency, Harding carried the North and the West and won 37 states. He even prevailed in Tennessee, the first time a Republican had carried that state. Many northern urban voters cast ballots for Harding out of resentment toward southern "drys" who supported Prohibition. Other Americans had been frightened by the paranoiac "Palmer raids" conducted by Wilson's attorney general, A. Mitchell Palmer, to expose alleged communist subversives. Perhaps most important, the election results signaled American rejection of Wilson's internationalism. The Democrats even lost their support among ethnic groups. German Americans and Irish Americans in cities, opposed to the Versailles Treaty, voted Republican or stayed away from the polls, which allowed the Republicans to capture New York City, Boston, and Baltimore. The election results killed any chance of American approval of the Versailles Treaty or participation in the League of Nations. "We have torn up Wilsonism by the roots," gloated Henry Cabot Lodge of Massachusetts, Wilson's political archnemesis.

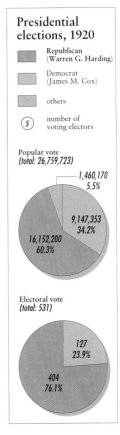

The Election of 1924

Calvin Coolidge
1872–1933
Though a quiet, dour-
faced man with a
passive approach to
the presidency,
Coolidge enjoyed
great popularity when
he ran for a full term,
as Americans
associated his
leadership with the
nation's prosperity.

Warren Harding's administration was one of the most scandal-ridden in history, but in 1923 he was spared public mortification over the corruption when he died of a heart attack. Calvin Coolidge became the nation's thirtieth president. "Silent Cal" was the stereotype of an austere, reserved New Englander and became best known for his public reticence. He also took a lackadaisical approach to the presidency, enjoying long naps in the afternoon and whiling away evenings seated in a rocking chair on the White House porch. He almost never devoted more than four hours a day to his executive duties. Despite his inactivity, Coolidge was a popular president, largely due to a booming economy. His pithy remarks revealed his worship of wealth and broadcast his support of American industry: "The business of America is business"; "Civilization and profits go hand in hand."

In June 1924, when Republicans held their national convention in Cleveland, Coolidge easily won the nomination. His vice presidential candidate was Charles Dawes, budget director under Harding and the architect of a postwar reparations plan for Germany. The presence of Dawes, a banker by profession, on the ticket reflected the probusiness orientation of the Coolidge administration.

The Democrats met in New York City, and the two wings of the party became locked in a bitter fight. The older, more traditional wing of the party was filled with rural southerners and westerners who were influenced by the revitalized Ku Klux Klan and its nativist, anti-immigrant views; this segment of the party supported William McAdoo of California, treasury secretary under Wilson. The northern, urban wing backed New York Governor Alfred Smith, an Irish Catholic who had advanced in New York politics with the support of the Tammany Hall political machine. The two wings angrily attacked each other, the urbanites calling the rural Democrats "rubes and hicks," and the populist Democrats denouncing the city dwellers as corrupt and venal. In a sweltering New York heat wave, the Democrats suffered through 103 ballots. Hundreds of New York City police officers stood guard to prevent the groups from erupting in violence. In total, the Democratic convention lasted 17 days.

Finally, both McAdoo and Smith withdrew, and the exhausted convention delegates settled on John Davis, a Wall Street lawyer who had served as a congressman from West Virginia and ambassador to Great Britain under Wilson. Davis's running mate was Charles Bryan, younger brother of William Jennings Bryan and the governor of Nebraska, whose presence on the ticket was intended to attract the rural vote. But the convention had seriously damaged the Democratic Party, and Davis later recalled that after all the squabbling, "the nomination wasn't worth purchase by anybody."

The election of 1924 brought the Progressive Party back to life. Backed by socialists, farmers, and labor, the party focused on reducing corporate monopolies. Meeting in Cleveland in July, the party nominated 61-year-old Robert "Battle Bob" LaFollette, a feisty Republican senator from Wisconsin. In a break from traditional practice, LaFollette picked his running mate, Democratic Senator Burton Wheeler of Montana. The Progressive platform espoused far-reaching reforms, including nationalization of the railroads, public ownership of utilities, an end to child labor, and election of the president by popular vote.

Davis campaigned widely, criticizing Coolidge's "vast, pervading silence"and reminding voters of the sordid scandals of the Harding administration. Coolidge did little campaigning. He shied away from speeches, and the tragic death of his son in the summer further curtailed his public activities. His most emphatic position was his probusiness orientation. "I am for economy. After that I am for more economy. At this time and under present conditions, that is my conception of serving the people," he declared. The formula sufficed. Coolidge won in a landslide. Davis's 28.9 percent of the popular vote was the lowest of any Democratic presidential nominee in the twentieth century. Coolidge won both the East and West coasts and even prevailed in many agricultural states, where rising agricultural prices buoyed the Republicans.

The election reconfirmed the strength of the GOP and the disarray of the Democrats. The Republicans attracted the majority of northern voters, who continued to view the party as the savior of the Union during the Civil War and as the party of emancipation. Business interests also allied themselves with the Republicans, which gave the party virtually unlimited financial resources and more prestige. Republicans, simply put, had greater socioeconomic status than Democrats.

Davis's dismal showing was due in part to the presence of the Progressive Party; LaFollette won 16.6 percent of the popular vote, the third-best showing for a third-party candidate in the twentieth century. He won his home state of Wisconsin and its 13 electoral votes and came in second in 11 states in the western half of the country. In the cities LaFollette's support was especially significant, for he won immigrant votes and peeled away blue-collar workers from the GOP, thus paving the way for their movement toward the Democratic Party. Like many third-party movements, the Progressive Party of 1924 was short-lived, vanishing after LaFollette's death in 1925, but it prefigured an important shift in the American electorate.

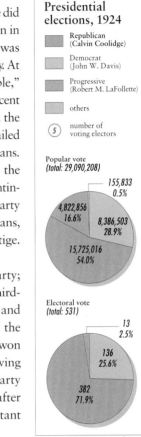

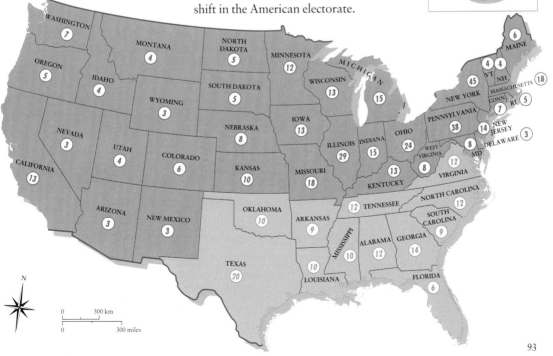

The Election of 1928

Herbert Hoover
1874–1964
Although the
presidency was the
first elective office he
had ever sought,
Hoover was a familiar
figure to many
Americans after his
successive tenure as
U.S. food
administrator during
World War I and
commerce secretary in
the Harding and
Coolidge
administrations.

Calvin Coolidge was popular enough that he could have won another full term as president, and most Americans expected him to run in 1928. But Coolidge kept tight-lipped about his intentions. On August 2, 1927, he held a press conference at a high school near his summer home in South Dakota. At the beginning of the meeting, Silent Cal quietly gave each reporter a handwritten note consisting of a single sentence: "I do not choose to run for president in nineteen twenty-eight."

The path lay open for a new Republican candidate, and when the Republicans met in Kansas City, they nominated on the first ballot Herbert Hoover, food administrator during World War I and secretary of commerce in the Harding and Coolidge administrations. To assuage farmers, who viewed the business-oriented Hoover as insensitive to agricultural interests, the party chose as its vice presidential candidate Senate Majority Leader Charles Curtis of Kansas.

The Democrats held their convention in Houston, the first party convention in the Deep South. The urban element of the party wanted to nominate Al Smith, the four-time governor of New York State, who had missed the nod in 1924. This time the Democrats needed just one ballot. They nominated Smith and selected as his running mate Senate Minority Leader Joseph Robinson of Arkansas.

Hoover was a cheerless, laconic man. He had studied engineering at Stanford University and had worked as a federal administrator. The presidency was the first elective office he had ever sought. Hoover was also a painfully awkward public orator who gave only seven speeches during the entire campaign. But he epitomized the self-made man, an orphan who became a millionaire. Republicans stressed his rags-to-riches story and portrayed him as the "Great Engineer." Hoover's election portended a "chicken in every pot and two cars in every garage," Republicans declared. "We in America today are nearer to the final triumph over poverty than ever before in the history of our land. The poorhouse is vanishing from among us," Hoover intoned in his acceptance speech.

In contrast to Hoover, Smith was a colorful character whose quick wit and brown derby hat became his trademarks as he actively campaigned throughout the country. Franklin Roosevelt dubbed him the "Happy Warrior," and the moniker quickly caught on. But Smith could not promise prosperity as convincingly as the Republicans. In trying to win broad support, he also had the handicap of being a Catholic New Yorker. His New York accent went over poorly on radio, and his lack of education, evident in his poor grammar, contrasted with the college-educated Hoover. Smith once joked that he did not know what states lay west of the Mississippi River. What further hurt Smith in the South, a traditional Democratic stronghold, was his personal opposition to Prohibition (which flew in the face of the Democratic platform, which supported it). As a "wet" he incurred the suspicion of "dry" southerners, and his position cemented his image as a liquor-loving Catholic—"Al-coholic Smith," as some people called him. Smith was the Democratic Party's first Catholic presidential nominee, and some Protestant Americans feared that he would be under the Pope's thumb.

Hoover won 40 states and became the first Republican since Reconstruction to make appreciable inroads in the Solid South, winning Florida, North Carolina, Tennessee, Texas, and Virginia. Smith won only seven states, six in the South plus Massachusetts. Hoover even beat Smith in his home state of New York. Hoover's lopsided victory confirmed the 1920s as a decade of Republican landslides.

Although the Democrats took a drubbing in this election, a fundamental realignment of the electorate was at work, one that would ultimately help make the Democratic Party the majority party in the country. In this respect, Smith's defeat was more historically significant than Hoover's victory. Smith represented the urban working class and gave voice to their feelings and concerns, especially those of Catholics and immigrants, and the Democratic Party began to act as the political home for these Americans. In 1924 the Republicans had won the country's 12 largest cities, but during the election of 1928 Smith captured them all. Smith's strong showing in Boston, the ninth-largest city in the country and home to many Irish Catholics, was especially significant because it allowed him to win Massachusetts, marking the first time a Democrat had won there in recent history. Meanwhile, many midwestern farmers who had voted for LaFollette in 1924 cast ballots for Smith, and more and more farmers generally abandoned the Republican Party, distrustful of Hoover and upset with the federal government's withdrawal of price supports under Coolidge. Although Smith won fewer states than John Davis had in 1924, he received almost twice as many popular votes as Davis. Smith's loss foreshadowed a significant shift in the American electorate, and the Democratic Party began to look for a magnetic personality who could draw together its urban and rural elements and welcome even more Americans into the party.

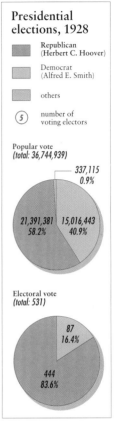

Presidential elections, 1928

Republican (Herbert C. Hoover)

Democrat (Alfred E. Smith)

others

⑤ number of voting electors

Popular vote (total: 36,744,939)

337,115 0.9%

21,391,381 58.2%

15,016,443 40.9%

Electoral vote (total: 531)

87 16.4%

444 83.6%

The Election of 1932

Franklin D. Roosevelt
1882–1945
During the 1932
campaign, Roosevelt
criticized Hoover's
"Destruction, Delay,
Despair and Doubt,"
and astonished aides
with the energy he
displayed in traveling
the country.

The prosperity of the 1920s ended with a jolt. On October 29, 1929, the stock market crashed, obliterating the savings and confidence of millions of Americans, and by the following spring the country was mired in the worst economic depression in its history. The nation's banking system collapsed, businesses failed, wages and prices plummeted, and by 1932 unemployment had reached 25 percent. Many Americans blamed Herbert Hoover, whose name became indelibly associated with the misery of the times. Jobless men and women were reduced to living in crude shacks in shantytowns called "Hoovervilles"; yesterday's newspaper was a "Hoover blanket"; a "Hoover flag" was a pants pocket turned inside out, indicating no spare change. As the 1932 campaign approached, the Republicans met in a joyless convention in Philadelphia. Only a miracle could stave off Hoover's defeat, and the Republicans knew it. But they did not want to repudiate their president, and no other Republican emerged as a viable alternative. Hoover won renomination.

The Democrats met in a hopeful, suspense-filled convention in Chicago. Whomever they nominated stood a good chance of defeating the hapless Hoover, and that man became Franklin Delano Roosevelt. Born into a wealthy New York family and educated at Groton Academy and Harvard, Roosevelt had grown up idolizing his distant cousin, Theodore Roosevelt, and in 1905 married Eleanor Roosevelt, Theodore's niece. In 1920 he gained national exposure when he ran as the Democratic vice presidential candidate, but his promising political career seemed to have been cut short the following year when he contracted poliomyelitis, which paralyzed his legs. Although unable to walk, Roosevelt relied on grit, determination, and an unflagging optimism to climb back into the political ring. In 1928 he was elected governor of New York, bucking a national trend that witnessed most Democrats, including presidential candidate Al Smith, take a beating. As governor of New York State, Roosevelt had won a reputation as a reformer with a liberal imagination, advocating old-age pensions, conservation, and aid for the jobless.

Democrats selected House Speaker John Nance Garner of Texas as Roosevelt's running mate. In a dramatic gesture, Roosevelt broke precedent by personally appearing at the convention to accept his nomination. (Until this time, nominees gave their acceptance speeches after the convention, usually at a celebration in their hometown.)

Despite—or perhaps because of—his handicap, Roosevelt proved a peerless campaigner. Polio had made Roosevelt understand human suffering, and he emerged from this chapter of his life with his sunny disposition intact. The ebullient "Happy Days Are Here Again" was Roosevelt's campaign song, and his cheer lifted the spirits of many people who regarded him a welcome relief from Hoover's solemnity. This campaign featured the first widespread broadcasts over radio, and here again Roosevelt had an advantage over Hoover, his mellifluous voice contrasting favorably with Hoover's somber tones. Roosevelt also took a railroad tour to the Pacific coast and back, during which crowds saw a healthy and vigorous candidate.

One of the most remarkable aspects of Roosevelt's campaign was that he hid his inability to walk. He never wanted the American people to see him in a wheelchair or with crutches, for he knew those things were the political kiss of death. The press abided by a gentlemen's agreement not to publish any photographs of Roosevelt in a wheel-chair. Cartoonists even depicted him walking or running. The result of this illusion was that for a long time many Americans were unaware that Roosevelt could not walk.

Roosevelt was vague about what he would do to alleviate the Depression, and that was no accident. Privately his plans were still unformed. But Roosevelt was more pragmatic and disposed toward experimentation and improvisation than Hoover. Once he became president, Roosevelt told his staff, "Take a method and try it. If it fails, try another. But above all try something."

On Election Day, the American people were eager not so much to vote for Roosevelt as to vent their frustrations against Hoover. Roosevelt buried the president in a landslide. The tables cruelly turned on Hoover: just four years earlier he had enjoyed a spectacular triumph by winning 41 states; in 1932 he won only 6 states, all in New England. Hoover's percentage of the popular vote was the lowest a Republican candidate had earned since William Howard Taft in 1912, when the party was divided. Roosevelt's landslide cut across geographical sections, making him the first candidate since Franklin Pierce in 1852 to win national, rather than sectional, support. After having captured the House in 1930, the Democrats also won control of the Senate, to enjoy large majorities in both houses of Congress.

Some Americans wondered if capitalism's days in America were numbered. Before Roosevelt was inaugurated, one of his friends predicted that if he steered the country out of the Depression, he would be remembered as the greatest president in history. Roosevelt told his friend: "If I fail, I shall be the last one." Yet the election showed that the American people, although in a deep state of despair, wanted a solution not a revolution. They were not willing to seek answers outside the pale of a democratic, free-market state. The Socialist candidate, Norman Thomas, received just 882,000 votes.

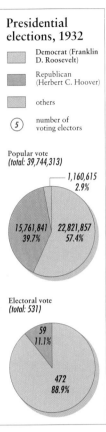

Presidential elections, 1932

- Democrat (Franklin D. Roosevelt)
- Republican (Herbert C. Hoover)
- others
- ⑤ number of voting electors

Popular vote
(total: 39,744,313)

- 1,160,615 2.9%
- 15,761,841 39.7%
- 22,821,857 57.4%

Electoral vote
(total: 531)

- 59 11.1%
- 472 88.9%

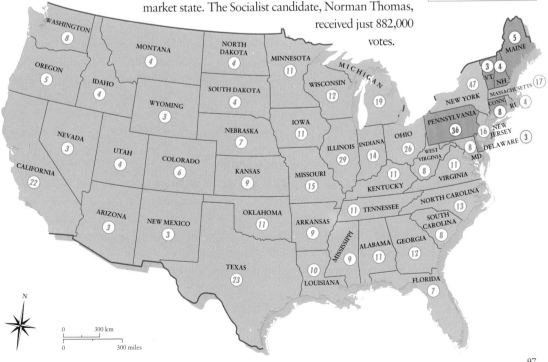

The Election of 1936

When he accepted the 1932 Democratic nomination for president, Franklin Roosevelt had declared, "I pledge you, I pledge myself, to a new deal for the American people." From this statement came the name for Roosevelt's domestic program designed to combat the Great Depression. With solid Democratic majorities in Congress, Roosevelt was able to pass an extraordinary amount of legislation aimed at ameliorating the economic crisis. In his whirlwind first 100 days as president, he established new agencies such as the Agricultural Adjustment Administration, the Securities and Exchange Commission, the Federal Deposit Insurance Corporation, the Civilian Conservation Corps, and the National Recovery Administration. Although the New Deal's momentum slackened after Roosevelt's first year in office, the Democrats increased their congressional majorities in 1934, and Republican governorships were reduced to just 7 states. From 1935 to 1936, Roosevelt presided over another wave of sweeping legislation that included the National Labor Relations Act, the establishment of the Works Progress Administration, and the landmark Social Security Act.

While national employment and the gross national product both improved during Roosevelt's first term, and bread lines and Hoovervilles began to disappear, none of the New Deal initiatives ended the Great Depression; some had only the mildest of palliative effects. Certain measures aroused opposition: the Supreme Court declared the Agricultural Adjustment Act and the National Recovery Administration unconstitutional because of their alarming expansion of government power.

One of the most important effects of the New Deal was emotive. Its programs boosted the sagging morale of many Americans, and by expanding the government's role as a relief agent and creating a welfare system, the New Deal effected a fundamental transformation in the relationship between the federal government and American citizens. Roosevelt was immensely popular, and as the election of 1936 approached, he was a shoo-in to win reelection. When the Democratic National Convention met in Philadelphia, they renominated Roosevelt and John Garner. (At this gathering, the party abandoned the rule, instituted in 1832, requiring a two-thirds majority for nomination. Henceforth Democratic candidates required a simple majority.) The president gave a stirring acceptance speech in which he proclaimed that Americans had a "rendezvous with destiny" in saving the country and its government.

The Republican National Convention was held in Cleveland; needing to select a candidate from the Midwest, an area where the Democrats had thrashed the GOP in 1932, the party nominated Governor Alf Landon of Kansas, a former Bull Moose Progressive. His running mate was Frank Knox, publisher of the *Chicago Daily News* and another former Bull Mooser. As governor, Landon supported some New Deal measures but also distinguished himself as a fiscal conservative who had balanced his state's budget. While Landon and the Republicans charged that New Deal programs were spendthrift ("willful waste," as Landon said) and created budget deficits and a bloated bureaucracy, they also embraced some of its principles, such as old-age pensions, aid for farmers, and federal help for the jobless. They resolved to continue such programs, although they promised to do so in ways that abided by the Constitution, respected private enterprise, and exercised fiscal responsibility. Business as well as the newspaper media described Landon as a "liberal Coolidge," meaning that he would tend to the nation's social needs without spending much federal money.

The Works Progress Administration (WPA) originally perceived as a humanitarian measure that might jump-start the economy, also functioned as a huge national patronage device on behalf of the Democratic Party.

Popular challenges to the New Deal came from three prominent Americans: Senator Huey Long, who enjoyed almost dictatorial power in Louisiana; Father Charles Coughlin, a Detroit Catholic priest who attracted a large following through his radio broadcasts; and Dr. Francis Townsend, a California physician who proposed a special pension for the elderly. These demagogues appealed to the fears and bewilderment of lower-middle-class Americans. After the assassination of Huey Long in 1935, Reverend Gerald L. K. Smith took up the cudgels as Long's successor, and joined with Coughlin and Townsend to form the Union Party. The party nominated Congressman William Lemké of North Dakota as their presidential candidate. Lemké, a listless speaker, mounted an ineffective campaign and was notable perhaps only for his unusual appearance. With a glass eye and bald head dotted with yellow freckles, he was what H. L. Mencken called "the most astonishing looking candidate that I have ever seen."

Landon won the support of many members of the business community and most newspapers, who charged that the New Deal infringed on individual liberty and threatened the free-market system. Businessmen bitterly resented the increased government regulation and taxes of the New Deal and the feeling

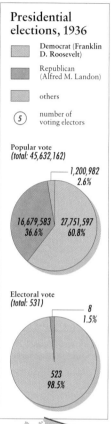

Presidential elections, 1936

Democrat (Franklin D. Roosevelt)

Republican (Alfred M. Landon)

others

(5) number of voting electors

Popular vote (total: 45,632,162)

1,200,982 2.6%

16,679,583 36.6%   27,751,597 60.8%

Electoral vote (total: 531)

8 1.5%

523 98.5%

that they, after enjoying an exalted status in 1920s America, were being eclipsed by the federal government. The well-to-do charged that Roosevelt was a "traitor" to his class. (Interestingly, during elections Roosevelt usually lost his hometown of Hyde Park, New York, a haven for wealthy citizens, who grew to loathe him. When Roosevelt visited Harvard University, his alma mater, the students booed him.) Conservative Democrats, including former presidential candidates John Davis and Al Smith, worried aloud that Roosevelt was careening toward socialism, and endorsed Landon.

Compared to the president, Landon was a small-time politician. The governor of a relatively small Midwestern state, he lacked the president's magnetic charm and smooth radio voice. Landon knew that though the president had his critics, he was invincible. Roosevelt, with a united party behind him, enjoyed the high road in the campaign and never even mentioned his opponent by name. He won 60.8 percent of the popular vote, even more than Harding's 60.3 percent in 1920. It was the greatest victory in American electoral history, to be surpassed only by Lyndon Johnson's landslide in 1964. Landon's 36.6 percent was the second-worst showing by any Republican candidate in the twentieth century. Roosevelt won every state except Maine and Vermont, beating Landon in the electoral college 523 to 8, the most lopsided electoral victory since James Monroe. Maine had been a bellwether state, voting for the winning candidate since 1860, which led to the expression, "As Maine goes, so goes the nation." But after this election, Democratic National Chairman James Farley joked, "As Maine goes, so goes Vermont." Landon even lost his home state of Kansas, which had voted Republican in every election since its entry into the Union in 1861.

The Democrats increased their majorities in Congress;

in the House the Republicans were reduced to 89 representatives, and in the Senate to 16. The Union Party polled 1.9 percent of the popular vote and quickly withered away. While the Great Depression was far from over, the New Deal had imbued Americans with hope. Roosevelt proposed to lead the way toward economic recovery, and most Americans were content to follow him.

During the 1920s the Democratic Party had been split between its urban, northern wing and its rural, southern wing. The former tended to be Catholic and "wet" and had supported Al Smith in 1924 and 1928; the latter tended to be Protestant and "dry" and had supported William McAdoo in 1924 and had to swallow hard to accept Smith as a nominee in 1928. The eclipse of these two men lessened the acrimony between the two wings, and the Great Depression represented a new, urgent issue that united the two sides, who had settled on Roosevelt as their nominee in 1932. The Depression was a chance for Democrats to break the Republican majority in America, and they seized the opportunity, transforming themselves into the majority party within only a few years.

Roosevelt built a broad Democratic coalition. Class played an important role in this election, unlike in previous elections, where region was a dominant factor. As a Democrat, Roosevelt could already count on the Solid South. But to this region he added an alliance comprising different classes and groups. Roosevelt became the enemy of the privileged and the defender of the downtrodden. He relished the role, lashing out against big business and monied interests. He told one crowd that the friends of "organized money are unanimous in their hate for me, and I welcome their hatred." The underprivileged and jobless gratefully supported him, as did urban voters, industrial workers, labor unions, liberal intellectuals, and farmers in the South and West. The elderly, thankful for the Social Security Act and its old-age pensions, voted for Roosevelt in large numbers. Roosevelt won three-quarters of the black vote: African Americans, voting mostly in northern cities, switched their political allegiance en masse to the Democratic Party. While the New Deal offered little in the way of civil rights for blacks, it offered economic relief to the unemployed, many of whom were black. The departure of African Americans from the party of Abraham Lincoln represented a historic political shift.

This election witnessed another historic transformation. By reelecting Roosevelt so resoundingly, Americans signaled their acceptance of an expanded federal role in their lives, with the Democratic Party as the vehicle to effect it. This was ironic, for Democrats since the time of Thomas Jefferson had supported states' rights and a weak central government. Meanwhile, the Republican Party, which had been founded on the principle of a strong central government and federal assistance to stimulate the economy, contradicted many of its founding principles in opposing Roosevelt's New Deal. With its new defining principles and new coalition of voters, the Democratic Party became the majority party in the country. It would dominate American politics for the next generation.

The Election of 1940

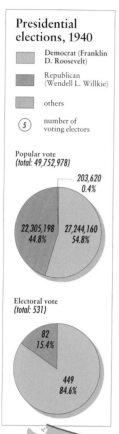

The election of 1936 represented the apogee of the New Deal. During 1937 and 1938, the nation's economic recovery slid off track as industrial production, after a partial recovery, declined and unemployment worsened. Conservative southern Democrats became disenchanted with the New Deal legislation that increased the power of labor and decreased the strength of southern planters. During the 1938 midterm elections, the Republicans picked up seats in both houses of Congress. The results represented the first significant GOP gains since the onset of the Great Depression, and were all the more impressive in view of the pounding the party had taken just two years earlier. Meanwhile, the president was forced to look toward foreign policy.

In September 1939, World War II broke out in Europe. In the United States, isolationist sentiment was at flood tide. Although Roosevelt adhered to a policy of official U.S. neutrality, his administration—and most Americans—clearly favored the Allied nations, and Roosevelt provided economic and military aid to the Allies, circumventing restrictions imposed by neutrality acts passed during the mid-1930s.

The European war injected itself into the 1940 presidential campaign. Considerable speculation centered on the question of whether Roosevelt would break with tradition and run for a third term. He delighted in the job and its trappings and performed deftly as president. The most important factor influencing Roosevelt's decision to seek a third term was the war overseas. Without this international crisis, Roosevelt might have been tempted to retire, but now he felt compelled to remain in office. He sent out word to Democrats that he would accept a "draft" at their Chicago convention in July.

Roosevelt won the nomination on the first ballot. But this time he needed a new running mate: Vice President John Garner, a conservative, had soured on the New Deal and wanted out. During this convention, Roosevelt initiated the practice of personally selecting a running mate, abandoning the tradition—

more than a century old—whereby convention delegates picked the nominee. The delegates were stunned at Roosevelt's choice: Henry Wallace, a former Republican whose views, such as his ardent support of labor unions and civil rights for blacks, were too liberal for many Democrats, and whose aloof personality had won him few friends. Delegates booed at the mention of Wallace's name, but Roosevelt insisted on his choice, and Eleanor Roosevelt went to Chicago to assuage the conventioneers' concerns. The delegates reluctantly accepted Wallace but resented the manner in which Roosevelt had forced his wishes upon them.

On June 28, the Republican National Convention, televised for the first time in history, began in Philadelphia. The most eminent prospects were New York State District Attorney Thomas E. Dewey, the apparent front-runner even though he was just 37 years old and politically inexperienced; Robert Taft, a senator from Ohio and son of the twenty-seventh president; and Senator Arthur Vandenberg of Michigan. All three men, especially Taft, leaned toward isolationism. But a dark-horse candidate emerged and won the nomination: Wendell Willkie, a Wall Street lawyer and president of a private utilities company. Willkie had been a Democrat until 1939 and had never held public office. He was the paradigmatic political novice, but precisely the kind of candidate the GOP needed—colorful, charismatic, and capable of rousing public interest. His running mate was Senator Charles McNary of Oregon, whose isolationist beliefs contrasted with Willkie's internationalism and who would, the Republicans hoped, attract Americans wary of involvement in another European war.

Wendell Willkie notification ceremony, Ellwood Indiana, 17 August, 1940.

Willkie had the backing of wealthy businessmen and many journalists. He ran an ambitious campaign, visiting 34 states and delivering 540 speeches. Although energetic, Willkie was a poor campaigner and public speaker. An even greater problem was that he found few issues on which to assail Roosevelt. He tried to alert the electorate to the dangerous precedent of a third-term president. He also assailed the New Deal for its failure to end the Great Depression. Neither issue evoked much attention. By October Willkie had shifted to foreign policy. While he was an internationalist who believed that Roosevelt's policy of aiding Great Britain was correct, he warned Americans that Roosevelt would involve the U.S. in the European war. "If you reelect him you may expect war in April 1941," Willkie predicted.

For most of the fall Roosevelt carried on his presidential duties without answering Willkie's charges. Only in late October did Roosevelt finally enter the fray, giving a series of speeches that defended his administration and attacked the Republican Party for "playing politics" with national defense and security. On October 30, just days before the election, the president gave an emphatic rejoinder to Willkie's most strident charge: "I have said this before, but I shall say it again and again and again: Your boys are not going to be sent into any foreign wars."

Roosevelt coasted to another easy victory. But in 1936, he had won 60.8 percent of the vote; this time, 54.8 percent. Maine and Vermont stayed in the Republican column; Willkie also won Michigan and Indiana, as well as six midwestern farm states: Colorado, Iowa, Kansas, Nebraska, North Dakota, and South Dakota. After the election, the president and the challenger swiftly patched up their differences, and Willkie urged the country to unite behind Roosevelt amid the growing international crisis.

The Election of 1944

The election of 1944 was only the third to take place during wartime. In December 1941, after the Japanese attack on Pearl Harbor, the U.S. entered World War II. President Franklin Roosevelt made it clear that the war effort would supersede the New Deal, telling reporters that "Dr. Win-the-War" was replacing "Dr. New Deal."

Meeting in Chicago, the Democrats nominated Roosevelt for an unprecedented fourth term. But their opposition to Henry Wallace had crystallized; they were unwilling to stomach the vice president for another term because of his stridently liberal views. Roosevelt, concerned about splitting the Democratic Party, agreed to drop Wallace from the ticket, and turned to a moderate senator from Missouri, Harry Truman. While Truman was far from a Senate luminary, he had gained national recognition as chairman of the Senate War Investigation Committee, where he acted as a defender of the public interest by rooting out waste and corruption in war contracts and thereby saving taxpayers' money. Truman initially balked at the idea of becoming vice president, a job he considered thankless. When Roosevelt learned of Truman's reluctance, he barked out, "Well, tell him if he wants to break up the Democratic Party in the middle of the war, that's his responsibility." Truman accepted the nomination.

The Republicans approached the election of 1944 with hopes of finally slaying the political giant in the White House. Anxiety over the war and resentment over wartime domestic controls allowed the Republicans to make gains in the 1942 midterm elections, an increase of 10 seats in the Senate and 47 in the House. The Republicans hoped their momentum would carry them to the presidency. Their Chicago convention nominated Thomas Dewey, who had been elected governor of New York just two years earlier as part of the impressive Republican midterm showing. Dewey had a reputation for progressive internationalism and, in order to balance the ticket, the convention picked Governor John Bricker of Ohio, a conservative internationalist, to run with him. Dewey was just 42 years old, and even four years earlier had been a top contender for the Republican nomination. At the time, Roosevelt's acerbic secretary of the interior, Harold Ickes, commented that Dewey had "thrown his diaper into the ring."

Dewey tried to turn his youth to his advantage. He could not attack the president's conduct of the war without appearing unpatriotic, so he chose instead to reiterate the familiar charges of Democratic inefficiency, waste in government, and excessive concentration of power. But Dewey also contrasted his own youthful vigor with the president's declining health and lengthy tenure in office. It was "time for a change," Dewey emphasized, time to replace the "tired old men" of the Roosevelt administration. Stories circulated that Roosevelt was gravely ill, and his pale, haggard mien all but confirmed the rumors. At 62 years of age, Roosevelt was indeed beset with a host of health problems, including heart disease and hypertension.

For a time the campaign seemed to have stimulated Roosevelt's competitive juices. As usual, he began the campaign late, with a kickoff speech on September 23. The speech was one of the most hilariously feisty in American history. After attacking the Republicans for their defense policies and alleged indifference to labor and the poor,

Roosevelt claimed that the GOP had even stooped to picking on his Scottish terrier, Fala. With mock indignation, the president chided, "These Republican leaders have not been content with attacks on me, or on my wife, or on my sons. No, not content with that, they now include my little dog Fala. Well, of course, I don't resent attacks and my family doesn't resent attacks, but Fala does resent them." Roosevelt had set the right tone of battle, and the speech helped to galvanize Democrats. In order to dispel speculation about his failing health, Roosevelt made vigorous campaign appearances in October, including a five-hour ride through New York City in an open car during a cold, driving rain. This display of fortitude impressed voters, but over the long term it further drained the president of his strength.

Roosevelt won a fourth term, but the election of 1944 was the closest of his four presidential contests. The New Deal coalition held firm for the president, who increased his support from the cities and from organized labor. Labor union strength had grown from 10 million to 15 million during the war, and the new Political Action Committee of the Congress of Industrial Organizations (CIO) registered millions of workers, who voted for Roosevelt in force. In addition to the New Deal coalition, Roosevelt received substantial support from the American servicemen fighting overseas, who voted by absentee ballot. The American people signaled their approval of Roosevelt's wartime leadership and did not want to "change horses in midstream," a concern that the president's supporters voiced. Americans wanted him to bring the war to its successful conclusion and shape the peace that would follow. But in April 1945, five months before the war's formal conclusion, Roosevelt died of a cerebral hemorrhage. An outpouring of national grief followed for the man whom many citizens felt they knew personally and who, for many young Americans, had been their only president.

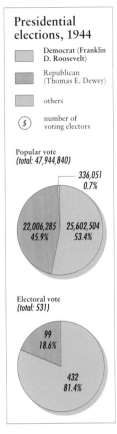

Presidential elections, 1944

Democrat (Franklin D. Roosevelt)

Republican (Thomas E. Dewey)

others

(5) number of voting electors

Popular vote
(total: 47,944,840)

336,051
0.7%

22,006,285
45.9%

25,602,504
53.4%

Electoral vote
(total: 531)

99
18.6%

432
81.4%

The Election of 1948

Harry Truman
1884–1972
Roosevelt picked
Truman as his running
mate because the
senator had supported
New Deal policies and
had gained national
attention by
investigating national
defense contracts,
unearthing fraud and
waste, and saving
taxpayers billions of
dollars.

The atomic bomb brought an unexpectedly sudden end to World War II. As president toward the close of the war, Harry Truman initially enjoyed great popularity, and partisanship was subordinated to the national effort to win the war. But the quick conclusion of the war caught the national economy off guard, and once the nation was thrust into the stresses of reconversion, Truman's standing with the American people fell dramatically. Taxes remained high, inflation surged to double digits, and key goods such as meat, automobiles, and appliances were in short supply. Wages could not keep up with soaring prices, which led to labor unrest. In 1946, an epidemic of strikes swept through the country, affecting major industries such as coal mining, railways, and steel. Americans blamed Truman for the problems, and he seemed unable to bring order to the economic chaos. Meanwhile, around the world events seemed to be spinning out of control. The U.S. and the U.S.S.R., once wartime partners, saw their alliance crumble after the war, and Eastern Europe fell under Soviet control. The cold war between the free and the communist worlds cast a pall of fear and uncertainty over Americans.

After the war, partisanship and old realignments reemerged, with conservatives and Republicans trying to block any expansion of the liberal welfare state that had grown during the New Deal. In the fall of 1945 Truman promulgated a series of legislative initiatives that he labeled the "Fair Deal," which included proposals for a higher minimum wage, national health insurance, a federal guarantee of full employment, and public housing. Congress's brusque rejection of the Fair Deal reflected the nation's conservative mood.

As the 1946 midterm elections approached, with conservative forces prevailing in Congress and inflation raging throughout the country, Truman was politically vulnerable. Critics portrayed him as a man struggling in water far over his head, unable to meet the demands of the presidency or measure up to FDR's example. Republicans developed two of the most satirical political slogans in history: "To Err Is Truman" and the simple question, "Had Enough?" Capitalizing on the Red Scare and reports of graft in the White House, they charged that the Truman presidency was one of "confusion, corruption, and communism." The Republicans won a thumping victory in the midterm elections, taking control of both houses of Congress. In a move designed to revenge FDR's unprecedented 12 years in office, the new Congress passed the Twenty-second Amendment in 1947, which limited a president to two terms.

Republicans saw their first real chance of winning the presidency since Herbert Hoover's victory 20 years earlier. Meeting in Philadelphia, they nominated New York Governor Thomas E. Dewey as their presidential candidate. Although he had lost to FDR in 1944, Dewey had made a respectable showing and had since established impressive credentials as a progressive governor, cutting taxes and banning discrimination in employment.

Many Democrats, including the Americans for Democratic Action, wanted to abandon Truman and nominate instead World War II hero General Dwight D. Eisenhower, but the general refused to run. The Democrats were stuck with

Truman, who seemed destined to lose. The nation lacked confidence in his leadership, and his standing in public opinion samplings was appallingly low. (An April 1948 poll showed that only 36 percent of respondents approved of his performance as president.) Moreover, the Democratic Party was splintered. The party's left wing broke away to protest Truman's harsh anti-Soviet foreign policy. These dissidents formed the Progressive Party and nominated former Vice President Henry Wallace. The Progressive Party blamed Truman for the cold war, denounced the policy of "containing" communism, and called for the elimination of America's nuclear arsenal. America's Communist Party endorsed Wallace, and its members flocked to his crusade.

At the Democratic National Convention in Philadelphia, the party developed another split, this one from its right wing. Hubert H. Humphrey, the mayor of Minneapolis, introduced a strong civil rights plank for the party platform, which the convention adopted and which Truman had endorsed. Southern delegates began to protest but found that their microphones had been shut off. Furious, the delegates from Alabama and Mississippi stormed out of the convention. Southern Democrats subsequently met in Birmingham and formed the States' Rights Party, more commonly known as the "Dixiecrats," and nominated South Carolina Governor J. Strom Thurmond as their candidate. The Dixiecrats openly advocated "segregation of the races" and denounced what they considered federal encroachment on states' rights. The loss of southern support was a crushing blow to Truman, who otherwise could have counted on the Democratic South.

With the Democratic party badly splintered and Truman unpopular, the Republicans anticipated a cakewalk. Their ticket was strong and, with California Governor Earl Warren as the vice presidential candidate, geographically balanced. (By contrast, Truman's running mate was Alben Barkley, a 71-year-old senator from Kentucky, which neighbored Truman's home state of Missouri.) Moreover, Dewey was well-educated, a graduate of the University of Michigan and Columbia University Law School, whereas Truman had never gone to college. Few Democrats thought that Truman would win, and the atmosphere at their national convention resembled that of a wake. "You could cut the gloom with a corn knife," Barkley later recalled. "The very air smelled of defeat."

Truman was undaunted. "I'm going to fight hard. I'm going to give 'em hell," he pledged at the convention. The pugnacious but fetching remark gained widespread attention, and during the campaign crowds frequently yelled, "Give 'em hell, Harry." The 64-year-old president put on a remarkable display of energy and determination. During September and October he traveled 22,000 miles by train, delivering ten or more speeches a day. His train stopped not only at large cities but at small towns as well. Republicans scorned these "whistle-stops" as a waste of time, but they became a badge of honor for Truman. In the curious alchemy of a political fight, the Truman camp adopted the term "whistle-stop," which the Republicans had intended as pejorative, to describe their campaign tour.

Truman portrayed himself as an ardent foe of communism and had evidence to prove it. In June 1948 Soviet Premier Josef Stalin had imposed a blockade of West Berlin, trying to pressure the Western Allies into abandoning that city. Truman reacted forcefully with an airlift that flew supplies around the clock into West Berlin. The blockade and the airlift were both in full force throughout 1948 and provided a stark display of Truman's commitment to combating Soviet aggression. Truman's dismissal of Henry Wallace from the cabinet had also offered further proof of his rigid anticommunism, and the presence of Communists in the Progressive Party tarnished Wallace's campaign.

During the campaign Truman deflected blame for the country's domestic ills by using the Eightieth Congress as a whipping boy. Known for his salty language, Truman used words like "rotten" and "poppycock" to lambaste GOP policies, called Republicans "gluttons of privilege" and "bloodsuckers with offices in Wall Street," and referred to the "do-nothing, good-for-nothing" Congress. He scolded Congress for its antilabor and antipoor positions, and in order to contrast himself with the Republicans and cement his appeal among the New Deal coalition groups, Truman advocated liberal proposals, calling for a higher minimum wage, repeal of the antilabor Taft-Hartley Act, and more public housing.

Despite Truman's energetic campaign, all of the polls and pundits predicted that he would lose. In September, the Roper polling organization, certain that Dewey would win, stopped taking polls. An October Gallup poll showed Dewey with a comfortable lead over Truman, 49.5 percent to 44.5 percent. All the major newspapers and magazines endorsed Dewey and forecast his victory. *Newsweek* predicted a Dewey "landslide"; *Life* magazine pictured Dewey with the inscription, "The next President of the United States"; the *Los Angeles Times* had the acid comment, "Mr. Truman is the most complete fumbler and blunderer this nation has seen in high office in a long time." The election results seemed a foregone conclusion.

But Truman pulled off the greatest upset in the history of presidential elections. He won 24 million votes (49.5 percent) and 24 states compared to Dewey's 22 million (45.1 percent) and 16 states. The electoral vote count was 303 to 189. Even though Dewey doubled his 1944 electoral vote, he had 36,000 fewer popular votes.

Neither of the splinter parties fared well. Thurmond and Wallace each won a little over one million votes, which translated to 2.4 percent of the popular vote. Although Wallace received no electoral votes, Thurmond won 39 from Alabama, Louisiana, Mississippi, and South Carolina. But Thurmond did little damage to the president, for the rest of the South went solidly to Truman. Had the splinter parties not been present, Truman's victory would have been even more stunning, for he likely would have won the four states Thurmond did and, without Wallace in the race, he might have won Maryland, Michigan, and perhaps even New York. As a crowning touch to Truman's victory, the Democrats also wrested both houses of Congress from the Republicans. From Truman's victory came the legendary photograph of him, grinning broadly, holding up a copy of the *Chicago Tribune* with the erroneous heading, "Dewey Defeats Truman."

Most Americans found Truman's personality and character more attractive than Dewey's. Of the four candidates aiming for the White House, the president was by far the best campaigner. Truman came across as a feisty underdog, someone the average American could understand and appreciate. Truman showed "the kind of courage the American people admire," commented Republican Senator Arthur Vandenberg of Michigan.

Dewey had few such attributes. His personality was stale and his manner stiff. Alice Roosevelt Longworth, a daughter of Theodore Roosevelt, said that Dewey reminded her of "the little man on the wedding cake." Dewey's campaign tactics were also ill-advised. Believing that he had erred in waging too aggressive a campaign in 1944, Dewey was determined to show more mild, statesmanlike behavior this time. Deliberately vague and less combative than Truman, he mortgaged policy specifics to the future, when he would presumably be sitting in the Oval Office. What glimpses of Dewey's personality Americans did see were not always attractive. Once, when he was speaking from the rear of his campaign train, it suddenly lurched backward. Dewey exploded in wrath, cursing the train engineer.

One of the most important factors in Truman's stunning victory was the strength of the Democratic coalition. The various groups that embraced the Democratic Party during the New Deal cast ballots for Truman: labor, the elderly, urban residents, ethnic groups, farmers, and African Americans. Northern blacks came out in force to support Truman, which offset the drain of Democratic votes in the South that Thurmond's campaign caused. Truman won an even greater percentage of the African-American vote than had FDR. With this powerful coalition intact, Truman proved that a Democrat could win a presidential election even without the Solid South.

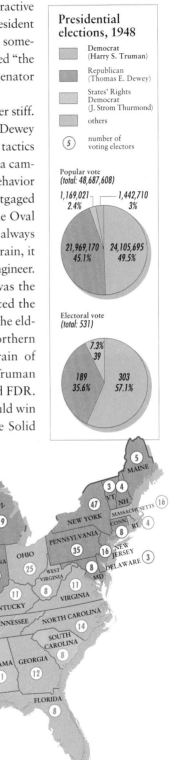

Presidential elections, 1948

- Democrat (Harry S. Truman)
- Republican (Thomas E. Dewey)
- States' Rights Democrat (J. Strom Thurmond)
- others

⑤ number of voting electors

Popular vote
(total: 48,687,608)

1,169,021 — 1,442,710
2.4% — 3%

21,969,170 — 24,105,695
45.1% — 49.5%

Electoral vote
(total: 531)

7.3%
39

189 — 303
35.6% — 57.1%

The Election of 1952

Dwight D. Eisenhower
1890–1969
Eisenhower's victory
in 1952 came as a
great relief to
Republicans who
feared that their party
might be permanently
weakened by the
Democrats' long hold
on the White House.

In 1952 the Republicans finally saw hope for victory. Harry Truman's popularity had plummeted, and setbacks in the cold war dampened Democratic prospects for retaining the White House. In August 1949, Americans were alarmed to learn that the Soviets had exploded their first atomic bomb years before most American scientists thought possible. Two months later, Mao Zedong's Communists gained control of China. Republicans excoriated Truman and Secretary of State Dean Acheson for "losing China." And the first military conflict of the cold war was turning into a quagmire: the Korean War, which had begun in 1950, was stalemated.

After World War II, General Dwight D. Eisenhower rode a wave of popularity, for during the war he had been the supreme commander of the Allied forces in Europe and led the June 1944 D-Day invasion of Europe. Both political parties courted him as a potential presidential nominee, but after the war he kept his political affiliation a secret. In truth, Eisenhower, a native of Kansas, had been a lifelong member of the GOP, and when he served as president as Columbia University after the war, he cultivated his connections with the Republican Party's eastern establishment.

In January 1952, Eisenhower publicly declared that he was a Republican, and when the party held its national convention in Chicago, support for "Ike" (as Eisenhower was affectionately known) was strong. His principal challenger was Senator Robert Taft of Ohio. The struggle reflected a long-standing division in the Republican party. Taft was a conservative and almost an isolationist, Eisenhower a moderate and internationalist. The possibility of Taft's becoming the Republican nominee was a major factor in inducing Eisenhower to seek the nomination. Although Taft emerged from the Republican primaries with more delegates than Eisenhower, at the convention most of the remaining delegates declared for Eisenhower. He won the nomination on the first ballot.

Eisenhower selected Senator Richard Nixon of California as his running mate. Nixon's presence on the ticket pleased Republican conservatives and Taft supporters, especially because Nixon boasted strong anticommunist credentials after having gained national attention for his relentless investigation of accused Communist spy Alger Hiss. Moreover, Nixon's youth—he was 39 years old—would offset Eisenhower's 61 years, and his West Coast roots balanced Eisenhower's East Coast connections.

Even though Truman was unpopular, most observers in 1952 thought that he would run for another term, but he withdrew from the race in March after a stunning loss in the New Hampshire primary to Tennessee Senator Estes Kefauver, who had built a national reputation opposing organized crime. Harboring no affection for Kefauver, who had harshly criticized his administration, Truman urged Illinois Governor Adlai Stevenson (the grandson of Grover Cleveland's second-term vice president) to run for the nomination. The Democratic National Convention, held in Chicago, nominated Stevenson, who picked Senator John Sparkman of Alabama as his running mate.

The Democrats promulgated the slogan, "You never had it so good," but Eisenhower challenged their claims of economic prosperity, arguing that the Democrats had achieved the good times only through war and high military expenditures. "The Democrats could purchase full employment only at the price of dead and mangled bodies of young Americans," he charged. Eisenhower criticized the high taxes and high prices that accompanied rearmament and promised to achieve military security and economic prosperity without a large defense establishment. He carried this message across the country in an ambitious campaign, traveling 33,000 miles and visiting 44 states (all but Missouri, Nevada, Maine, and Vermont).

The Republicans developed a slogan that hit the Democrats where they were vulnerable: "K1C2," meaning "Korea," "communism," and "corruption." First of all, the Korean War was going badly. Secondly, the Republicans charged that the Truman administration was soft on communism, pointing to cold war setbacks such as the "loss" of Eastern Europe and China. Finally, the Republicans pointed to evidence of corruption in the Truman administration.

During the campaign Nixon worked as Eisenhower's attack dog, charging the Truman administration with a "scandal a day." He questioned Truman's and Stevenson's commitment to the anticommunist crusade, calling the nominee "Adlai the Appeaser." But Nixon's strictures against Truman administration corruption boomeranged on him when, on September 18, the *New York Post* trumpeted a front-page story that 66 California millionaires had maintained a secret fund of more than $18,000 for Nixon that he used for personal—rather than political— purposes. The story was not strictly true: while contributors had indeed established a fund for Nixon, he had used the money solely for political purposes to defray the considerable expenses associated with being a senator from California. But the allegation grabbed national headlines, and most of Eisenhower's advisers urged him to dump Nixon from the ticket.

Nixon fought back. On September 23, he went on national television to explain the fund to the American people. The largest television audience in history at that time, 58 million viewers, tuned in and watched as Nixon defended the fund. "Every penny of it was used to pay for political expenses that I did not think should be charged to the taxpayers," he declared. Nixon mentioned a cocker spaniel dog that a political supporter had given his family as a gift. Nixon explained that one of his daughters had named the dog "Checkers," and he vowed, "And you know the kids, like all kids, love the dog, and I just want to say this right now that regardless of what they say about it, we are going to keep it." Nixon's detractors thought that the "Checkers speech," as it quickly became known, was maudlin and cynical, but millions of Americans were moved by it. The Republican National Committee received hundreds of thousands of letters and telegrams supporting Nixon. Eisenhower decided to keep Nixon on the ticket.

The other dramatic moment in the campaign came in late October. With American troops still fighting the Korean War and with peace negotiations getting nowhere, most opinion polls indicated that Americans saw the war as the most important issue in the campaign. On October 24 in Detroit, Eisenhower made the sudden announcement that if elected, "I shall go to Korea." The promise immediately enthralled the nation, for Eisenhower's international prestige and stature as a war hero seemed to promise a speedier resolution to the conflict. Stevenson could offer nothing similar, and the announcement widened Eisenhower's lead in the polls.

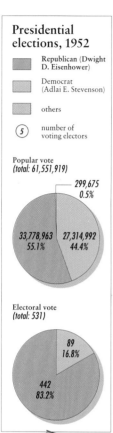

Presidential elections, 1952

- Republican (Dwight D. Eisenhower)
- Democrat (Adlai E. Stevenson)
- others

⑤ number of voting electors

Popular vote
(total: 61,551,919)

299,675
0.5%

33,778,963
55.1%

27,314,992
44.4%

Electoral vote
(total: 531)

89
16.8%

442
83.2%

During the 1952 campaign the Republicans also paid studious attention to women, who now voted in equal numbers with men. The Republican Party emphasized traditional family values that were fractured by the Great Depression and World War II: a male breadwinner, a supportive wife, and happy children. The GOP suggested that General Eisenhower would end a war in Korea that was disrupting family life and robbing Americans of husbands and fathers. Pollster Lou Harris observed that women "were more disturbed about the Korean War than men in 1952. In fact, there is evidence to indicate that women were among the real prime movers in making the Korean War a major and decisive influence in the outcome of the election." On Election Day, a majority of women voted for Eisenhower.

Stevenson proved no match for the popular war hero. He had recently divorced his wife, which not only hurt his personal image but also detracted from the Democrats' ability to appeal to the family values so important in the 1950s. Stevenson was also perceived as a staid intellectual "egghead" whose speeches—often witty and eloquent—were abstract, failing to evoke an emotional response from his audience.

Eisenhower won a resounding victory, 55.1 percent to 44.4 percent. He claimed the entire North and West, and won 39 out of 48 states, even capturing Stevenson's home state, Illinois. Stevenson won states only in the South. Significantly, Eisenhower won Florida, Tennessee, Texas, and Virginia. He thus began to create cracks in the monolithic South, a historic process that would continue over the next generation. In fact, the New Deal coalition hemorrhaged votes across the country. Not only did southerners bolt from the Democratic Party to vote for Eisenhower, but so did minorities, labor union members, and farmers. African Americans were the only minority to remain loyal to the Democrats; Stevenson received 81 percent of the black vote (more than Truman's 64 percent in 1948).

The Election of 1956

In September 1955, President Dwight D. Eisenhower suffered a heart attack. As Vice President Richard Nixon presided over cabinet meetings at the White House, Eisenhower recovered at an Air Force hospital in Denver, finally gaining enough strength by November to move to his farm in Gettysburg, Pennsylvania. The following month he returned to Washington. Eisenhower had not yet announced his candidacy for 1956. Throughout his first term he affirmed that he would serve only one term as president, and his age (he was 66) and his heart attack combined to make his health a prime concern among voters. Yet he felt that he needed another term to complete the work he had begun, especially on improving relations with the Soviet Union. Finally, in February 1956, Eisenhower announced that he would seek a second term.

Rumors circulated that Richard Nixon might not be Eisenhower's running mate. Many Republican insiders urged the president to dump Nixon, and Eisenhower had always harbored reservations about his vice president, whom he viewed as too political and immature. Eisenhower suggested to Nixon that he take a cabinet post to broaden his political experience, but Nixon promptly declined. In public, the president said little, which only fueled speculation about Nixon's place on the ticket. But at the GOP national convention in San Francisco—the first major party convention held in California—the Republicans renominated both Eisenhower and Nixon.

Three men jumped into the race for the Democratic nomination: Governor Adlai Stevenson, Senator Estes Kefauver, and New York Governor Averell Harriman. Meeting in Chicago, the Democrats turned once again to Adlai Stevenson, who added drama to the convention by throwing the choice of the vice presidential nominee to the convention delegates instead of selecting one himself. "The choice will be yours," he told the delegates, "the profit will be the nation's." A hard-fought contest took place between Kefauver, who had been Stevenson's main rival in the primaries, and John Kennedy, a young senator from Massachusetts who had won election to the Senate just four years earlier. Kefauver won the struggle, and Kennedy's gracious acceptance of the loss instantly made him a prospect for the 1960 nomination.

This campaign was the first in which the candidates relied more on air transportation than on trains. Stevenson traveled extensively, and was more strident than he had been four years earlier. He chided Eisenhower for his alleged detachment from a rigorous job, calling him a "part-time leader." The image was inaccurate, and Eisenhower's health crises—which included an attack of ileitis in June—rather than sowing doubts in the minds of Americans, elicited sympathy, making him even more politically bulletproof. Like Eisenhower, Stevenson's greatest interest was foreign policy, and two cornerstones of his campaign were his pledge to suspend all hydrogen bomb tests and his determination to end the military draft and transform the military into an all-volunteer, professional force. But historian Malcolm Moos has observed that "in tangling with a military hero in the White House on the H-bomb, draft, and national defense issues, he was challenging the one area in which people believed Eisenhower to have the greatest judgment and competence."

In contrast to Stevenson, Eisenhower traveled just 14,000 miles and visited 13

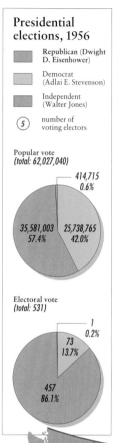

Presidential elections, 1956

- Republican (Dwight D. Eisenhower)
- Democrat (Adlai E. Stevenson)
- Independent (Walter Jones)
- (5) number of voting electors

Popular vote
(total: 62,027,040)

414,715
0.6%

35,581,003
57.4%

25,738,765
42.0%

Electoral vote
(total: 531)

1
0.2%

73
13.7%

457
86.1%

states in this campaign. But his use of television commercials was more skillful than Stevenson's, and he was also able to vaunt the achievements of his first term, such as the 1953 Korean War armistice and economic growth. "America is happier than it was four years ago" was a constant Eisenhower refrain during the campaign. Two foreign crises, including one around Election Day, also encouraged Americans to support the president. Earlier in the year the Soviet Union had invaded Hungary to crush a rebellion there; and in late October, Israel, supported by British and French troops, invaded Egypt to force that country to relinquish the Suez Canal, which it had seized. With concern over a possible Suez war running at fever pitch, the beneficiary of the crisis was Eisenhower. Americans rallied around their president, and polls additionally revealed that most Americans trusted Eisenhower more than Stevenson in the handling of foreign policy.

The election of 1956 lacked the drama of 1952's contest. Both men were known quantities, and the outcome seemed preordained. Eisenhower won another landslide, an expression of his immense popularity and of Americans' approval of his leadership during cold war crises and his stewardship over the economy. His victory was even more resounding than in 1952. He won 41 states, a tally that once again included some in the Deep South: Florida, Louisiana, and Texas (Louisiana went for a Republican presidential candidate for the first time since 1876). As in 1952, Stevenson's states were all in the South.

In 1952, Eisenhower's landslide had extended to Congress, as the Republicans captured both houses of Congress. But his coattails were short, and voters were more attracted to the person than his party. In 1954 the Democrats had regained control of both houses of Congress, and in 1956 they held firm there. Unlike Franklin Roosevelt, Eisenhower was unable to translate his personal popularity into a larger movement to strengthen and broaden the appeal of his party.

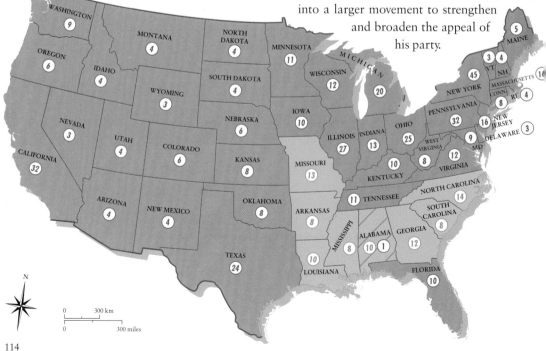

The Election of 1960

Dwight D. Eisenhower would have been tempted to run for a third term in 1960, but the Twenty-second Amendment prohibited him from doing so. At the GOP national convention in Chicago, the nomination went to Ike's heir apparent, Vice President Richard Nixon. His running mate was Henry Cabot Lodge, Jr., American ambassador to the United Nations and a former U.S. senator from Massachusetts who had been defeated in his 1952 reelection bid by John F. Kennedy.

Kennedy was the front-runner in the 1960 Democratic primaries. During World War II, he had commanded a patrol boat that was sunk by a Japanese destroyer, an incident that he publicized to portray himself as a war hero. Curiously, his career in the U.S. Senate had been unimpressive. He sponsored no major legislation, had a poor attendance record, and seemed bored by senatorial duties. But in 1956 he rose to national prominence when his book *Profiles in Courage* won a Pulitzer Prize. The award established Kennedy's reputation as an intellectual and set him apart from other politicians, thus positioning him as a credible candidate for president in 1960.

Other factors helped Kennedy as well. At the 1956 Democratic National Convention, he had almost won the vice presidential nomination, and since then he had maintained a high profile and an aggressive speaking schedule. Kennedy's father, Joseph, who had served as U.S. ambassador to Great Britain under Franklin Roosevelt, was one of the wealthiest men in America, and he threw his financial resources into supporting his son's campaign. Moreover, Kennedy's appearance improved. In 1960 he began receiving cortisone injections to compensate for an adrenal gland deficiency that had given him an alarmingly gaunt countenance. The shots filled out his face, giving him a healthy appearance and movie-star good looks.

Kennedy scored convincing victories in the Democratic primaries, forcing rival Hubert Humphrey, a senator from Minnesota, to withdraw from the race. Kennedy briefly faced a stumbling block when Senate Majority Leader Lyndon Johnson declared his candidacy just five days before the Democratic National Convention, held in Los Angeles. Kennedy won the nomination on the first ballot, which helped to establish the importance of primaries in securing a party's nomination. He resented the Johnny-come-lately challenge from Johnson, but the Texan's clout in the Senate and in the Democratic Party, his age (he was nine years Kennedy's senior) and the geographical balance he would add to the ticket led Kennedy to pick Johnson as his running mate. The two men formed an uneasy partnership.

Many Protestant Americans were concerned about Kennedy's religion, fearing that if he became president, as a Roman Catholic he would be subject to the influence of the Vatican. Kennedy tried to dispel the concerns with an eloquent appeal to Protestant ministers in Houston. He pledged to resign if his religion ever conflicted with his duties as president. "I am not the Catholic candidate for president. I am the Democratic Party's candidate for president, who happens also to be a Catholic," he declared.

Although he did not mention the popular Eisenhower by name, Kennedy charged that the Eisenhower administration had been remiss in allowing Cuba to

*John F. Kennedy
1917–1963
Kennedy displayed his celebrated wit throughout the 1960 race. At one campaign stop, where throngs of enthusiastic children appeared to greet him, he quipped, "If we can lower the voting age to nine, we are going to sweep the state."*

fall into communist hands in 1959. One of his most effective accusations was that the administration had let American missile production falter, enabling the Soviet Union to achieve superiority in its missile arsenal. This charge of a "missile gap" between the U.S. and the U.S.S.R., although subsequently proven inaccurate, alarmed Americans.

Although only four years younger than Nixon, the 43-year-old Kennedy was 27 years younger than Eisenhower, and he hammered away at the tired, old appearance of the Eisenhower administration, referring to its "horse and buggy policies." "Let's Get This Country Moving Again" was the Kennedy campaign slogan, evoking the promise of young, activist leadership.

Kennedy and his handlers crafted a masterful image of an athletic, erudite war hero and a devoted family man. It was a winning formula, even if the reality often belied the image. Although Kennedy was physically active, he was often wracked by back pain. *Profiles in Courage* had been ghostwritten, and his conduct as a patrol boat commander during World War II was spotty, if indisputably courageous. He appeared happily married to Jacqueline Bouvier, and the couple had a young daughter (a son was born later in 1960), yet his philandering was almost insatiable, although publicly unknown. Despite the apparent contradictions, the image worked, and contrasted effectively with that of Nixon, who lacked Kennedy's charm, wit, and athletic grace.

Where the Kennedy image really shone through was on television, which had superseded both radio and newspapers as the most important news medium in America, and which helped to emphasize style over substance. Kennedy challenged Nixon to debate on national television, and the vice president agreed. But during the first debate, on September 26, Nixon looked wan and haggard from an illness and a strenuous campaign schedule. He had lost so much weight that his clothes looked ill-fitting, and he also made the critical mistake of refusing proper television makeup. Without it, he looked sweaty and unshaven, an appearance that, combined with his dark eyes, made him look almost sinister. By contrast, Kennedy looked tan and relaxed. More than 70 million television viewers watched the debate, and they saw a poised and articulate Kennedy, an image that instantly contravened Nixon's charge that the young senator was inexperienced.

Two weeks before the election, Kennedy called Coretta Scott King to convey his concern for her husband, civil rights leader Martin Luther King, Jr., who had just been jailed in Atlanta. Later, Kennedy's brother, Robert, persuaded the judge involved to release King on bail. On the Sunday before the election, Kennedy's father paid for two million leaflets recounting the incident to be distributed at black churches throughout the country. By contrast, Nixon was silent during King's ordeal, partly because he did not want to appear to be pandering to the black vote or interfering with a legal case, and partly because he did not want to alienate southern whites. After his son's release from jail, Martin Luther King, Sr. —who had been supporting Nixon—promised, "I have a suitcase full of votes and I'm going to take them to Mr. Kennedy and dump them in his lap."

Lyndon B. Johnson being sworn into office on the flight back to Washington from Dallas after the assassination of John F. Kennedy in November 1963.

The 1960 election was the closest election in the twentieth century, and had the highest voter participation of the century as well, with a turnout of 64 percent. Kennedy's margin of victory was just 119,450 votes.

This election was the first in which citizens of Alaska and Hawaii voted, as both states had been admitted to the Union in 1959, bringing the total number of states in the Union to 50. Nixon won more states than Kennedy did, 26 to Kennedy's 24, and dominated the West, losing only Nevada in the far West. Kennedy, the first New Englander to run for the presidency since Franklin Pierce in 1852, derived his principal support from the Northeast and the South, and Kennedy became the last candidate from the Northeast to win a presidential election in the twentieth century. His closest and most controversial victories were in Illinois and Texas; the electoral vote count was close enough that if he had lost those two states, he would have lost the election. Charges of voter fraud in those two states were persistent, directed especially at Chicago Mayor Richard Daley, who had personally promised to deliver Illinois to Kennedy. (In an election-night telephone conversation with Kennedy, Daley reportedly told him that "with a little bit of luck and the help of a few close friends, you're going to carry Illinois.") Nixon faced considerable pressure to demand a recount, but he refused, fearing that such a measure would be a long, divisive process that would snarl government operations. Nixon sent his formal concession statement to Kennedy via telegram, declining to read it over television, the medium that more than any single factor had tipped the balance in favor of his opponent. Kennedy thus became the thirty-fifth president; he was the only candidate besides Warren Harding to move directly from the Senate to the presidency. He was also the youngest man ever elected to the office, and he succeeded at that time the oldest man ever to leave the presidency (Eisenhower was 71).

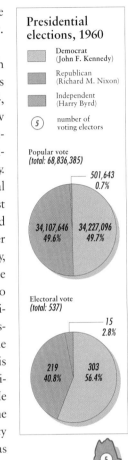

Presidential elections, 1960

Democrat (John F. Kennedy)

Republican (Richard M. Nixon)

Independent (Harry Byrd)

⑤ number of voting electors

Popular vote (total: 68,836,385)

501,643 0.7%

34,107,646 49.6%

34,227,096 49.7%

Electoral vote (total: 537)

15 2.8%

219 40.8%

303 56.4%

The Election of 1964

*Lyndon B. Johnson
1908–1973
Although Johnson
campaigned as a
unifier in 1964, his
term in office became
one of the most
divisive four-year
periods in the nation's
history, forcing him to
abandon his hopes for
another full term.*

In 1964 the Democratic Party was united by the tragedy of John F. Kennedy's assassination. Many Democrats wanted President Lyndon Johnson to pick as his running mate Attorney General Robert Kennedy. (Feelings were so fervent for the younger Kennedy that Democrats gave him a 22-minute standing ovation at the 1964 Democratic National Convention.) But Johnson detested Robert, who reciprocated the sentiment. George Reedy, Johnson's press secretary, compared the two men to dogs who came into a room and growled at each other. Johnson thought that Kennedy was little more than a spoiled rich kid—brash, cocky, and deceitful. When the Democrats began to dun him with requests to put Bobby Kennedy on the ticket, Johnson dug in his heels. "I'd waited for my turn. Bobby should've waited for his," he later explained. Instead, at the Democratic National Convention in Atlantic City, Johnson selected Hubert H. Humphrey, the senator from Minnesota, for the number two spot.

The tranquil, eight-year Eisenhower presidency had temporarily papered over the long-running feud between the Republican Party's conservative and moderate wings. In 1964 the feud broke open. The moderate forces in the GOP were too disorganized and feeble to advance a viable candidate. Nixon was out of the question; his 1960 presidential loss had been compounded by his 1962 defeat in the California gubernatorial race, after which he snarled at reporters, "You won't have Nixon to kick around anymore because, gentlemen, this is my last press conference." The only other viable GOP moderate was New York Governor Nelson Rockefeller; however, his reputation had been tarnished by a recent divorce and remarriage. When Rockefeller attempted to speak at the 1964 GOP convention in San Francisco, conservative delegates drowned him out with a thundering chorus of boos.

The conservative forces, better organized and more determined than the moderates, nominated Arizona Senator Barry Goldwater. Elected to the Senate in 1952, Goldwater had quickly established conservative credentials by criticizing Eisenhower's moderate brand of Republicanism and supporting Senator Joe McCarthy, the Wisconsin senator who spearheaded anticommunist hysteria. Goldwater's *Conscience of a Conservative* (1960) laid bare his beliefs: free enterprise, a reduction of federal power, a return to states' rights, and a relentless pursuit of the cold war. Goldwater selected as his running mate William Miller, a conservative congressman from upstate New York. The selection of Miller gave geographical balance to the ticket but added little political heft and, moreover, tilted it far to the right.

Goldwater's nomination bore eloquent testimony to the burgeoning political and economic strength of the South and the West, the fastest-growing regions of the country. A lifelong resident of Arizona, Goldwater epitomized the feelings common among westerners in the United States, namely, an anti-East animus and a sharp distrust of the federal government. Westerners loved Goldwater's acid-tongued attacks on the federal government and on the East; he once even declared that he wanted to saw off "the Eastern Seaboard [to] let it float right out into the Atlantic."

While such talk delighted western conservatives, it alarmed most Americans. After he won the nomination, moderates from both political parties denounced

Goldwater as an extremist, and he embraced the image. "[E]xtremism in the defense of liberty is no vice ... moderation in the pursuit of justice is no virtue," he declared in his acceptance speech.

Goldwater sounded his caustic rhetoric throughout the campaign and, in a nuclear age, his views on foreign policy were especially troubling. He favored the U.S. role in Vietnam and even proposed using nuclear weapons. "I'd drop a low-yield atomic bomb on the Chinese supply lines in North Vietnam or maybe shell 'em with the Seventh Fleet," he once suggested. He also wanted to cut off diplomatic relations with the Soviet Union and spoke casually about "lobbing [a nuclear bomb] into the men's room of the Kremlin." The remarks appeared reckless.

Republican conservatives proudly declared that Goldwater represented "A Choice, Not An Echo" and advanced the shibboleth, "In Your Heart You Know He's Right." The Democrats countered with the slogans, "Yeah, Far Right," and "In Your Guts You Know He's Nuts." In one of the most effective—and chilling—advertisements in American campaign history, the Johnson camp unveiled a television commercial that showed a little girl innocently counting petals on a daisy. The camera suddenly zoomed in on her eye, and the image of an atomic explosion and a mushroom cloud filled the screen. Johnson's voice then told viewers, "These are the stakes. We must learn to love one another, or surely we shall die." The commercial ran only once, but that was enough to do inestimable damage to Goldwater.

Whereas Goldwater cut a bellicose image, Johnson soared above the fray. "Extremism in the pursuit of the Presidency is an unpardonable vice," he declared. At the same time, however, Johnson was eager to dispel any intimation that he was soft on the Vietnamese communists, and an opportunity came in August 1964. After an alleged North Vietnamese attack on two U.S. destroyers off the Vietnamese coast, he exerted presidential muscle in getting Congress to pass the Gulf of Tonkin Resolution authorizing him to take "all necessary measures" to prevent attacks on American armed forces in the region. Now Republicans could not impugn Johnson's commitment to fighting communism.

The president built an image of a unifier who preached moderation and stability and who tried to bring Americans together under the large Democratic umbrella. Following in the footsteps of his political idol, Franklin Roosevelt, Johnson had proposed an ambitious legislative program, the "Great Society," and he appealed to the traditional elements of the New Deal coalition, suggesting that under him, the federal government would care for everybody. He stated, "The farmer in Iowa, the fisherman in Massachusetts, the worker in Seattle, the rancher in Texas have the same hopes and harbor the same fears. ... [T]hey share a fundamental unity of interest, purpose, and belief."

Goldwater never had a chance. Johnson won the greatest popular majority in American history. He won 44 states and an even higher share of the popular vote, 61.0 percent, than Roosevelt's 60.8 percent in 1936. Goldwater, with just 38.4 percent, was buried. The Democrats also added to their majorities by picking up 38 seats in the House and 2 in the Senate. Johnson no longer felt haunted by the Kennedy legacy; he had won the presidency in his own right and had an overwhelming mandate to proceed with his legislative program, the Great Society.

While Goldwater won only six states, his victories were politically significant. All of the states he won (except his home state, Arizona) were in the Deep South: Alabama, Georgia, Louisiana, Mississippi, and South Carolina. Goldwater thus continued the historic process, begun by Eisenhower in the 1950s, of breaking up the Solid South and wrenching it from Democratic control that had lasted a century. The senator and his campaign staff employed a deliberate "southern strategy" that accepted the support of southern racists, thereby capitalizing on a white backlash in the South against the civil rights movement and the Democratic Party for introducing the Civil Rights Act of 1964, even if Republicans helped to pass it. Goldwater carefully avoided overt racist appeals and instead addressed concerns about the increase in crime and lawlessness, which whites often blamed on blacks. The shift was monumental: after 1964, Republicans controlled the southern white vote.

Goldwater campaign aide and biographer Lee Edwards called him the "most important loser in American history," because his doomed campaign marked not the end but rather the beginning of the American conservative movement. Returning to the Senate and accepting defeat with equanimity, Goldwater recognized that the time was not ripe for his ideas, commenting, "When you've lost an election by that much, it isn't the case of whether you made the wrong speech or wore the wrong necktie. It was just the wrong time."

The right time was to come two decades later, when Ronald Reagan—a former actor who first attracted political attention by speaking for Goldwater in 1964—made conservatism more attractive by softening the harsh edges that Goldwater had sharpened. At the 1984 Republican National Convention that renominated Reagan for a second term, Goldwater was a featured speaker, and he unabashedly spoke the same words about extremism that had seemed so unnerving 20 years earlier.

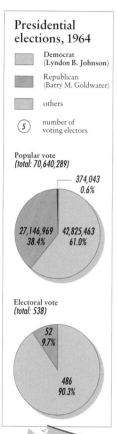

Presidential elections, 1964

- Democrat (Lyndon B. Johnson)
- Republican (Barry M. Goldwater)
- others

⑤ number of voting electors

Popular vote
(total: 70,640,289)

374,043
0.6%

27,146,969
38.4%

42,825,463
61.0%

Electoral vote
(total: 538)

52
9.7%

486
90.3%

The Election of 1968

During 1968 America's domestic situation deteriorated alarmingly. The major issue was the Vietnam War, which aroused increasing domestic opposition and produced large-scale demonstrations. There were other domestic disturbances. The assassinations of Martin Luther King and Robert Kennedy, who was campaigning for the Democratic nomination, left Americans stunned, shattering a sense of hope and justice in America. There was a backlash against liberalism. The Great Society programs were vast in their scope and costly to the American taxpayer, yet seemed to lack tangible results. The majority of Americans felt that Lyndon Johnson's administration, too ambitious on civil rights, was ripping rather than mending the nation's social fabric. These feelings had seemed confirmed when, five days after Johnson signed the momentous Voting Rights Act of 1965, a riot and fire nearly destroyed Watts, a black ghetto in Los Angeles. Violent crime increased at an alarming rate, and Johnson appeared unwilling to clamp down on the domestic unrest. Americans sought a leader who could offer safety and security.

Richard Nixon
1913–1994
Nixon's capture of the Republican nomination and his election victory represented a stunning political comeback, especially after his 1962 loss in the race for California's governorship, after which he declared he was leaving politics.

By 1968 Johnson had become a prisoner within the White House. He canceled all speaking engagements—except on military bases—because the jeers from antiwar demonstrators made every public appearance a miserable, humiliating, and dangerous experience. His long and storied political career now boiled down to one issue: Vietnam. In November 1967, Senator Eugene McCarthy of Minnesota announced that he would enter the Democratic primaries as an antiwar candidate.

At first, McCarthy seemed harmless. He was a little-known senator from a less populous state, and he was challenging an incumbent president and consummate politician. But in January 1968, North Vietnam launched the Tet Offensive, catching South Vietnamese and American troops off guard and gaining control of several South Vietnamese cities, even briefly occupying the American embassy in Saigon. While South Vietnamese and American forces were finally able to repel the assault, Americans sustained heavy casualties, and the aggressiveness and tenacity of the North Vietnamese belied the reports from the Johnson administration and the U.S. military that the enemy was all but vanquished. With the rude shock of the Tet Offensive as a backdrop, the McCarthy campaign picked up steam as the first primary, on March 12 in New Hampshire, approached.

Political pundits gave McCarthy little chance in the primary, saying that 20 percent of the vote would be a good showing against the president. McCarthy stunned the country by winning 42.4 percent, surprisingly close to Johnson's 49.5 percent. McCarthy's showing was tantamount to a victory. As McCarthy revealed Johnson's political vulnerability, a more formidable challenger rushed into the campaign. Robert Kennedy, Johnson's nemesis and now a senator from New York, announced that he would seek the Democratic nomination as an antiwar candidate.

Johnson had to do something about the morass in Vietnam. He instructed his speechwriters to prepare an address announcing his intention to de-escalate the war. As they tried to craft a conclusion to the speech, Johnson told them, "Don't worry, I may have a little ending of my own." On March 31, Johnson went on national television to announce that he would limit the bombing of North Vietnam, and then shocked the nation by announcing, "I shall not seek, and I will not accept, the nomination of my party for another term as your president."

On April 27, Vice President Hubert Humphrey entered the presidential race, which was now to be a slugfest between him and Kennedy. But on June 5, 1968, after celebrating his victory in the California primary, Kennedy was assassinated. The murder only added to the widespread impression that the fabric of American society was unraveling. Instead of boosting the prospects of McCarthy, the other avowed antiwar candidate, the murder drained McCarthy's campaign of energy and enthusiasm. The way was clear for Humphrey to claim the nomination at the Democratic National Convention, scheduled for late August in Chicago.

The convention proved to be one of the most acrimonious and self-destructive in history. The Youth International Party, or Yippies, a group of antiwar protesters, gathered to demonstrate against the party of Lyndon Johnson. Chicago Mayor Richard Daley assembled a large phalanx of police officers to contain the protesters, and for days the demonstrators and the Chicago police clashed in the streets, culminating in a brutal confrontation on nomination night. A national television audience watched in horror as police viciously beat demonstrators and dragged them into police vans.

The convention nominated Humphrey, who picked Senator Edmund Muskie of Maine as his running-mate. But the nomination was overshadowed by the events in Chicago's streets, which seemed to confirm that Democratic politicians fostered lawlessness. The convention, which Humphrey called a "catastrophe," shattered the party, left it demoralized, and haunted Humphrey for the rest of the campaign.

In contrast to the Democratic debacle, the Republican National Convention in Miami was harmonious. Delegates there witnessed the culmination of the most remarkable political comeback in American history. After losing the 1960 presidential election and the 1962 California gubernatorial race, Richard Nixon had been left for politically dead. But he never gave up. He moved to Manhattan, where he worked as a lawyer and cultivated his Republican Party connections. By 1968 he was the clear front-runner for the nomination, beating back a field of hopefuls that included the governors of three large states: Nelson Rockefeller of New York, Ronald Reagan of California, and George Romney of Michigan.

There was no question that Nixon would win the GOP nod. The only shock to the smooth convention came when he announced his running mate: Spiro Agnew, the governor of Maryland. Agnew was a political cipher, and convention delegates began to joke, "Spiro Who?" But Nixon picked him for a reason. After the urban riots nationwide following Martin Luther King's assassination, Agnew had come down hard on Baltimore's black leadership, blaming them for the unrest and berating them for doing nothing to stop the riots in that city. In Nixon's political calculus, Agnew's hard line would appeal to southern whites.

Nixon was under special pressure to attract the votes of southern whites because of the presence of a third-party candidate. George Wallace, the segregationist governor of Alabama, was running for the American Independent Party. He claimed that the "communist movement is behind the civil rights movement" and, repairing to the old doctrine of states' rights, pledged that as president he would not use federal money to achieve integration. Promising to restore law and order, patriotism, and respect for authority, Wallace struck a responsive chord with blue-collar and lower-class whites, who were frustrated and scared by lawlessness in the nation. Capitalizing on the disillusionment with Great Society programs and with liberalism generally, he denounced intellectuals and liberals as "pointy-heads" and commented, "Liberals, intellectuals, and long hairs have run the country for too long. When I get back to Washington, I'll throw all these phonies and their briefcases into the Potomac."

Nixon was determined not to repeat past mistakes. In this campaign he conducted himself with a statesmanlike decorum, leaving the dirty work to Agnew, whom critics dubbed "Nixon's Nixon." Taking the high road, Nixon cultivated the image of a "New Nixon," a man more mature and dignified than the one Americans had known before. Because television had hurt him in his first run for the White House, Nixon refused to accept Humphrey's challenge to debate on national television, prompting Humphrey to call him "Richard the Chicken-Hearted." Nixon also limited his campaigning. Instead of visiting all 50 states as he had done in 1960, he concentrated on the 7 most populous ones: California, Illinois, Michigan, New York, Pennsylvania, Ohio, and Texas.

Nixon built his campaign around traditional conservative values. He billed himself as the "law and order" candidate and appealed to the "forgotten Americans," quiet citizens left frightened and bewildered by the upheavals of the 1960s. These citizens were "the non-shouters, the non-demonstrators," as he described them, and they obeyed the nation's laws and respected authority. In shrewd political posturing that echoed Barry Goldwater's "southern strategy," Nixon also used racist fears and the appeal of the states' rights doctrine to attract votes from white southerners, thus pulling this group out of the Democratic fold and embracing them as Republicans. To attract white southerners, Nixon declared, for example, that he advocated the principle of integration but would move slowly in enforcing integration of southern schools.

Although he concentrated primarily on domestic issues (an irony, since his first love was foreign policy), Nixon also promised that he would end the Vietnam War. Vague in specific details, he only intimated that he would scale back American troop involvement in the war and use his world contacts and diplomatic skills to end the war soon.

The war was Humphrey's bête noire. He was vice president for the administration that had escalated American involvement in the war, and he could not repudiate the administration's war policy—unpopular as it was—without appearing disloyal to his own president. In September, Humphrey finally divorced himself from administration policy by proclaiming that as president, he would stop the bombing of North Vietnam to induce the North to pursue peace in earnest. On October 31, Johnson gave Humphrey a huge boost by announcing the suspension of all bombing in North Vietnam so as to speed peace talks. The pronouncements lifted Humphrey in the polls, and he began receiving numerous endorsements, including from Eugene McCarthy.

Nixon thought that he would lose the presidency for a second time. But he won a narrow plurality, 43.4 percent of the popular vote, compared to Humphrey's 42.7 percent. The margin of victory was just 500,000 votes, although Nixon's lead in a number of states (he won 32 to Humphrey's 14) and in the electoral college was more com-

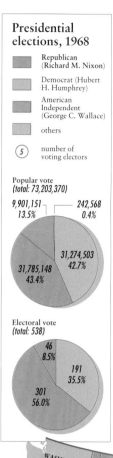

Presidential elections, 1968

Republican (Richard M. Nixon)

Democrat (Hubert H. Humphrey)

American Independent (George C. Wallace)

others

(5) number of voting electors

Popular vote (total: 73,203,370)

9,901,151 — 242,568
13.5% — 0.4%

31,274,503 42.7%

31,785,148 43.4%

Electoral vote (total: 538)

46 8.5%

191 35.5%

301 56.0%

manding. Nixon dominated the Midwest and the West, plus part of the South, and benefited from the electoral votes of California, Illinois, and Ohio. Humphrey's states were concentrated in the Northeast and New England, and he won the populous states of Michigan, New York, Pennsylvania, and Texas, the electoral votes of which normally propel a candidate to victory. Wallace won 13 percent of the popular vote.

Nixon was a minority president. In the twentieth century, only Woodrow Wilson—coincidentally, the president whom Nixon admired the most—had a flimsier mandate, 41.9 percent in 1912 (in an even more bitter three-way race). Though Nixon had won 4 million more votes than Goldwater had in 1964, he received 2.3 million fewer votes than he had in 1960. Moreover, the Democrats retained their majorities in both houses of Congress, marking the first time since Zachary Taylor in 1848 that an incoming president's party did not control at least one house of Congress.

The election of 1968 continued a transformation of the southern electorate that had begun a decade earlier. The South deserted the Democratic Party, as most white southerners voted for either Nixon or Wallace; Humphrey won only 10 percent of the southern white vote. Clearly, Nixon's "southern strategy" paid off, as he was able to win Florida, Georgia, and Tennessee. The change was historic: the Solid South was no longer Democratic.

More generally, in the election of 1968 Americans rejected liberalism. The combined popular vote for Nixon and Wallace was 56.9 percent, which represented a repudiation of the Johnson administration. Americans seemed eager to forget the Great Society's social engineering and the upheavals associated with the liberal reform impulse. Many conservative, middle-class Americans were fed up with federal power, the Vietnam War, social protests and violence, the counterculture, and all the turmoil of the decade. Their fear of and disgust with these elements ushered in the beginnings of a new conservative movement, the first tremors of which were signaled by Nixon's election.

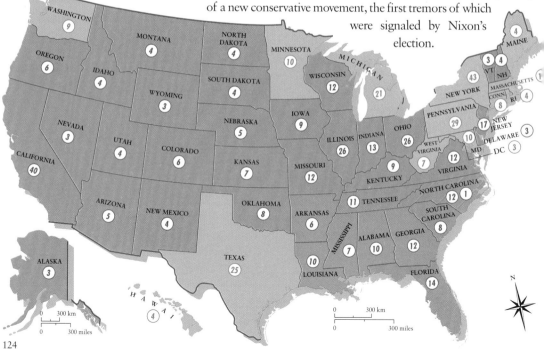

The Election of 1972

Prior to 1972, only a third of Democratic or Republican delegates were chosen through state primaries. After the Democrats' disastrous 1968 convention, where Hubert Humphrey won the nomination without entering any primaries, disgruntled Democrats charged that party bosses dictated the party nominee and platform. To enlarge rank-and-file participation at the 1972 convention, the Democratic Party decided to hold more state primaries. The Republicans did likewise, so that in 1972 both parties selected a majority of their delegates through these primaries. Henceforth, presidential hopefuls faced a grueling and expensive series of state primaries, a season of political combat that often stretched longer than the general campaign in the fall. And as the importance of the primaries increased, the national nominating convention became an event more to christen rather than to select a nominee. Unlike during the nineteenth and early twentieth centuries, modern candidates always win the nomination on the first ballot.

By 1972 Senator Edward Kennedy of Massachusetts, the last surviving brother of the legendary political family and one of the Democratic Party's best prospects for the nomination, had had his hopes dashed. In 1969 he drove his car off a bridge near Chappaquiddick Island in Massachusetts. Kennedy escaped but his young female passenger drowned. Kennedy's failure to report the accident, and his subsequent admission that he had panicked, suggested his unsuitability for the presidency.

Another Democratic prospect was Senator Edmund Muskie of Maine, the party's 1968 vice presidential nominee. He won the New Hampshire primary but failed to generate deep, enthusiastic support among the Democratic faithful. His campaign derailed entirely after he broke down in an emotional defense of his wife, who had been the subject of newspaper criticism. Another Democratic contender, Governor George Wallace of Alabama, was shot while campaigning in Maryland. Wallace, paralyzed, withdrew from the race.

With the conservative and moderate Democrats out of contention, the way was clear for a more liberal candidate, and so emerged Senator George McGovern of South Dakota. The former American history professor and Methodist minister won the nomination on the first ballot. McGovern's supporters fashioned a party platform that took extremely liberal positions, alarming Democratic moderates. The platform advocated an immediate withdrawal of American troops from Vietnam and proposed amnesty for draft dodgers. It also advocated school busing to integrate public schools, and a ban on handgun sales. McGovern's obvious sympathy for the underrepresented and underprivileged concerned moderate Democrats, but the plank that was most troubling asserted Americans' right "to make their own choices of lifestyles and private habits without being subject to discrimination or prosecution." To conservatives and moderates, this plank expressed an intention to tolerate loose sexual mores, drug experimentation, and more.

The pluralistic structure of the party convention itself also alienated moderate Democrats. After the disastrous 1968 convention, the party adopted reforms that allowed a quota for minority representation at the 1972 convention (which was held in Miami Beach, site of the Republican convention in both 1968 and 1972). The reforms resulted in more Hispanics, women, and blacks among the delegates, but traditional Democrats—such as urban bosses and labor unions—believed their influence was being diluted.

McGovern's candidacy got off to a rough start. When his running-mate, Senator Thomas Eagleton of Missouri, disclosed that he had received electroshock treatments for depression, McGovern handled the news clumsily, at first declaring himself "1,000 percent" behind Eagleton, and then abandoning him. As a replacement, he picked R. Sargent Shriver, a Kennedy brother-in-law and the former director of the Peace Corps. But McGovern's abrupt about-face on Eagleton raised questions about his decision-making abilities and made his campaign look amateurish.

Richard Nixon waves goodbye after resigning the office of president.

Nixon's reelection effort ran smoothly. With George Wallace gone, Nixon had a firm hold on conservative voters, especially in the South. His reelection a virtual certainty, Nixon made few campaign appearances and declined to debate McGovern. His record as president spoke of notable achievements, especially in foreign policy. In February 1972, he had made a landmark trip to China, the first visit to that country by an American president. Another major diplomatic breakthrough came in June when Nixon traveled to the Soviet Union to sign the Strategic Arms Limitation Treaty. Secretary of State Henry Kissinger bolstered Nixon's reelection prospects with his announcement just two weeks before the election that "peace is at hand" in Vietnam.

But the Nixon camp went to bizarre, and ultimately self-destructive, lengths to ensure the president's reelection. A special group, CREEP (the Committee to Reelect the President), raised hundreds of thousands of dollars, often illegally. On June 17, five members of CREEP were arrested at the Watergate office complex in Washington, where they were caught trying to bug the Democratic National Headquarters. McGovern cried foul and characterized the break-in as "the kind of thing you expect under a person like Hitler." Nixon denied any White House knowledge of the episode, dismissing it as a "third-rate burglary." The incident had no effect on the 1972 election, but two years later the extent of White House involvement become apparent, bringing down the Nixon presidency.

McGovern's extreme liberalism (he was nicknamed "the Goldwater of the Left") offended many elements of the New Deal coalition, especially white blue-collar workers and conservative southerners. Catholics in the North made a strange-bedfellow alliance with Protestants in the South as both denominations found McGovern's social agenda alarming. All of these groups voted for Nixon in large numbers; for example, while only 34 percent of blue-collar workers had voted for Nixon in 1968, 55 percent cast ballots for him in 1972. The Twenty-sixth Amendment, which had been adopted in 1971, lowered the minimum voting age to 18, but instead of backing the Democratic candidate, half of all young voters supported Nixon. The GOP was able to break the grip that the Democratic Party had on many Americans who had called that party their political home since the New Deal.

Nixon won by a landslide, collecting 520 electoral votes and garnering 49 states. He had surpassed Franklin Roosevelt's 1936 record of losing only two states; McGovern won only Massachusetts, with its strong liberal constituency, and the District of Columbia. His electoral vote total was a scant 17. Nixon's 60.7 percent of the popular votes was the highest percentage of any Republican in history.

Presidential elections, 1972

- Republican (Richard M. Nixon)
- Democrat (George S. McGovern)
- others
- ⑤ number of voting electors

Popular vote
(total: 77,727,590)

1,385,620
1.8%

47,170,179
60.7%

29,171,791
37.5%

Electoral vote
(total: 538)

1
0.2%

17
3.1%

520
96.7%

The Election of 1976

On August 9, 1974, Nixon stepped down from office in the wake of his involvement in the Watergate scandal, the only president to resign from office. Gerald R. Ford became the nation's thirty-eighth president and the first who had not been elected either to the presidency or to the vice presidency. In December 1973, he had become vice president through the Twenty-fifth Amendment, succeeding Spiro Agnew, who had resigned three months earlier after pleading no contest to having received bribes while Maryland governor and as vice president.

In an effort to salve the wounds created by Watergate and the Nixon resignation, Ford took one of the most controversial acts of his presidency just one month after entering office. On September 9, 1974, Ford granted Nixon "a full and unconditional pardon" for any crimes he might have committed as president. A storm of protest erupted, and many Americans angrily accused Ford of having struck a "deal" with Nixon to exchange the presidency for a pardon. Controversy over the pardon bedeviled Ford as the 1976 campaign approached.

By 1976, Ford had gained neither enthusiastic support from the nation nor the full backing of his party. The GOP's conservative wing was restive and vociferous, and particularly upset over Ford's appointment of liberal Republican Nelson Rockefeller as vice president. Worried that Rockefeller's presence on the 1976 ticket would be a liability, Ford declared that Rockefeller would not be his running mate. The move failed to appease former California governor Ronald Reagan, who challenged Ford for the nomination. In the bitter primaries that ensued, Reagan hammered away at the Ford administration, especially claiming that it had been soft on the Soviet Union. By the time of the Republican National Convention in Kansas City, Ford's and Reagan's delegate totals were nearly even. The president eventually won on the first ballot, and for his running mate picked Senator Bob Dole of Kansas, who was acceptable to conservatives, including Reagan.

In the Democratic primaries, former Georgia governor Jimmy Carter emerged victorious from a crowded field that included senators Birch Bayh, Henry Jackson, and Frank Church, Congressman Morris Udall, and governors George Wallace and Jerry Brown. At the Democratic National Convention in Manhattan, Carter won on the first ballot and picked Senator Walter Mondale of Minnesota as his running- mate.

A former peanut farmer, Carter was a virtual unknown when he began his quest for the presidency. But he had propelled himself above the other Democratic hopefuls by announcing his candidacy early, in December 1974, and campaigning vigorously throughout 1975. Carter was an outsider to Washington politics and had served only one term as Georgia governor, but he turned his outsider status and inexperience to his advantage, as many Americans were disgusted with the poisoned atmosphere of post-Watergate, post-Vietnam Washington. Carter built a campaign around his honesty. "Trust me," he promised, "I will never lie to you." Carter pledged to devote more attention to the unemployed, a promise that resonated strongly with millions of jobless Americans who had recently suffered through a severe recession in 1974–75. Ford was more focused on fighting inflation rather than unemployment, but his apparent inability to alleviate the suffering of those Americans who were out of work contributed to a perception that he was insensitive to their suffering.

In August Ford trailed Carter by as much as 20 points in the polls. Trying to boost his campaign, he challenged Carter to a series of nationally televised debates. During the first debate Ford outperformed Carter and cut into his challenger's lead in the polls, but during the second debate Ford committed a gaffe that hurt him. Speaking about U.S.–Soviet relations, he declared, "There is no Soviet domination of Eastern Europe and there never will be under a Ford administration." This odd remark, which Ford did not recant for three days, stripped him of the momentum he had been building.

Jimmy Carter
1924–
After assuming office, Carter tried to soften some of the presidency's imperial trappings, symbolized by his decision to walk down Pennsylvania Avenue at his inauguration rather than ride in a limousine.

The Ford-Carter face-offs established debates as a staple of presidential elections, and the campaign also featured the first-ever vice presidential debate, during which Mondale outclassed his opponent. Dole had a reputation for being caustic, and the debate bore it out. He came across as vitriolic, and when he referred to the "Democratic wars" of the twentieth century, Mondale shot back, "Does he really mean that there was a partisan difference over our involvement in a fight against Nazi Germany?" Journalist Jules Witcover, watching Dole's performance, described him as "dark, brooding, sarcastic, even mean," and commented that Dole's behavior reminded him of Nixon.

Despite the political burdens of Watergate, the Nixon pardon, and a sluggish economy, Ford staged a remarkable comeback and by Election Day Carter's once insurmountable lead had vanished. The two contestants were in a virtual dead heat. Confidence in Ford's stewardship of the country as well as doubt about Carter's abilities and experience allowed Ford to close the gap separating him from his challenger.

But in the end Carter won a close contest. Although Ford won more states than Carter—27 to 23—Carter benefited from the support of northeastern and southern states, which swung solidly behind the Georgia native. Geographically, the election results seemed almost to have divided the country in two. Ford won most of the western half of the country, while Carter took the East. Although Ford won populous states whose electoral votes have historically ensured victory—California, Illinois, and Michigan—Carter triumphed in the critical states of Florida, New York, Ohio, Pennsylvania, and Texas.

Ford attracted the Republican constituency of affluent, well-educated, suburban voters, and Carter won the support of the fading New Deal coalition of African Americans, labor, the elderly, and the underprivileged.

African Americans remained especially loyal to the Democratic Party, with 95 percent of the black votes going to Carter, a civil rights advocate. The black vote enabled Carter to edge out Ford in key states such as New York, Pennsylvania, and Maryland; more than any single group, African Americans delivered victory to Carter.

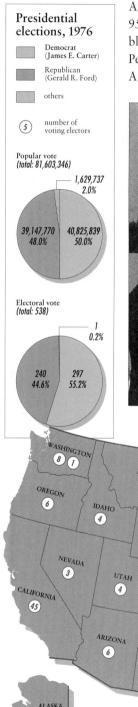

Presidential elections, 1976

Democrat (James E. Carter)

Republican (Gerald R. Ford)

others

⑤ number of voting electors

Popular vote
(total: 81,603,346)

1,629,737
2.0%

39,147,770
48.0%

40,825,839
50.0%

Electoral vote
(total: 538)

1
0.2%

240
44.6%

297
55.2%

The high tide of the Carter administration was the successful conclusion of the Camp David Accords. But it was not enough to secure a Democratic victory in 1980.

WASHINGTON ⑧ ①

OREGON ⑥

MONTANA ④

IDAHO ④

NORTH DAKOTA ③

MINNESOTA ⑩

MAINE ④

VT ③ ④ NH

NEVADA ③

UTAH ④

WYOMING ③

SOUTH DAKOTA ④

WISCONSIN ⑪

MICHIGAN ㉑

NEW YORK ㊶

MASSACHUSETTS ⑭ RI ④ CONN ⑧

CALIFORNIA ㊺

COLORADO ⑦

NEBRASKA ⑤

IOWA ⑧

ILLINOIS ㉖ INDIANA ⑬

OHIO ㉕

PENNSYLVANIA ㉗

NEW JERSEY ⑰

DELAWARE ③

ARIZONA ⑥

NEW MEXICO ④

KANSAS ⑦

MISSOURI ⑫

KENTUCKY ⑨

WEST VIRGINIA ⑥

MD ⑩ DC ③

VIRGINIA ⑫

OKLAHOMA ⑧

ARKANSAS ⑥

TENNESSEE ⑩

NORTH CAROLINA ⑬

SOUTH CAROLINA ⑧

TEXAS ㉖

LOUISIANA ⑩

MISSISSIPPI ⑦

ALABAMA ⑨

GEORGIA ⑫

FLORIDA ⑰

ALASKA ③

HAWAI ④

0 300 km
0 300 miles

0 300 km
0 300 miles

N

The Election of 1980

For decades political conservatives struggled but failed to make their message attractive. But during the 1970s a conservative mood crept over the country. This change partly stemmed from the disillusionment with the panoply of Great Society programs, which failed to cure social ills and bloated the federal budget. To some, "liberalism" had become a nasty epithet, a code word for government spending for minorities. Voters were tiring of high taxes and government regulation, and wanted relief from both. During the 1960s and even into the 1970s, the nation seemed to have lost its moral bearings, and Americans who emphasized traditional values lamented legalized abortion, the prohibition of voluntary school prayer, and other social policies that liberals had endorsed. The conservative upsurge also resulted from conservatives' concerted efforts after Barry Goldwater's humiliation at the polls in 1964.

Ronald Reagan 1911–

While running for president, Reagan promised a 30 percent across-the-board tax cut and a tough line against Moscow, which appealed to Americans weary of high taxes and alarmed by the recent Soviet invasion of Afghanistan.

Late in the 1970s, conservatism found an effective spokesman in Ronald Reagan. A former movie actor, Reagan had been elected governor of California in 1966 and had served two terms. After losing the 1976 Republican nomination to Gerald Ford, Reagan moderated his rhetoric and reassured listeners that he would not scuttle social programs or start a war. Moreover, the Californian had a warm smile and a friendly demeanor, and his acting skills allowed him to use television effectively. Coming from a western state made him all the more attractive to Republicans who distrusted the eastern establishment.

Reagan cruised through the Republican primaries, beating back a field that included George Bush, senators Bob Dole and Howard Baker, former treasury secretary John Connally, and Congressman John B. Anderson. In April, Anderson, a liberal Republican who found himself at odds with the increasingly conservative bent of his party, announced that he would continue his bid for the White House as an independent candidate, calling his effort the "National Unity Campaign." Although victory was improbable for a third-party candidate, Anderson had reason to hope for a respectable showing, because by early summer public opinion polls showed that 25 percent of the electorate supported him.

In August Reagan won the Republican nomination in Detroit; at age 69, he was the oldest man ever to be nominated by a major party. After former president Ford turned down the number two spot on the ticket, Reagan picked his closest competitor in the primaries, George Bush, a wise choice because it united the squabbling eastern and western wings of the party.

Jimmy Carter was in trouble. During the primaries he faced a challenge from Senator Edward Kennedy of Massachusetts. Although Carter prevailed, the intraparty fight was bruising. Moreover, inflation had reignited during the preceding year and was running at double-digit levels. The country had simultaneously slumped into a recession, and the jobless rate hit 7.8 percent in July.

Another of Carter's burdens was in foreign affairs. On November 4, 1979, Iranian religious militants, protesting U.S. support for the autocratic Shah of Iran, seized the American embassy in Teheran, taking American hostages. Fifty-two Americans were held hostage after the embassy takeover, and they were to remain there for over a year. Carter denounced the Iranian action as "an act of terrorism totally outside the bounds of international law," but he appeared helpless. While the country initially rallied around the president, as the hostage crisis wore on, Americans complained of Carter's feckless leadership.

In December 1979, just one month after the Iranian incident, the Soviet Union invaded Afghanistan. The invasion exacerbated cold war tensions and increased the insecurities of Americans. Again, Carter appeared helpless. To protest the invasion, he imposed a grain embargo against the Soviets and led the U.S. and other Western nations in a boycott of the 1980 Summer Olympics in Moscow, a move that won him instant critics and was of doubtful efficacy.

Amid palpable signs of American decline at home and abroad, Reagan promised new hope and displayed a sunny optimism and confidence. Excess government, Reagan asserted, had hamstrung the free-market economy, and he promised to cut taxes, to reduce the waste and abuse in the government's welfare programs, and "take government off the backs of the great people of this country." Reagan was especially harsh on Carter's foreign policy.

A televised debate between Carter and Reagan was a decisive event in this campaign. With more than 100 million viewers watching, Reagan spoke smoothly and effectively. He had a particularly memorable line when he chided the president, "There you go again," after Carter claimed that Reagan opposed Medicare. At the close of the debate, Reagan repeated his standard but highly effective campaign question: "Are you better off than you were four years ago? Is it easier to buy things in the stores than it was four years ago? Is there more or less unemployment in the country than there was four years ago? Is America respected throughout the world as it was?" For many Americans, to ask these questions was to answer them.

By Election Day the race was a statistical dead heat, with Reagan leading Carter in the polls by only a few points. But the country went decisively for Reagan. The numbers for Carter looked so bad that he conceded to Reagan even before the polls on the West Coast had closed. John B. Anderson won only 6 percent of the popular vote and received no electoral votes.

The magnitude of Reagan's victory came as a surprise. Apparently, a large bloc of undecided voters went for Reagan on Election Day. His coattails were long enough to pull in a Republican-controlled Senate, the first since 1952, with a gain of 11 seats. Although the Democrats retained control of the House, the Republicans picked up 33 seats.

Carter won only 6 states and the District of Columbia. Even southern states and traditionally Democratic states like New York went to Reagan. The 1980 election made clear a process that had been at work for more than a decade: the fragmentation of the New Deal coalition. The genius of this coalition had been in welding together disparate groups with sometimes competing interests. But the coalition experienced mass defections, as blue-collar workers, ethnic whites, and urban voters voted for Reagan in large numbers. The only New Deal group to remain overwhelmingly loyal to Carter was African Americans, who cast 85 percent of their votes for him.

Carter's defeat was the most resounding of an incumbent since Herbert Hoover lost to Franklin Roosevelt by 18 percent in 1932. It reflected fundamental flaws in his campaign as well as a deep dissatisfaction with his presidency. Carter engaged in negative campaign tactics that made him appear desperate and were unworthy of a man who touted his own integrity and character. Even more important, Carter was an unpopular president. During the summer of 1980, a Gallup poll registered Carter's job approval rating at 21 percent, the lowest ever for a sitting president. The *New York Times* observed, "On Election Day, Mr. Carter was the issue." Voters scored him especially for incompetent economic stewardship. Since prices had risen dramatically during the past two years, most voters cited inflation as their primary concern. Yet Carter could do little to stop inflation, adding to the perception of a weak leader. The 1980 election represented a departure from customary voter predilections, as most Americans had traditionally trusted the Democrats to deal more effectively with domestic economic issues, while entrusting foreign policy stewardship more to the Republicans. The new conservative movement placed a deliberate emphasis on pocketbook issues, and Reagan had consistently shown himself more attuned to these concerns.

Voters had no more confidence in Carter's foreign policy than in his economic leadership. America's international prestige had suffered as the country endured a series of humiliating reversals around the world, most notably in Iran. Americans overwhelmingly disapproved of Carter's handling of the hostage crisis, and his administration was unable to pull off an "October surprise" and secure the release of the hostages in time for the election. As it was, the doleful first anniversary of the embassy takeover fell on Election Day. The overwhelming Reagan victory resulted from pent-up frustrations that Americans felt over Carter's leadership in both domestic and foreign policy.

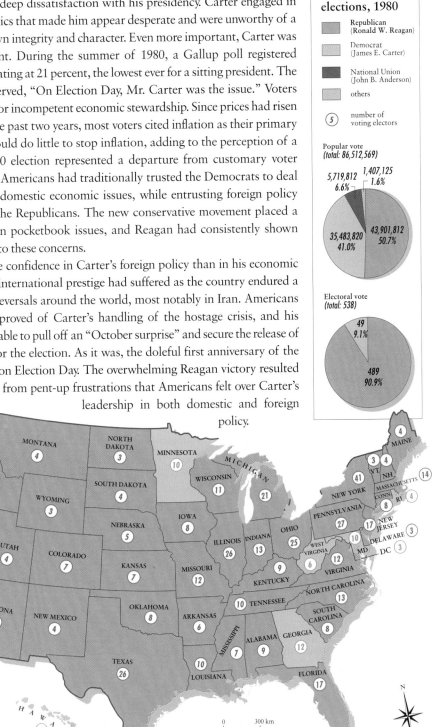

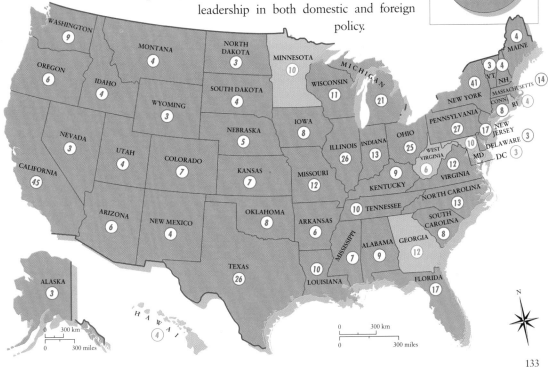

The Election of 1984

In the 1984 primaries, Democratic aspirants for the White House included former Vice President Walter Mondale, Senator John Glenn of Ohio, Senator Gary Hart of Colorado, and civil rights leader Jesse Jackson. At the Democratic National Convention in San Francisco, Mondale emerged as the nominee and made history by picking the first woman ever to be nominated as the vice presidential candidate of a major party, Representative Geraldine Ferraro of New York.

The Republican Party held its national convention in Dallas, the first such gathering in Texas, one of the fastest-growing states in the nation. The GOP was solidly united behind Reagan. He had earned the nickname the "Teflon president" because criticism would not stick to him, and he seemed to have restored power and prestige to an office that, as pundits observed, had destroyed a succession of men dating back to the 1960s. Reagan won the GOP nomination unchallenged, and the Republicans exulted in the revival of patriotism that the country had experienced during Reagan's first term. Reagan stoked feelings of national pride by emphasizing the country's power and success and by painting a glorious future for America. During the campaign, he exhorted crowds, "Trust the American people. The shadows are behind us, and the bright sunshine of hope and opportunity lies ahead." Enjoying advantages of at times more than 20 points in the polls, Reagan took an easy approach to the campaign, rarely discussing specific goals for a second term, seldom mentioning Mondale by name, and campaigning only two or three days a week.

Even Mondale gave Reagan credit for the increased patriotism in the country. But he warned of a darker side to the Reagan presidency. He criticized what he viewed as the abrasive social policies of the Reagan years, denouncing their "official cruelty." Characterizing Reagan's government as one "of the rich, by the rich, and for the rich," Mondale leveled a common criticism against "Reaganomics" (as Reagan's economic policies frequently—and often pejoratively—came to be known), namely, that it widened the gap between the rich and the poor. Mondale also warned against the large federal budget deficits that had occurred under Reagan's watch, and promised to reduce the deficit by two-thirds. In his speech accepting the Democratic nomination, he struck at the president's alleged disingenuousness by boldly declaring: "Mr. Reagan will raise taxes, and so will I. He won't tell you. I just did." Mondale's promise to raise taxes, however forthright, was political poison.

From the moment of his nomination, Mondale trailed Reagan badly in the polls. The president was popular, and his television speeches throughout his first term had been so effective that he had earned the nickname, "The Great Communicator." By contrast, Mondale spoke in a monotone, and Ferraro failed to generate the excitement he had anticipated. The Democrats' only glimmer of hope came after the first of two television debates with Reagan, during which the president gave an uncharacteristically lackluster performance; Mondale's popularity rose slightly. Reagan's halting, unfocused behavior bred doubts about whether, at age 73, he would be equal to the task of serving another term. But he appeared in command during the second debate, the most memorable moment of which came after a questioner raised the issue of age, and Reagan quipped, "I am not going to exploit, for political purposes, my opponent's youth and inexperience."

Reagan won 49 states, losing only Mondale's home state of Minnesota. He equaled Nixon's 49-state sweep of 1972, and his landslide in popular vote rivaled the four other landslides of the century: 1920, 1936, 1964, and 1972. Mondale fared much worse than Carter had against Reagan, and did not have the disadvantage—as Carter did—of a third-party candidate to draw away Democratic votes. Unlike in 1980, however, Reagan's coattails were short. The Republicans gained only 14 seats in the House and lost two Senate seats. The failure of Reagan's victory to translate into broader gains for the Republican Party indicated that his triumph was a personal one that did not represent a more fundamental shift in the nation.

The West followed its usual voting pattern and went solidly for the Republican Party, and even New York and Massachusetts went for Reagan. The South continued its pattern, begun in the 1960s, of voting Republican behind the solid backing of southern whites, who voted for Reagan 71 to 29 percent. Ferraro's presence on the ticket seemed to have hurt Mondale, particularly in the South, where conservatives were discomfited by the prospect of a woman, especially one from New York City, becoming vice president. Additionally, voters nationwide could not fail to note her lack of charisma —even abrasiveness—and lack of experience in national office (she had served three terms as a congresswoman).

Once again, Reagan made impressive inroads into the New Deal coalition, attracting a majority of votes from blue-collar workers and from women. He also attracted broad support from all age groups—young, middle-aged, and old. Many Democrats—dubbed "Reagan Democrats"—crossed political lines to vote Republican. Especially noteworthy was the president's attraction among young voters, age 18 to 24, who had traditionally voted Democratic. Almost two-thirds of this group cast ballots for the president, an outcome that suggested a potential realignment of the electorate, as the younger generation was increasingly attracted to the Republican Party. As in 1980, only two groups remained unswervingly loyal to the Democratic candidate: African Americans, with more than 90 percent casting their ballots for Mondale, and workers earning less than $10,000 a year.

As *Time* magazine saw it, "The campaign was dominated by four Ps: Prosperity, Peace, Patriotism, and Personality." In 1980, voters had elected Reagan largely to rectify the country's decadelong economic problems, and four years later, the majority of voters apparently felt that he had suc-

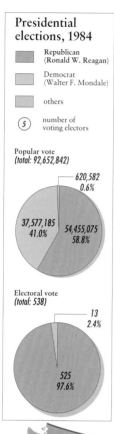

Presidential elections, 1984

- Republican (Ronald W. Reagan)
- Democrat (Walter F. Mondale)
- others

(5) number of voting electors

Popular vote
(total: 92,652,842)

620,582
0.6%

37,577,185
41.0%

54,455,075
58.8%

Electoral vote
(total: 538)

13
2.4%

525
97.6%

ceeded. He had delivered on his promise of tax cuts, the economy was expanding, unemployment was low, and prices had stabilized. While Mondale had decried the large federal budget deficits that Reagan had presided over, the issue was too remote or abstract to most Americans, who were enjoying personal prosperity. Reagan had rebuilt pride in the country, enhanced its military strength, and kept the country out of war. Voters perceived him as a strong and decisive leader, and a likable one as well. He had bravely survived a 1981 assassination attempt and displayed peerless communications skills. The magnitude of Reagan's victory established him as the most popular president since Dwight D. Eisenhower.

Walter Mondale and Geraldine Ferraro on the campaign trail. Ferraro was the first woman to be nominated for high office by any major party.

The Election of 1988

Many contestants in the 1988 Democratic primaries were unknowns, such as former governor Bruce Babbitt of Arizona, Massachusetts Governor Michael Dukakis, Tennessee Senator Al Gore, Illinois Senator Paul Simon, and Missouri Congressman Richard Gephardt. Jesse Jackson ran again, but two other well-known candidates were forced to quit amid controversy. Colorado Senator Gary Hart withdrew from the race after the *Miami Herald* published details of the 52-year-old senator's adulterous affair with a 29-year-old model, Donna Rice. Senator Joe Biden of Delaware pulled out after a disclosure that he had plagiarized portions of a speech. (The incidents vividly illustrated how important character had become in American politics.) The Democrats held their national convention in Atlanta, and the nomination went to Dukakis, who had pointed proudly to his state's economic turnaround—the "Massachusetts Miracle." Dukakis chose Texas Senator Lloyd Bentson as his running mate. The Democratic convention was often caustic, with participants indulging in ad hominem attacks against Vice President George Bush, the prospective Republican nominee. The attacks set the tone for the rest of the campaign.

George Bush
1924–
In an effort to overcome what Time *magazine dubbed "The Wimp Factor"— his image as a weak leader—Bush campaigned aggressively in 1988, advocating capital punishment, forswearing new taxes, and attacking his Democratic opponent.*

Bush viewed the presidency as the capstone to a long career in public service, during which he had served as a congressman, chairman of the Republican National Committee, ambassador to the United Nations, envoy to China, CIA director, and finally, vice president. In the primaries, Bush faced challenges from Senator Bob Dole, former secretary of state Alexander Haig, and television evangelist Pat Robertson. Dole was Bush's chief rival, and the contest between the two men was often bitter. Like Dukakis, Bush became the front-runner after winning big on "Super Tuesday," a cluster of southern state primaries held on March 8. At the party's national convention in New Orleans, Bush won the nomination on the first ballot. His acceptance speech contained the memorable phrase, "I want a kinder, gentler nation," which reflected widespread unease with the economic inequities that Reaganomics had allegedly exacerbated, and the even more memorable pledge, "Read my lips: no new taxes." Not known for oratorical panache, Bush delivered the speech with a surprising earnestness and eloquence.

But Bush surprised—and dismayed—the Republican convention with his choice for the ticket's second spot, Dan Quayle, a conservative senator from Indiana. Just 41 years old, Quayle hardly seemed presidential timber. His easygoing, blithe personality, combined with boyish looks, prompted cartoonists to depict him as a little kid. The misgivings over Quayle only increased when an account surfaced that he had used family influence to join the National Guard and avoid wartime service in Vietnam. Bush was under immediate pressure to withdraw his choice. While he stood by Quayle, in his diary he penned private regret about his vice presidential pick, writing that "it was my decision, and I blew it."

In the spring of 1988, before the political conventions, Bush trailed Dukakis by 16 points. But Dukakis proved a poor campaigner and lost his lead. His personality seemed cold. In fact, one of his nicknames was "The Ice Man," and Americans, who knew little about him, could not identify with him emotionally. His campaign refrain, "Good jobs at good wages," fell flat. During the second of two televised debates against Bush, Dukakis lost a golden opportunity to display passion when he stoically stated, in response to a question, that he would not advocate the death penalty for someone who had raped and murdered his wife. Bush appeared more likable than his opponent, and his extensive experience in government made him attractive.

Bush and his political handlers mounted a blistering attack that made Dukakis the campaign's prime issue and focused on themes reminiscent of Richard Nixon's 1968 campaign: liberalism, patriotism, and crime. The vice president derided Dukakis as a "liberal," and the Bush campaign aired aggressively negative commercials attacking Dukakis. Bush impugned Dukakis's patriotism by lambasting him for a 1977 veto of a bill that would have required Massachusetts schoolchildren to recite the Pledge of Allegiance. The most notorious attack advertisement, sponsored by independent Republican group, criticized Dukakis for a prisoner furlough program in Massachusetts. It showed the face of convicted murderer Willie Horton, an African American who had assaulted and raped a woman while on a weekend furlough. The racist appeal of the advertisement, while not overt, was nonetheless clear.

The negative campaigning was dreary but effective. Bush's attacks on Dukakis painted an unflattering picture of the Massachusetts governor and drove up his negative ratings. Though distressed by the attacks, Dukakis turned the other cheek rather than fight back. Where he tried to dispel critics, the results were sometimes misbegotten. After Republicans said he was soft on defense, Dukakis visited a General Dynamics plant and rode in a tank. He looked ludicrous in oversize military headgear with his head poking up out of the turret.

In tarring Dukakis so mercilessly, Bush showed how artful and image-driven presidential campaigning had become. The ever-increasing importance of television imagery, combined with the long season of primary contests, encouraged candidates to hire professional political consultants. These experts conducted public opinion polls, interviewed "focus groups" to determine the concerns of the average American, designed hard-hitting television commercials, and choreographed candidate appearances. Political consultants now exerted a powerful influence and manipulated public opinion to an unprecedented degree.

Bush won a decisive victory over Dukakis, with 53.4 percent versus 45.7 percent of the popular vote, and 426 electoral votes to Dukakis's 111. Bush's strengths were in the South and the Rocky Mountain states, and he even won most New England states (except for Rhode Island and Dukakis's native state of Massachusetts) and Pennsylvania, where Dukakis had campaigned earnestly and where he had gone to college. Most of Dukakis's states were traditionally Democratic ones, such as New York. (Bush's loss of the Empire State and its rich lode of electoral votes marked the first time since 1948 that the Republicans lost the state but won the election.) Dukakis won another traditionally Democratic area, the cities, while Bush outpolled Dukakis in the suburbs, a growing region of the country that was increasingly the domain of the Republicans, where more affluent and better-educated Americans lived, a core GOP constituency. African Americans continued strongly to support the Democrats, giving Dukakis 90 percent of their votes.

Bush had staged a remarkable comeback against Dukakis. He had benefited especially from a strong economy. An expansion that had begun in 1983 was still going strong; more than 15 million jobs had been created, and unemployment was at its lowest level in 14 years. As the vice president and heir apparent to the Reagan legacy, Bush rode the political and economic momentum that his popular predecessor had generated. In some respects, his victory represented a third term for Ronald Reagan.

Bush became the first sitting vice president since Martin Van Buren to win the presidency. Although his victory was clear, his precise mandate was not, for Bush had made Dukakis the issue and campaigned against him, without expressing concrete goals for a Bush presidency. Moreover, after three decisive Republican presidential election victories, the Democratic Party still showed its strength and majority status in the country, since Dukakis won a greater percentage of the popular vote than either Carter or Mondale had, and both houses of Congress remained in Democratic hands.

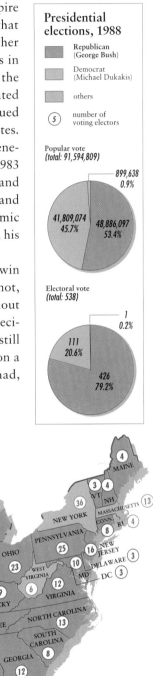

Presidential elections, 1988

Republican (George Bush)
Democrat (Michael Dukakis)
others
5 number of voting electors

Popular vote (total: 91,594,809)
899,638 0.9%
41,809,074 45.7%
48,886,097 53.4%

Electoral vote (total: 538)
1 0.2%
111 20.6%
426 79.2%

The Election of 1992

Bill Clinton
1946–
In the 1992 primaries and general election, Clinton overcame a cascade of character revelations by focusing on the economy and by practicing centrist politics, appealing to moderate Republicans as well as to Democrats.

George Bush's presidency witnessed seismic changes in foreign affairs. Around the world, communism crumbled: the Berlin Wall came down, East and West Germany reunified, and the Soviet Union collapsed. World tensions eased as the cold war finally came to a close, and Bush proudly pointed to a "New World Order." The Persian Gulf War of early 1991, during which mostly American forces easily overwhelmed Iraq, added a stunning foreign policy success to Bush's record. After the war, he looked politically unbeatable. His public approval rating hit 91 percent, an unimaginable summit for any president. But domestic worries soon clouded the glow of wartime victory. The nation slipped into a recession, and in mid-1991 unemployment hit almost 8 percent.

As the economy foundered, Bush's standing in the polls dropped, too, sinking to 29 percent by early August. The recession not only punctured George Bush's seeming political invincibility but also highlighted his inattention to domestic problems. As a political thinker, Bush was emphatically more interested in foreign policy, and his first term was largely barren of domestic achievements. While he had originally promised to be the "education president" and the "environmental president," those pledges had withered away. He openly professed an inability to articulate the "vision thing," an admission that was disquieting and even embarrassing. Political gridlock between the White House and Congress also tarnished the Bush presidency, as he faced a Democratic Congress with which he had an uneasy relationship.

Bush also alienated Republican conservatives by reneging on his "no new taxes" pledge from the 1988 campaign. In 1990 he agreed to a tax increase as part of a deficit reduction package that attempted to relieve the country of its federal deficit and mounting national debt (the deficit hit a record $290 billion in the 1992 fiscal year, while the debt stood at over $4 trillion by the end of Bush's presidency). Dissatisfaction with Bush within the Republican Party prompted conservative newspaper columnist and former Nixon speechwriter Patrick Buchanan to challenge him in the primaries. Although Buchanan never posed a significant political threat to Bush, his challenge not only reflected widespread conservative disaffection with Bush but also weakened party unity.

Bush's political strength after the Persian Gulf War, among other factors, had persuaded many prominent Democrats to sit out the 1992 race, including New York Governor Mario Cuomo and Tennessee Senator Al Gore. As a result, less known Democrats vied for the nation's highest office. Massachusetts Senator Paul Tsongas won the first primary, in New Hampshire, but thereafter Arkansas Governor Bill Clinton dominated the Democratic contests. Clinton, a Rhodes scholar and graduate of Yale Law School, had become the youngest governor in the nation in 1978 when he was elected at age 32. Two years later he lost his re-election bid but won another term in 1982, earning the nickname, "The Comeback Kid."

Another Clinton moniker was "Slick Willy," which referred to his penchant for shading the truth. At one point in the campaign, he admitted that he had tried marijuana as a youth but added the qualification that he "didn't inhale." Clinton was dogged by charges that he had dodged the draft during the Vietnam War and was unfaithful to his wife. Early in the primary season, Clinton's campaign was nearly capsized by Gennifer Flowers, a lounge singer who publicly revealed a 12-year affair with Clinton. That Clinton was able to withstand such charges of marital infidelity was due in part to the steadfastness of his wife, Hillary Rodham, whom he had met at Yale Law School and who had become an effective political partner. Partly, too, the American people appeared jaded by character issues.

At the Democratic National Convention in New York City, Clinton won the nomination and picked Tennessee Senator Al Gore as his running mate. Although Gore's presence added little geographic diversity, the instant popularity of the ticket illustrated not only Bush's political weakness but, more important, the successful Democratic strategy of nominating for national office southerners who could pull the region away from the Republicans while retaining traditionally Democratic areas such as the Northeast. Clinton and Gore, 46 and 44 years old, respectively, also represented a new generation of Americans, the baby boomers, whereas Bush represented the last of a generation of World War II veterans. Clinton accentuated his appeal among younger Americans by appearing on youth-oriented television networks and programs, such as MTV, even donning dark sunglasses and playing the saxophone on a television talk show. The Clinton campaign promised change and adopted the effective strategy of focusing on the economy, blaming Bush for the recession. A sign prominently displayed in the Clinton campaign headquarters' "war room" said it all: "The economy, stupid."

The 1992 campaign also witnessed the entry of a crotchety, eccentric Texan. H. Ross Perot, whose computer firm, Electronic Data Systems, had made him a billionaire, capitalized on popular disaffection with Washington. A diminutive man with a crew-cut and oversized ears, Perot struck a peculiar figure, but he had a plain-talking style and promised a direct, no-nonsense approach to repairing whatever was wrong with the national government. The businessman blazed the television talk show circuit and attracted a populist following, striking fertile ground among Americans who were fed up with Washington insiders and with the standard nostrums from politicians. But in July, Perot abruptly withdrew from the race, and equally perplexing, rejoined three months later.

Though erratic, Perot made his presence felt. His extraordinary wealth allowed him to spend his own money without stint, circumventing normal campaign finance restrictions, and he doled out more money on television advertising than either the Bush or Clinton campaigns. Perot's trademark became his prime-time, nationally broadcast "infomercials," half-hour- or hour-long advertisements in which Perot, armed with a pointer and charts, discussed issues such as the federal deficit. The sales pitches were surprisingly effective, as millions of viewers watched and Perot's popularity inched upward.

For Bush it was an unhappy race. Never one to enjoy campaigning, Bush appeared particularly unenthusiastic to hit the hustings one last time. After repulsing the Buchanan challenge, he won the nomination at a relatively insipid Republican convention that celebrated the vague theme of "family values" and failed to give him the usual boost in the polls (one poll showed that only 15 percent of voters saw family values as an important issue). By emphasizing social issues, the convention turned a blind eye toward the economic woes that worried the majority of Americans, making the Bush administration appear out of touch. Polls indicated that most voters felt that Bush did not understand the problems of the average American.

Unlike in 1988, when Bush flailed away relentlessly at Michael Dukakis, this time he had to defend his record as president, which Clinton—a much cannier opponent than Dukakis—skillfully attacked. Bush never outlined a clear agenda for a second term, and he trailed Clinton in public opinion polls from the start. The president tried to raise the issue of character and trust, where Clinton was vulnerable, but among most voters these issues seemed remote. To add to Bush's burdens, doubts about his vice president continued. Many Republican confidants urged Bush to drop Dan Quayle from the ticket, but he refused, even though Quayle was perhaps the most ridiculed vice president in American history.

In October the three presidential candidates met in three television debates; a debate among the three vice presidential candidates was also held. Bush gave generally uninspired performances, while his Democratic challenger appeared knowledgeable and articulate. Clinton made an especially strong showing in the second debate, which took the format of a "town hall meeting" and allowed him to roam the stage and show his empathy for the average American. By contrast, Bush appeared distracted and inattentive during this debate, and television cameras even caught him glancing at his wristwatch.

Only during the waning days of the campaign, when it was clear that his job was in peril, did Bush throw his heart into the campaign, although he sometimes appeared unpresidential. He repeatedly referred to Clinton and Gore as "bozos" and even ventured that the First Dog, Millie, knew more about foreign policy than the two Democrats.

On Election Day the palm went to Bill Clinton, although his mandate was hardly resounding and represented more a repudiation of Bush than a vote of confidence for the Democrats. Clinton garnered only a plurality of the popular vote, 42.3 percent, and won 370 electoral votes and 32 states. His mandate was the weakest since Woodrow Wilson's 41.9 percent in 1912, a year that also featured a bitter three-way race. Clinton became the seventeenth candidate in history to win the presidency without a majority of the popular vote. Bush won 37.4 percent of the popular vote, 168 electoral votes, and 18 states. Perot gave a strong showing, with 19 percent of the popular vote, though he failed to win any electoral votes. His was the strongest showing of a third-party candidate since Theodore Roosevelt in 1912, and his presence in the race probably prevented Clinton from winning a majority of the popular vote. The voter turnout in 1992, 55 percent, reversed a general trend of decline since 1960.

Clinton swept the Northeast and New England, even winning New Hampshire and California, traditionally conservative states that had not gone Democratic since Johnson's 1964 landslide. He was also able to regain some of the South for his party (Georgia, Louisiana, Tennessee, and his native state of Arkansas), which had been reliably Republican for a generation. The West Coast, which had been safe Republican territory since the 1950s, went Democratic. Clinton was able to win key groups over Bush and Perot, including independent voters, Reagan Democrats, 18- to 24-year-olds, and single parents, an increasingly large segment of the population that trusted the Democrats to secure the social programs that they depended on for survival. As expected, Clinton won the African-American vote, with 83 percent, compared to 10 percent for Bush and 7 percent for Perot.

Bush's fall from grace had been rapid. Foreign policy victories seldom translate into enduring popularity for presidents; Richard Nixon, a sideline observer during this election and the veteran of many foreign policy coups during his own presidency, had ruefully predicted after the Persian Gulf War that Bush would still lose the election because of a weak economy. Bush had also faced a politically adroit challenger. Unlike other recent Democratic candidates for president, who had relied on votes from the traditional Democratic constituency of liberals, urban voters, and lower-class Americans, Clinton established a connection with the suburban middle class, promising help for them while avoiding hints of excessive government activism. He continued the traditional Democratic emphasis on equality and social fairness, but he shrewdly positioned himself as a centrist Democrat who would avoid expensive government programs while at the same time reversing the effects of Reaganomics.

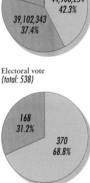

Presidential elections, 1992

Democrat (William J. Clinton)

Republican (George H. Bush)

Independent (H. Ross Perot)

others

⑤ number of voting electors

Popular vote
(*total: 104,421,811*)

670,149
1.4%

19,741,065
18.9%

44,908,254
42.3%

39,102,343
37.4%

Electoral vote
(*total: 538*)

168
31.2%

370
68.8%

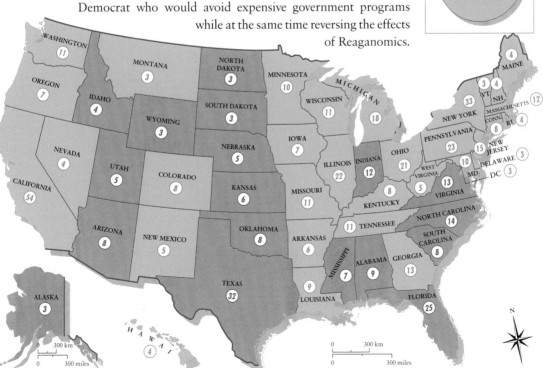

The Election of 1996

In the 1994 midterm elections, the Democratic Party suffered an ominous setback when the Republicans gained control of the House and Senate, marking the first time the GOP controlled both houses of Congress since Dwight D. Eisenhower's first term. With a Democrat in the White House, the situation represented a surprising reversal of the political pattern since World War II, namely, Republican dominance in the presidency and Democratic strength in Congress. The congressional Republicans declared an aggressive legislative package that they dubbed their "Contract with America." In April 1995, Bill Clinton's presidency seemed to have sunk to a nadir when he insisted during a news conference that he was "relevant" to the governing process.

But the "Comeback Kid" was able to claw his way back to contention for the 1996 election. Much of Clinton's renewed strength rested on the country's economic boom. Signs of America's prosperity were everywhere—increased productivity, low unemployment, stunning technological advances (especially in communications, including the explosive growth of the Internet), increased exports, a soaring stock market, and sharp reductions in the federal budget deficit. Almost miraculously, inflation remained low during these boom times (whereas in the past a robust economy often experienced inflationary pressures). Clinton became the obvious beneficiary of the economic prosperity.

No Democrat challenged the president in the primaries, which allowed Clinton to husband his energy and financial resources and to concentrate early in 1996 on beating any Republican challenger. The Democrats enjoyed a harmonious convention in Chicago. (The situation contrasted vividly with the debacle the last time their convention was held in that city, in 1968. The 1996 Chicago convention marked the twenty-fifth time the city had hosted a major party convention, a record.) Clinton adopted a strategy called "triangulation," in which he distinguished himself from liberals and conservatives and portrayed himself as a moderate, thus capturing the center of the political spectrum. In doing so, he was not afraid to renounce orthodox Democratic tenets. In his January 1996 State of the Union address, he proclaimed that the "era of big government is over," a rebuke of traditional Democratic fiscal policy that cemented his appeal among many moderates and fiscal conservatives. He also embraced the goal of a balanced budget, a position that drew supporters of Ross Perot back into the Democratic fold. Clinton fashioned a position that co-opted Republican ideals while preserving Democratic ones; he preached fiscal responsibility while also defending the government's social services.

Senate Majority Leader Bob Dole led the Republican primaries in what was his third run for the presidency. He beat back contestants such as Pat Buchanan and businessman Steve Forbes, whose campaign attracted attention because he proposed an unconventional but simplifying tax code called "flat tax." The upcoming campaign figured to pit the president against the majority leader, two men who knew each other well and who had worked together closely on legislation for almost four years; not since 1960 had a campaign featured two candidates who were so familiar with each other. Having locked up the nomination early in the primary season, in May Dole made the dramatic announcement that he would resign from the Senate to devote his attention full-time to winning the presidency. It was a bold gambit to energize a floundering campaign. By leaving his post as Senate majority leader he was "giving all and risking all," he said, and he promised that he "will seek the presidency with nothing to fall back on but the judgment of the people and nowhere to go but the White House or home."

For Dole, his third bid for the White House got him further than ever before, as he won the GOP nomination. At the Republican National Convention in San Diego, he picked as his running mate Jack Kemp, a former Buffalo Bills quarterback, former congressman, and secretary of Housing and Urban Development in the Bush administration. But the Dole-Kemp campaign was ineffective from the start. Part of Dole's problem was the bad luck of facing an opponent who, in addition to his formidable political skills, was presiding over flush economic times. Dole's age also worked to his disadvantage: at 73 years old, he was facing a 50-year-old incumbent who represented the baby boom generation, while Dole represented the World War II generation. Clinton jogged in Washington, while Dole had recently battled prostate cancer; Clinton spoke of building a "bridge to the twenty-first century," while Dole reflected on the leadership of World War II veterans.

In addition to these inherent handicaps, Dole never successfully articulated a message or an agenda for a Dole presidency. He tentatively tested various slogans, such as touting his character and steady leadership or criticizing the moral blots on the Clinton administration, but none had efficacy or staying power. A shadow of impropriety had hung over the Clinton White House during the past four years, as questions cropped up surrounding Bill and Hillary Clinton's involvement in the money-losing Whitewater land deal in Arkansas, the failure of a savings-and-loan bank run by the Clintons' business partners, and the dismissal of several White House travel office workers. Dole scored the scandals and "the sleaze factor" of the Clinton White House, and when the American people appeared indifferent, he implored, "Where is the outrage?" Struggling to find a defining issue, Dole proposed an across-the-board 15 percent tax cut, but the idea failed to excite voters, and appeared inconsistent with his past emphasis on balanced budgets in the Senate. Two television debates against Clinton failed to give his candidacy a boost, and in the vice presidential debate, the normally exuberant Kemp appeared uncharacteristically tentative against Vice President Al Gore.

Shrewd Democratic advertising kept Dole pinned down and on the defensive. Clinton television commercials saturated the country and depicted Dole as a political ally of controversial House Speaker Newt Gingrich, thus making Dole appear a callous opponent of Medicare and Medicaid. Clinton plumped himself as the protector of these sacred entitlements, and Dole never effectively countered the advertisements. Absent was the sharp tongue that Dole had displayed in previous national campaigns, making his campaign less exciting.

Ross Perot once again ran as the nominee of the Reform Party, but he was never more than a footnote. Although he again used his own money lavishly for advertising, his media strategy was less focused than in 1996, and his message was less clear. Unlike in 1992, this time he was excluded from the presidential debates on the grounds that he had no realistic chance of winning.

This political contest was one of the least dramatic in the twentieth century, an indication of which was the low voter turnout on Election Day, just 49 percent, the lowest showing since 1924. One of the only moments of excitement was Dole's decision to conclude his campaign with a marathon, nonstop 96-hour finale. But it did him little good. Clinton won 49.2 percent of the popular vote and 379 electoral votes, compared to Dole's 41 percent and 159 electoral votes. Perot won only 9 percent, less than half of his share from four years earlier, and he once again failed to win a single electoral vote. Clinton triumphed handily with two groups, women and young voters, beating Dole among these groups by 26 and 19 points, respectively. Clinton became the first Democratic president since Franklin Roosevelt to win reelection. But like Jimmy Carter, the only other Democrat to win the White House since Roosevelt, Clinton's support lacked depth or fervency, as he was unable to win an absolute majority.

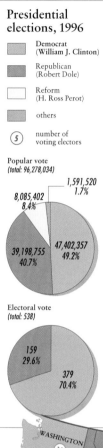

Presidential elections, 1996

- Democrat (William J. Clinton)
- Republican (Robert Dole)
- Reform (H. Ross Perot)
- others
- (5) number of voting electors

Popular vote
(total: 96,278,034)

1,591,520 1.7%
8,085,402 8.4%
47,402,357 49.2%
39,198,755 40.7%

Electoral vote
(total: 538)

159 29.6%
379 70.4%

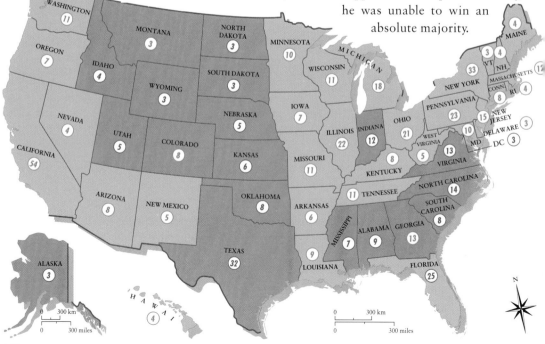

The Election of 2000

Scandal rocked Bill Clinton's presidency during his second term. In December 1998, the Republican Congress impeached him for his misconduct after a sexual affair with a White House intern. Although the Senate acquitted him in the subsequent trial, Clinton was only the second president to be impeached. The sordid affair left a deep moral stain on his presidency and handed the Republicans an issue for the 2000 presidential race.

The two GOP front-runners were Texas Governor George W. Bush and Senator John McCain of Arizona, a Vietnam veteran who had spent five and a half years in a Hanoi prison. Bush, the eldest son of the former president, was the candidate of the Republican establishment and had a considerable advantage in endorsements, organization, and money. A former businessman and a relative newcomer to politics—he was elected Texas governor in 1994—Bush styled himself as a "compassionate conservative," a moderate who would soften the perceived harshness of Republican social policies. Bush was the presumptive nominee, but the New Hampshire primary, in which McCain trounced Bush by 19 points, left the Texan's campaign reeling. Bush rebounded, partly by appealing to the GOP's right wing, and by March he had clinched the nomination.

George W. Bush
1946–
In defeating an
incumbent vice
president, Bush
benefited from family
connections, a well-
financed campaign,
and Republican
determination to win
the White House after
eight years of
Democratic rule.

Former senator and professional basketball player Bill Bradley of New Jersey challenged Vice President Al Gore, Clinton's handpicked successor, for the Democratic nomination. In response to the Bradley challenge, Gore retooled his campaign and revamped his image. He moved his campaign headquarters from Washington to his home state of Tennessee, hired new strategists, and attacked Bradley's policy proposals. Criticized for a wooden speaking style, Gore tried to appear more animated on the campaign stump. Bradley failed to win a single primary, and by March Gore had secured the nomination.

Both Bush and Gore broke with tradition by announcing their running mates before their party conventions. Bush picked Dick Cheney, whose extensive political experience included ten years as a Wyoming congressman and four years as defense secretary during George H. Bush's presidency. The Republican convention in Philadelphia was a harmonious, multicultural pageant at which the party tried to emphasize racial and ethnic diversity. Just before the Democratic National Convention in Los Angeles, Gore chose Senator Joseph Lieberman of Connecticut as his running mate. Lieberman's nomination marked the first time a major party had placed an Orthodox Jew on a national ticket. A senator since 1989, Lieberman had been a harsh critic of Clinton during his sex scandal.

By Labor Day, Gore had a slight lead over Bush in the polls. The Texas governor lost traction in September, partly because of his campaign's own gaffes, such as his use of profanity to describe a reporter, a remark caught by a live microphone. But October's three presidential debates allowed Bush to regain

his footing. During the first debate, Gore appeared pedantic, interrupting Bush and sighing audibly while his opponent spoke. Gore's behavior reinforced his image of an unlikable man, while Bush appeared more knowledgeable than most observers had expected.

Both contestants battled on. Gore led a populist campaign in which he portrayed himself as the champion of the people. "I want to fight for you," he boomed out at audiences. On the preeminent issues of the day—health care, Social Security, and prescription drugs for the elderly—voters trusted Gore more than Bush, who championed more for the issues of education, national defense, and tax reduction. With a quarter-century of experience in national office, Gore came across as having a firm grasp of detail. By contrast, Bush labored under the image of an intellectual lightweight. But Gore's dull, didactic personality was legendary, as was his tendency toward self-aggrandizement. Critics cited his overly generous claim that he had taken the initiative in creating the Internet. And whereas Gore pledged to fight for the working class, Bush retorted, "We've had enough fighting. It's time to unite." Additionally, he promised to restore integrity to the White House.

By early November, the race was a dead heat. On election night, the television networks projected Bush as the winner, and the vice president telephoned the Texas governor to concede. But then the vote in Florida, a state that the television networks first called for Gore, appeared too close to declare a winner. Without the state's 25 electoral votes, the election could not be determined, and in a highly unusual move Gore called Bush to retract his concession. The election was thus left hanging, with Bush having 246 electoral votes and Gore with 267, just three votes shy of the winning number. What followed was a protracted legal battle that centered on Florida, where Bush clung to a lead of fewer than one thousand votes out of six million cast. A state law required an automatic recount for an election this close. In addition, the Gore campaign demanded hand recounts of the vote in four of Florida's 67 counties, arguing that machines did not properly count ballots or that ballots had confused voters.

Both campaigns tussled in courts over the recounts. Bush protested the Florida law that had allowed the hand recounts, maintaining that they were unreliable, and protested their taking place only in selected counties. On November 26, the state of Florida certified Bush as the winner of the state's electoral votes, having edged Gore by just 537 popular votes. Gore appealed the decision to the Florida Supreme Court, which ordered the recount to proceed beyond the legal certification deadline. The case went all the way to the U.S. Supreme Court, and on December 14, in a 5–4 ruling, the Court stopped the Florida recount on the grounds that it violated the Constitution's equal protection clause. The decision dashed Gore's hopes for the presidency. He went on national television to concede to Bush, declaring, "While I strongly disagree with the Court's decision, I accept it."

The closeness of the election indicated that the two parties were at almost equal strength, and the results also illustrated national voting patterns. Gore won the traditional Democratic constituencies: a majority of women, Hispanics, urban residents, and union workers voted for him, and he won more than 90 percent of the African-American vote. Bush's support came largely from rural voters, men, and white Americans. Bush swept a broad band of conservative states running in an L shape from Montana and the Dakotas through the Southeast. Gore claimed the Northeast, the West Coast, and the Upper Midwest, the populous areas rich in electoral votes. His triumphs in California, New York, and Illinois made him the first candidate in history to win those states yet lose the election.

The election of 2000 became the fourth race in history in which the electoral vote winner lost the popular vote. Bush became the first son of a president to win the White House since John Quincy Adams in the election of 1824, another race in which the winner had lost the popular vote. The confusing and controversial 2000 contest aroused voter concerns not only over the electoral college and its sometimes inaccurate reflection of the people's will but also over the various methods that localities used to record votes. In an electronic age, voting districts still relied on antiquated devices such as lever machines, punch cards, and paper ballots, and the problems that surfaced in Florida revealed the deficiencies of these techniques. During the twenty-first century, new and improved procedures will develop, and the changes will have been stimulated in part by the election of 2000.

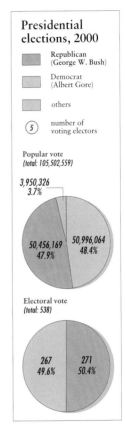

Presidential elections, 2000

- Republican (George W. Bush)
- Democrat (Albert Gore)
- others
- (5) number of voting electors

Popular vote
(total: 105,502,559)

3,950,326
3.7%

50,456,169
47.9%

50,996,064
48.4%

Electoral vote
(total: 538)

267
49.6%

271
50.4%

Presidents and Vice Presidents

Year	President	Vice President	Main Opponent *	Electoral Votes		Popular Vote	
				Winner	Main Opponent	Winner	Main Opponent
1789	George Washington (F)	John Adams	John Adams	69	34	No record	
1792	George Washington (F)	John Adams	John Adams	132	77	No record	
1796	John Adams (F)	Thomas Jefferson	Thomas Jefferson	71	68	No record	
1800	Thomas Jefferson (D-R)	Aaron Burr	Aaron Burr	73	73	No record	
1804	Thomas Jefferson (D-R)	Rufus King	Charles C Pinckney	162	14	No record	
1808	James Madison (D-R)	George Clinton	Charles C Pinckney	122	47	No record	
1812	James Madison (D-R)	Elbridge Gerry	De Witt Clinton	128	89	No record	
1816	James Monroe (D-R)	Daniel D Tompkins	Rufus King	183	34	No record	
1820	James Monroe (D-R)	Daniel D Tompkins	John Quincy Adams	231	1	No record	
1824	John Quincy Adams (N-R)	John C Calhoun	Andrew Jackson	84	99	108,740	153,544
1828	Andrew Jackson (D-R)	John C Calhoun	John Quincy Adams	178	83	647,286	508,064
1832	Andrew Jackson (D-R)	Martin Van Buren	Henry Clay	219	49	701,780	484,205
1836	Martin Van Buren (D)	Richard M Johnson	William Henry Harrison	170	73	764,176	550,816
1840	William Henry Harrison (W)	John Tyler	Martin Van Buren	234	60	1,275,016	1,129,102
1841	John Tyler (W)	(president after the death of William H. Harrison)					
1844	James K Polk (D)	George M Dallas	Henry Clay	170	105	1,337,243	1,290,062
1848	Zachary Taylor (W)	Millard Fillmore	Lewis Cass	163	127	1,360,099	1,229,544
1852	Franklin Pierce (D)	William R King	Winfield Scott	254	42	1,601,274	1,386,580
1856	James Buchanan (D)	John C Breckinridge	John C Frémont	174	114	1,838,169	1,341,264
1860	Abraham Lincoln (R)	Hannibal Hamlin	John C Breckinridge	180	72	1,866,452	847,953
1864	Abraham Lincoln (R)	Andrew Johnson	George B McClellan	212	21	2,213,665	1,805,237
1865	Andrew Johnson (R)	(president after the assassination of Abraham Lincoln)					
1868	Ulysses S Grant (R)	Schuyler Colfax	Horatio Seymour	214	80	3,012,833	2,703,249
1872	Ulysses S Grant (R)	Henry Wilson	Horace Greeley	286	—†	3,597,132	2,834,125
1876	Rutherford B Hayes (R)	William A Wheeler	Samuel J Tilden	185	184	4,036,298	4,300,590
1880	James Garfield (R)	Chester A Arthur	Winfield S Hancock	214	155	4,454,416	4,444,952
1881	Chester A Arthur (R)	(president after the assassination of James Garfield)					
1884	Grover Cleveland (D)	Thomas A Hendricks	James G Blaine	219	182	4,874,986	4,851,981
1888	Benjamin Harrison (R)	Levi P Morton	Grover Cleveland	233	168	5,439,853	5,540,309
1892	Grover Cleveland (D)	Adlai E Stevenson	Benjamin Harrison	277	145	5,556,918	5,176,108
1896	William McKinley (R)	Garret A Hobart	William J Bryan	271	176	7,104,779	6,502,925

Year	President	Vice President	Main Opponent*	Electoral Votes		Popular Vote	
				Winner	Main Opponent	Winner	Main Opponent
1900	William McKinley (R)	Theodore Roosevelt	William J Bryan	292	155	7,207,923	6,358,133
1904	Theodore Roosevelt (R)	Charles W Fairbanks	Alton N Parker	336	140	7,623,486	5,077,911
1908	William H Taft (R)	James S Sherman	William J Bryan	321	162	7,678,908	6,409,104
1912	Woodrow Wilson (D)	Thomas R Marshall	Theodore Roosevelt	435	88	6,293,454	4,119,207
1916	Woodrow Wilson (D)	Thomas R Marshall	Charles E Hughes	277	254	9,129,606	8,538,221
1920	Warren G Harding (R)	Calvin Coolidge	James M Cox	404	127	16,152,200	9,147,353
1924	Calvin Coolidge (R)	Charles G Dawes	John W Davis	382	136	15,725,016	8,386,503
1928	Herbert C Hoover (R)	Charles Curtis	Alfred E Smith	444	87	21,391,381	15,016,443
1932	Franklin D Roosevelt (D)	John N Garner	Herbert C Hoover	472	59	22,821,857	15,761,841
1936	Franklin D Roosevelt (D)	John N Garner	Alfred M Landon	523	8	27,751,597	16,679,583
1940	Franklin D Roosevelt (D)	Henry A Wallace	Wendell L Wilkie	449	82	27,244,160	22,305,198
1944	Franklin D Roosevelt (D)	Harry S Truman	Thomas E Dewey	432	99	25,602,504	22,006,285
1948	Harry S Truman (D)	Alben W Barkley	Thomas E Dewey	303	189	24,105,695	21,969,170
1952	Dwight D Eisenhower (R)	Richard M Nixon	Adlai Stevenson	442	89	33,778,963	27,314,992
1956	Dwight D Eisenhower (R)	Richard M Nixon	Adlai Stevenson	457	73	35,581,003	25,738,765
1960	John F Kennedy (D)	Lyndon B Johnson	Richard M Nixon	303	219	34,227,096	34,107,646
1964	Lyndon B Johnson (D)	Hubert H Humphrey	Barry M Goldwater	486	52	42,825,463	27,146,969
1968	Richard M Nixon (R)	Spiro T Agnew	Hubert H Humphrey	301	191	31,785,148	31,274,503
1972	Richard M Nixon (R)	Spiro T Agnew	George McGovern	520	17	46,740,323	28,901,598
1974	Gerald R Ford (R)	(Nominated to the vice-presidency after the resignation of Spiro Agnew, 1973. Became president on the resignation of Richard Nixon in 1974.)					
1976	Jimmy Carter (D)	Walter F Mondale	Gerald R Ford	297	240	40,825,839	39,147,770
1980	Ronald Reagan (R)	George Bush	Jimmy Carter	489	49	43,901,812	35,483,820
1984	Ronald Reagan (R)	George Bush	Walter F Mondale	525	13	54,455,075	37,577,185
1988	George Bush (R)	J Danforth Quayle	Michael S Dukakis	426	111	47,946,000	41,016,000
1992	William J Clinton (D)	Albert Gore, Jr.	George Bush	370	168	44,908,254	39,102,343
1996	William J Clinton (D)	Albert Gore, Jr.	Bob Dole	379	159	45,590,703	37,816,307
2000	George W Bush (R)	Dick Cheney	Albert Gore, Jr.	271	266	50,456,169	50,996,064

* See individual elections for data on all major candidates.

† Greeley died before Electoral College voted.

Source: National Archives and Records Administration Federal Register.; Congressional Quarterly's Guide to U.S. Presidential Elections.

Sources for Further Reading

GENERAL

Batchelor, John. *"Ain't You Glad You Joined the Republicans?" A Short History of the GOP.* New York: Henry Holt and Company, 1996.

Boller, Paul, Jr. *Presidential Campaigns.* New York: Oxford University Press, 1996.

Congressional Quarterly. *Presidential Elections, 1789–1996.* Washington: Congressional Quarterly, 1997.

Congressional Quarterly. *Historical Review of Presidential Candidates from 1788 to 1968.* Washington: Congressional Quarterly, 1969.

Dinkin, Robert. *Campaigning in America: A History of Election Practices.* New York: Greenwood Press, 1989.

Dover, E. D. *Presidential Elections in the Television Age, 1960–1992.* Westport, Connecticut: Greenwood Press, 1992.

Fischer, Roger. *Tippecanoe and Trinkets Too: The Material Culture of the American Presidential Campaign, 1828–1924.* Champaign: University of Illinois Press, 1988.

"If Elected…": Unsuccessful Candidates for the Presidency, 1796–1968. Washington: Smithsonian Institution Press, 1972.

Jamieson, Kathleen Hall. *Packaging the Presidency: A History and Criticism of Presidential Campaign Advertising.* New York: Oxford University Press, 1984.

Lorant, Stefan. *The Glorious Burden: The History of the Presidency and Presidential Elections from George Washington to James Earl Carter, Jr.* Lenox, Massachusetts: Authors Edition, Inc., 1976.

McGillivray, Alice and Richard Scammon. *America at the Polls: Harding to Eisenhower; A Handbook of Presidential Statistics.* Washington: Congressional Quarterly Press, 1998.

Melder, Keith. *Hail to the Candidate: Presidential Candidates from Banners to Broadcasts.* Washington: Smithsonian Institution Press, 1992.

Moore, John. *Elections A to Z.* Washington: Congressional Quarterly, Inc., 1999.

Morreale, Joanne. *The Presidential Campaign Film: A Critical History.* Westport, Connecticut: Greenwood Press, 1993.

Pierce, Neal. *The People's President: The Electoral College in American History and the Direct-Vote Alternative.* New York: Simon and Schuster, 1968.

Roseboom, Eugene. *History of Presidential Elections.* New York: The Macmillan Company, 1985.

Schlesinger, Arthur and Fred Israel (eds.). *History of American Presidential Elections, 1789–1984.* Vols. 1–4 and supplement. New York: Chelsea House Publishers, 1971–1986.

Schlesinger, Arthur, Jr., et. al. (eds.). *Running for President: The Candidates and Their Images.* Vols. 1 and 2. Simon and Schuster, 1995.

Shields-West, Eileen. *The World Almanac of Presidential Campaigns.* New York: World Almanac, 1992.

Southwick, Leslie. *Presidential Also-Rans and Running Mates, 1788–1980.* Jefferson, N.C.: McFarland and Co., 1984.

Stone, Irving. *They Also Ran: The Story of the Men Who Were Defeated for the Presidency.* Garden City, N.Y.: Doubleday, Doran and Company, Inc., 1945.

Warda, Mark. *100 Years of Political Campaign Collectibles.* Clearwater, Florida: Sphinx Publishing, 1996.

Wayne, Stephen J. *The Road to the White House, 1996: The Politics of Presidential Elections.* New York: St. Martin's Press, 1997.

Young, Michael. *The American Dictionary of Campaigns and Elections.* Lanham, MD: Hamilton Press, 1987.

Specific Elections

Bagby, Wesley M. *The Road to Normalcy: The Presidential Campaign and the Election of 1920.* Baltimore: Johns Hopkins University Press, 1968.

Drew, Elizabeth. *Portrait of an Election: The 1980 Presidential Campaign.* New York: Simon and Schuster, 1981.

Faber, Harold (ed.). *The Road to the White House: The Story of the 1964 Election by the Staff of the New York Times.* New York: New York Times, 1965.

Gammon, Samuel. *The Presidential Campaign of 1932.* Westport, CT: Greenwood Press, 1971.

Germond, Jack and Jules Witcover. *Blue Smoke and Mirrors: How Reagan Won and Why Carter Lost the Election of 1980.* New York: Viking Press, 1981.

——. *Mad as Hell: Revolt at the Ballot Box, 1992.* New York: Warner Books, Inc., 1993.

——. *Whose Broad Stripes and Bright Stars? The Trivial Pursuit of the Presidency, 1988.* New York: Warner Books, 1989.

Glad, Paul. *McKinley, Bryan, and the People.* Chicago: Ivan R. Dee, 1964.

Goldman, Peter, et. al. *Quest for the Presidency 1992.* College Station: Texas A&M University Press, 1994.

Gould, Lewis. *1968: The Election That Changed America.* Chicago: Ivan R. Dee, 1993.

Gullan, Harold. *The Upset That Wasn't: Harry S. Truman and the Crucial Election of 1948.* Chicago: Ivan R. Dee, 1998.

Kessel, John. *Goldwater Coalition: Republican Strategies in 1964.* New York: Macmillan, 1968.

McGinniss, Joe. *The Selling of the President, 1968.* New York: Trident Press, 1969.

Ogden, Daniel. *Electing the President: 1964.* San Francisco: Chandler Publishing Company, 1964.

Pomper, Gerald, et. al. *The Election of 1976: Reports and Interpretations.* New York: Longman, 1977.

Remini, Robert. *The Election of Andrew Jackson.* Philadelphia: J.B. Lippincott, 1963.

Ross, Irwin. *The Loneliest Campaign: The Truman Victory of 1948.* New York: New American Library, 1968.

Shram, Martin. *Running for President, 1976.* New York: Stein and Day, 1977.

Stacks, John. *Watershed: The Campaign for the Presidency 1980.* New York: New York Times Books, 1981.

Stroud, Kandy. *How Jimmy Won.* New York: William Morrow and Company, Inc., 1977.

Thompson, Hunter. *Fear and Loathing: On the Campaign Trail '72.* New York: Warner, 1983.

Wattenberg, Martin. *The Rise of Candidate-Centered Politics: Presidential Elections of the 1980s.* Cambridge: Harvard University Press, 1992.

Waugh, John. *Reelecting Lincoln: The Battle for the 1864 Presidency.* New York: Crown Publishing Group, 1998.

White, Theodore. *America in Search of Itself: The Making of the President, 1956–1980.* New York: Harper & Row, 1982.

White, Theodore. *The Making of the President, 1960.* New York: New American Library, 1967.

White, Theodore. *The Making of the President, 1964.* New York: Atheneum Publishers, 1965.

White, Theodore. *The Making of the President, 1968.* New York: Atheneum Publishers, 1969.

White, Theodore. *The Making of the President, 1972.* Atheneum Publishers, 1973.

Witcover, Jules. *Marathon: The Pursuit of the Presidency, 1972–1976.* New York: Viking Press, 1977.

Index

Acknowledgments

I wish to thank the many friends and colleagues who helped me to write this book. Series editor Mark C. Carnes has been a mentor since I first worked with him, over a decade ago, while I was in graduate school. Mark and Kevin Ohe, my editor at Routledge, gave steadfast encouragement, and their many suggestions on drafts of this book have sharpened its focus. Malcolm Swanston and Elsa Gibert gave valuable advice to keep the text congruent with the maps. Andrew Bailis, production editor, provided much-needed assistance, and Norma McLemore copy-edited expertly with a journalist's eye. Alan Brinkley and John A. Garraty, as always, gave expert guidance, directing me to sources and challenging me to present specific critical ideas. I gratefully acknowledge Dowling College's Long Range Planning and Development Committee, which granted course releases that helped me to devote more time to research and writing. Special thanks go to Michael S. Green of the Community College of Southern Nevada. Mike has been an inspiration since graduate school, a friend who has tirelessly answered my questions on history and listened to my ideas when I needed an audience. Mike took time away from his own research and teaching to review this manuscript and made many insightful comments to correct its errors and improve its flow.

Geir Gundersen and Kenneth Hafeli of the Gerald R. Ford Library and Jennifer Sternaman of the Ronald Reagan Library were especially helpful in obtaining photographs as well as data to construct maps. I would also like to thank Philip Scott and Linda Seelke of the Lyndon B. Johnson Library, Robert Bohanan of the Jimmy Carter Library, Susan Naulty of the Richard Nixon Library and Birthplace, and Amy Williams of the Harry S. Truman Library.

A number of friends gave support and inspiration, which I much appreciated. They include Barber B. Conable, Jr., Lou Munch and Sue Maloy, Jim North, Glenn Schleede, Paul Theis, and Patrick Williams.

The two best confidants and critics I have are my parents, Bogdan and Seiko Mieczkowski. They faithfully reviewed the manuscript, from first to final draft, checking my research, offering advice, and most of all, furnishing ideas and encouragement. To them and to my brothers, Van and Dean, I owe the deepest gratitude.

The publisher wishes to thank the following for their permission to reproduce the illustrations for this book.

Arcadia Editions Limited: 12, 18, 20, 24, 26, 29, 32, 37, 39 ,41, 42, 43, 47, 49, 52, 57, 58, 63, 65, 67, 68, 71, 75, 79, 83, 85, 90, 92, 94, 96, 106, 110, 115, 118, 121, 128, 129, 131, 137, 140, 147, 148
Betmann Achives: 43
Clements Library: 40
Courtesy of the Library of Congress: 14, 16, 44, 55, 59, 69, 73, 103
Courtesy of the White House Collection: 130
Culver Pictures: 76
Des Moines Register and Leader: 89
Lyndon Baines Johnson Library: 116
Magnum Photos: 126
National Gallery of Washington: 15
Peter Newark American Pictures: 99
Sygma: 136

Design: Malcolm Swanston

Cartography: Elsa Gibert with Jeanne Radford and Malcolm Swanston for Arcadia Editions Limited, England

Cover Design: Trudi Gershenov of Trudi Gershenov Design

Illustrations: Peter A.B. Smith

Typesetting: Jeanne Radford for Arcadia Editions Limited

Printing: R.R. Donnelley & Sons, Salem, Virginia, U.S.A.

Lake Wales Public Library
290 Cypress Garden Lane
Lake Wales, FL. 33853
(863) 678-4004

DEMCO

6-01